LOVE IS NOT FOR COWARDS

The Autobiography of Shirley Dyckes Kelley

as told to Elizabeth Gullander

PRENTICE-HALL, INC., *Englewood Cliffs, New Jersey*

To preserve the privacy of certain individuals, and because it was impossible to contact others for permission to use their names, in some cases names of people and places in this book are fictitious.

I accept full responsibility for the material in this book.

Shirley Dyckes Kelley

Love Is Not for Cowards: The Autobiography of Shirley Dyckes Kelley
by Shirley Dyckes Kelley as told to Elizabeth Gullander
Copyright © 1978 by Shirley Dyckes Kelley
All rights reserved. No part of this book may be
reproduced in any form or by any means, except
for the inclusion of brief quotations in a review,
without permission in writing from the publisher.
Printed in the United States of America
Prentice-Hall International, Inc., London
Prentice-Hall of Australia, Pty. Ltd., Sydney
Prentice-Hall of Canada, Ltd., Toronto
Prentice-Hall of India Private Ltd., New Delhi
Prentice-Hall of Japan, Inc., Tokyo
Prentice-Hall of Southeast Asia Pte. Ltd., Singapore
Whitehall Books Limited, Wellington, New Zealand
10 9 8 7 6 5 4 3 2 1

Library of Congress Cataloging in Publication Data
Kelley, Shirley Dyckes, Date
Love is not for cowards.
1. Kelley, Shirley Dyckes, Date   2.   United
States—Biography.   3.   Ex-nuns—United States
—Biography.   I.   Gullander, Elizabeth, joint
author.   II.   Title.
CT275.K4393A35   1978   973.92′092′4 [B]   77-26211
ISBN 0-13-541029-0

Contents

This book is dedicated to my husband
whose loving kindness and zest for life make every
day a joy and an adventure for me.

1

Butterfly in Cocoon

Tomorrow's headlines might banner, "FBI Director Marries Former Nun," but to me it would be, "Love Conquers All—Shirley and Clarence Make It!"

I turned in front of the mirror, inspecting my wedding dress. I had bought it in such a hurry that I had had to take it out of stock at Garfinckel's, and they had done a rush job of removing the train. I insisted on that! There was no time for tripping over ruffles! I was busy just trying to keep in touch with one of the fastest-moving men in America, and marrying him was something for which there scarcely seemed time.

I had known Clarence only a few months. Not easy months. It was 1976, a presidential election year. Politics bears down heavily on public officials during the campaigns. Clarence Kelley, as the Director of the FBI, had been under particularly heavy personal attacks from an unfriendly press, and especially from a self-righteous presidential candidate. He had also suffered serious physical stress from an old injury to his back. Our courtship had been scanty, scattered, and scary. Yes, scary! I had entered a world of serious-minded, gun-toting men who knew how to draw a gun as deftly as I knew how to draw on my lipstick. And a lot quicker! What was I getting into, marrying the Chief of the Cops in a world full of crackpots and robbers? But I was in love, as I had always wanted to be. And the man I loved, a very special man, needed me as much as I needed him.

At least, I thought happily, *this* time I had been able to choose my own wedding gown, and it had not been worn by countless others before me.

In a different way, I had lived through this day before. Once before I had worn a wedding gown and walked to the altar of my church with love in my heart to dedicate my life eternally. I had experienced a marriage service. How different it would be today! For the first ceremony had been an investiture as a sister of the Catholic order of the Holy Cross, and this time it was to enter into holy matrimony with one of the most powerful men in the United States.

To many, the very possibility of a woman having been a nun and later marrying was still a new thought. There were many misconceptions about the rites of the Catholic Church, and there had also been, in the past few years, many changes and attitudes within the Church.

I was not unaware of the ripples of curiosity caused by the announcement of my engagement. In the press I wore a label. I was "Former Nun." Not "Teacher," as I had been for the past seven years since my departure from the convent, and indeed, as I had been employed for thirteen years within the convent. Nor did they list my degrees in theology and history. I was "a nun." Or, I *had* been.

The choice of this way of life seemed to create mystery. Nuns set themselves apart from the complications of society the better to perform their work and to pray. It was as simple as that. The choice of being a nun was freely made. It was a privilege.

When I was growing up in Miami, though it was never said to me, I knew I had one inevitable course to follow. It led to only one door: to marriage, a *successful* marriage. I was educated at private schools, spent my spare time in carefully selected places, and associated with "the right" people. My family lived on a street in one of the prettiest areas of Miami.

My mother was a slim, pretty, rather quiet lady, exceedingly young looking, who always wore beautiful dresses and smelled delicious. I loved her, but of course had scrapes and scraps. I learned, however, never to permit these to develop after lunch. My mother's single threat to me was to "tell Daddy." If I had mischief in my heart, I scheduled it before my nap, so that it would be forgotten before my father returned home. I had a sister, Joyce, one year my junior. For many years we were so alike in our size and fair coloring that people mistook us for twins. We were treated equally by our parents.

Until his retirement, my father had for forty years been president of a chemical company. The people we met were of similar interests and expectations. There was no social climbing, or attempting to keep up with the Joneses. We were moderately wealthy and contented with our station.

It was expected that Joyce and I would continue in line. We would attend private school, earn college degrees, and meet and marry handsome, healthy, career-minded men with whom we would eventually create a minimum of two children each, preferably some of each sex.

That was the plan.

Life was supposed to be as uncomplicated as that.

From contemporary viewpoint, such a life is limited. But there were only two choices for girls of my background in the fifties—to marry or remain single. The first was touted as success; the second, failure. Even for men, that was the choice.

In the Catholic Church, of which my family are members, there are three vocations for which women may declare themselves: religious, single, or marriage. The religious life requires a commitment of chastity and poverty and life centered around the confinement of a convent. Single life is another means of dedication—perhaps to the care of aging parents or the welfare of an invalid, or a career in nursing or teaching. Marriage means a husband, home, and the care and rearing of as many children as God gives one.

Few Catholic women experience more than one vocation. Two or three could suggest turmoil and agonizing decision-making. I was to live all three.

To explain away part of the puzzle convent life seems to cause among outsiders, I would say that to the Catholic Church serving it is the richest of rewards—a visible expression of one's sincere belief in the Church, its purpose and workings. Choosing to be a nun or a priest is no different from deciding to make one's life work in any other profession which requires years of study and exacting discipline. It is like becoming a scientist or engineer, or even a doctor, who expects a life of twenty-four-hour-a-day service with few holidays. Except most doctors take Wednesdays off, and nuns don't.

Catholic parents are proud when one of their children decides to serve the Church. They may be initially sad, as my parents were. My mother, I later heard, quietly sorrowed for two years—but this passes, and eventually parents feel the honor and blessing espoused to their child. If the child makes such a choice, the Catholic parent considers it a grace which throws its light backward, reflecting on his own example and teaching of Christian life.

But I had no thought whatsoever of entering the convent as I was growing up. I had few serious thoughts. I was busy enjoying life, happy in an easy pattern of one day following the next, with little concern for the day after.

§≈

My family tree gives no hint of a religious vocation. There was frequent intermarriage between Catholics and Protestants which caused some intergeneration misunderstanding. My mother, Lillian Russell Hern, was a daughter of such a mixed marriage. My grandfather, Joseph Hern, named her for the famous singer and beauty, Lillian Russell, who was then the wife of one of his more famous legal clients.

Stanley Dyckes, my father, was also born to a family with a mixed religious background, but both he and my mother were raised in the Catholic Church. The foundation for my religious life had been laid before my birth, though no one imagined to what an extent I would carry it.

In the 1940s in Miami, many of the fine Catholic Church buildings had not yet been built, and there were not many Catholic schools. Our original parish was St. Mary's. Later, when a new parish was formed, we attended Mass in the auditorium on the campus of Barry College. Due to crowded conditions, I was not enrolled in St. Mary's Catholic grade school. Instead, Joyce and I spent many happy years at the Cushman School, a private institution.

When it became time for me to take instruction so that I might receive my First Communion, I attended classes, but memorizing the Apostles' Creed seemed, to me, a hopeless task. I accomplished it, but as soon as I had made my First Communion, I quickly forgot it. Some time later my mother once more conscripted us into attendance at Sunday School. There were two things I remember about those sessions, one

4

bad and one good. Sunday School was held in the classrooms of St. Mary's, where we knew no one. Before classes began all the little boys played in the dirt schoolyard under the hot sun. When they raced in, panting, perspiring, and smelling, it was more than my delicate nose could stand! At Cushman School, boys did not come to school in that condition.

The other memory is that Joyce and I participated in the St. Mary's procession in honor of the Blessed Mother. We had seen a sister making a beautiful white crown of flowers for the statue of the Mother of God. This statue was a favorite of mine, though for a long time I had not known it was supposed to be the Blessed Mother. I liked it because of the blue and white outfit she wore, and the way that she held her hands. Parading to honor Mary was fun, but to me the rest of churchgoing was awful. We finally had enough. No more Sunday School! Mother did not appreciate our attitude, but Church did not dominate our programs. Going to confession on Saturday and attending Mass on Sunday was not a prerequisite for family peace, although we usually received the sacraments.

As you can see, I was not preordained toward religious life, nor was I pressured in that direction. Even a sudden and dangerous experience at my home, when I was five, which might, in another family, have been used to direct my future, was not.

The street where we lived at the time was very quiet. There were only five houses on it. Across from our house were two belonging to Protestant ministers, Dr. Johnson of the Presbyterian Church and Dr. James, minister of White Temple Methodist Church. Joyce and I were allowed out only on this short street, and were never permitted to cross it without my mother standing on the sidewalk watching. My mother was loving, firm, and exceedingly protective of us.

Our house was a two-story stucco wrapped around a sun-filled patio. The yard was large and bright with tropical plantings, palm trees, hibiscus and oleander bushes, and lawns.

One forenoon I had been scrubbed and dressed in the fussiest dress my mother could find in my closet, and my blond hair was combed and beribboned. My mother's bridge club was coming for luncheon, and Joyce and I were to be little ladies. It was a warm day, and I would much have preferred playing barefoot in my underpants in the dirt of the vacant lot down the street. But I had been warned not to get dirty. I was to *stay inside*.

I *was* inside, but I was also as far outside as I could possibly be without totally disregarding orders. I leaned out on the screen door over the back steps. Overhead, I watched a small airplane stunting.

Behind me, in the kitchen, Joyce, her dress all bundled up in a huge apron, was helping my mother make strawberry shortcake.

Alongside our backyard the trashmen drove their banging, clattering truck, just as they always did on Tuesdays.

I waved to them shyly.

The driver of the truck smiled broadly and waved back at me.

For the first time in my life I noticed that the palm of his hand was pink. The rest of him was black.

I had been around black people all my life. We had a black maid who came in twice a week to help the housekeeper with the heavy cleaning. And of course every time I went for a drive, I saw countless other black people. I had always recognized that there was a difference between us, but I had never pinpointed what it was. On *that* morning, as the driver waved at me, I became aware of the real difference.

I hung out on the screen door over the steps overwhelmed by the discovery I had just made. *People had different-colored skins.* This was a most momentous piece of information.

I knew I must tell Joyce immediately.

Letting the door slam shut, I leaped off to go tell her.

As I raced away, the airplane that had been stunting overhead crashed down onto the steps. I had narrowly escaped being killed.

Immediately our yard became a maelstrom of ambulances, police, newspaper reporters, and cameramen. A wrecker came to gather up the remains of the aircraft.

Joyce and I were carefully shielded from the crowd of curious who gathered. My mother sat us on the top step in front of the French doors that led upstairs, and stationed herself between the reporters and us. No photographs were to be taken. No microphones could be thrust into our faces. No reporter might ask me, "How does it feel to be almost killed on your own back steps?" Under pressure, my mother finally submitted to the press a studio portrait of the two of us. But that was it. There would be no exploitation of her young daughters.

Joyce and I viewed the scene, our mother a buffer between us and reality. It was like watching a play. Now, as we live in an age of frequent violence, wherein children intimately share the griefs of the world through television, gory newspaper pictures, and through magazines and movies, I realize what a complete sheltering screen my mother erected around me. Even when tragedy came so close, I was able to remain detached from it.

I sat on the steps with Joyce and was so busy watching, I completely forgot what I was going to tell her when I so fortunately left the screen door and ran deep into the house. It was months before I remembered, and years before I realized, in effect, that two black men had made the difference between my living or dying at the age of five.

I have mentioned Cushman School. In preparing me for adult life, my parents had chosen my schools carefully. Private schools, of course. I attended the Cushman School for Boys and Girls from junior kindergarten through grade seven. This school was a blend of old-fashioned and progressive teaching methods. At the end of the day, as they said good-bye to their teachers, the young ladies curtsied, the young gentlemen bowed from the waist. There were no report cards. The official description of this fine school was "Distinctive for Character Development and Scholastic Achievement." Classes were run informally, which was easy to do with only ten to fifteen students. Connected to each classroom were two rest rooms, and when the necessity to visit one occurred, students did not have to ask permission to be excused but could quietly leave to use the facility. The Cushman School for younger students had a playhouse and its own playground with a pond stocked with goldfish.

My time out of school was spent largely in the company of Joyce, since we were so close in age. The third leg of our triumvirate, for many years, was Caryl James, the daughter of the Methodist minister who lived across the street. We three let our hair grow and braided it down our backs and soon we had braids we could sit on.

In the summer, Caryl attended the Bible School run by her father, and one year Joyce and I decided to join her, though not for truly altruistic reasons. Caryl wore a spectacular decoration she had received for regular religious attendance. Each year an additional bar was attached to it by loops. Since Caryl had been going to Sunday School practically since birth, this ornament seemed phenomenal to us little undecorated Catholics. We, too, wished to win and wear one. So, in spite of the disapproval expressed by my Irish and Catholic paternal grandmother, Joyce and I enrolled in class. We joined wholeheartedly in all the studies, games, hymn singing, and memorizing of Bible verses. Surely our efforts would be noted and rewarded! One day, however, we found out that Summer Bible School was not part of the regular church program. No attendance awards would be given. That ended Bible School. No pins. No ribbons. No Shirley!

One day Caryl announced that she was sick of washing dishes in her own house. She loved polishing my mother's cranberry glassware. On the other hand, I enjoyed listening to the Jameses' canary, Pretty Boy, sing, as I worked at her house. We began frequent exchanges of dishwashing.

It was in this situation that I entered a life of crime.

I stole.

All alone in the James house washing dishes, enjoying the music of Pretty Boy, I noticed a little white enamel pin painted with a red cross lying near the sink. I picked it up and pocketed it.

At home I removed my new treasure and stared at it lovingly.

Then a terrible truth came to me. I couldn't show it to anyone! Not to Joyce or my mother. If I did, I would have to return my prize and admit my theft!

In horror I realized what I had done. Stealing was wrong. It was a sin which was recognized on both sides of the street, by Protestants and Catholics alike. I hid the pin where no one would find it.

Day after day I worried about my stolen property, my conscience growing ever more heavy with guilt. At last I was able to return alone to the Jameses' kitchen and replace the pin where I had found it. I could not wait to get rid of it! For three days that tiny bauble had loomed the largest thing in my life. I realized then that crime was not for me. I would never again be tempted to steal.

Not only was I in and out of the James house on an almost daily basis, but I was a frequent visitor to the White Temple Church. I knew it far more intimately than I did any Catholic building, as we played hide-and-seek, and other games, amid its corners and closets. This seeming irreverence disturbed my Grandmother Dyckes, who had different ideas as to the purpose of sanctified places. Finally, when she could stand it no longer, she pointed this out to the Reverend.

Kindly man that he was, he assured her, "It's quite all right with God, Mrs. Dyckes. He understands children."

౭≈

Part of our summers were spent at the swimming pool on the second-floor terrace level of the beautiful landmark Roney Plaza Hotel in

Miami. Year after year we leased a cabana there, and Joyce, my mother, and I suntanned and relaxed by its purified waters. The years of World War II came and went. Joyce and I loved to lean over the balcony to watch the soldiers drilling in the street below. In their uniforms they all looked alike, and they marched so perfectly that they were like a huge machine, except they sang as they marched. From their throats sprang forth strong male voices lustily chorusing songs long familiar in America.

One of the platoons, from the Quartermaster Corps, had a wire-haired terrier named Topper as its mascot. Topper always wore a red blanket with a little brass castle, the symbol of the corps, pinned to it. When the troop left Miami, they presented him, along with his coat, to Joyce and me. We had him for many years.

ॐ

For my secondary education I entered Miami's well-known private girls' school, Miss Harris'. I was then in an all-girl climate. Most of the boys I had known were sent off to private schools or military academies. In the summers we each attended separate camps.

There were about two hundred girls enrolled in Miss Harris' from kindergarten through high school, which made very small classes.

One of my classmates was Irene Pawley, a daughter of William Douglas Pawley, ambassador to Peru and Brazil, 1945–46. For a time Irene kept us breathless with the inside scoop on a special interest of her brother, Bill. First he had a date with a young movie star named Elizabeth Taylor. Next, they were in love. Then about to become engaged! Denial! Engagement! Breakup!

Melody Raye, the talented daughter of Martha Raye, was enrolled at Miss Harris'. Janet Guthrie, the Indianapolis 500 racer, attended while Joyce was there.

Another schoolmate was Karen Wylie, daughter of Philip Wylie, author of many books, including *A Generation of Vipers*. At that time some people considered his books "dirty." Karen was always able to acquire copies, and would pass them out to the girls. I confess I honestly did not understand Wylie's books, or even like them, but as part of being a sophisticated high school girl, I never expressed my opinion.

My most important job during my high school years was having a good time. School was easy for me, and homework never a chore. Classes were in session just four hours, from 9:00 A.M. until 1:10. We would race out of school and rush to downtown Miami for lunch, and then spend the afternoon touring the shops, swiming, playing tennis, or lying around a cabana improving our ever-constant suntans.

One of the biggest complaints of my high school years, beyond a running argument about not being allowed to wear blue jeans downtown, or spending the night in a Miami Beach hotel during annual Sorority House Party Week, was my father's refusal to join the Bath Club, a favorite cabana club. True, we belonged to other clubs, but this was one I wanted to join. Why, my father countered, should he join a club where his daughters could order hamburgers at $1.20, when anywhere else on the street they could be had for $.50? On most other counts, he was generous with us, but on this, he was adamant.

In Miami, at that time, there were several high school sororities. I considered one with about thirty lively girls from both public and private high schools to be the greatest, and was delighted when they asked me to join. Our purpose in life was the next good time. We were always planning a picnic, party, or dance.

Once we held a car wash. It ended in wild confusion, but we had fun. There were too many cars, and not enough shade, which resulted in one tragedy. Janet MacIntosh brought her mother's new Cadillac to be washed. It was a gorgeous car, and we took pains to give it our personalized attention. However, we worked in the sun. Under its intensity, the soap caked and cooked into the paint, and worked havoc with the finish. In spite of this, my friendship with Janet did not lessen. Janet MacIntosh, now Mrs. Bill Reed, is the friend who introduced me to Clarence Kelley.

The sorority held countless slumber parties during which we stayed up all night. It was a group, but was composed of individuals. Anyone could do what she wanted. I loved to play bridge and would play until sunrise. Other games were played, or the girls chatted. One girl always brought her Bible, which she read before going to sleep. No one ever remarked on this practice, nor were we made to feel less "good" because we were not as devout as she. We had good times together, and yet did not assume a sorority mold. We were all very individually ourselves.

At these sessions, there was little discussion of sexual behavior. Talk of physical development, yes, but personal habits, no. One-to-one relationships with boys among us were rare. Few of us fell deeply in love. Only one girl became pregnant during my sorority years, and she married before the baby was born.

Through those years I had one close male friend, though I hesitate to say "boyfriend." Clark was a typical boy-next-door, more big brother than date. We both enjoyed concerts and ballet, and when Clark had tickets, he would ask me to go along. He also had a boat. Our relationship was so casual that my father actually permitted Joyce and me to cruise around Biscayne Bay with Clark unchaperoned! He was a loyal friend, though I found him so unexciting that I can remember praying, "Don't ever let me get so desperate for a husband that I settle for Clark."

There was little opportunity, and no desire, in my life for teen-age transgression. I did not drive a car. When I had been learning, a child darted out in front of me and I almost hit him. The shock of that near-miss dulled my interest. I did not get a driver's license. The next year, Joyce, who loved to drive, got hers. When I went somewhere, I was accompanied by Joyce, a friend, or my mother. Someone always knew where I was and whom I was with. My territory was always designated, and I stayed in it.

Some of our sorority sisters occasionally helped out at a child care center we had learned about through one of the mothers who was active in the Junior League. Of course, we did not attend on a regular basis. That would have made it seem like work! But as a change of pace from swimming or shopping or tennis, we could always go to the center and assist with the children. They were between the ages of three and six and were cared for while their mothers worked.

Once an emergency arose and my friend Janet Field and I had to return a child to her home, which was in a housing project. I had never been in such a place before, and the sameness of the buildings and the lack of beauty bothered me. In Florida flowers grew everywhere. They needed little more than water to bloom profusely. Yet the complex was colorless. For the first time, I recognized the barrenness in which some people existed.

ॐ

Much of my social life, as I was growing up, was an extension of the lives of my parents. They were young, and happy, and enjoyed dancing. Through the years they hired instructors to come to teach them and their friends the latest dance steps. Joyce and I watched, and later would enjoy gliding across the terrazzo floor of our porch with Daddy and his friends. On Thursday evenings we accompanied our parents to the country club for dinner. We were not two generations in one household. We were a family who did things together.

My childhood was comfortable. I accepted its ease without any sense of guilt about having more than others. At that time, I was not aware of how *much* more than others I had.

ॐ

I had no serious thoughts for the future, nor was I particularly aware of nuns, never having spoken seriously with one. They were people removed from me by yards of habit, their peaceful faces peering out from under starched white headdresses.

The Church required confession only once a year. My mother saw to it that we attended four or five times. Such frequency imposed upon my free time. I hated getting dressed up in the middle of a Saturday afternoon to go to church, but Mother insisted.

On our way there, she would begin telling us what to say.

"Now, Shirley, tell Father that you talked back to your mother and that you quarreled with Joyce."

Finally I grew old enough to say, "Mother, it is my conscience. I will tell the priest what I want to!"

One of the nuisances of confession was having to line up and await one's turn. After that inconvenience, one must again wait, on one's knees in the tiny confessional, for the Father to open his window. It was also necessary to know the number of days since one's last confession, and to give an accurate accounting; plus there was a proper form which one had to use to address the priest.

When it was over, I could never get out into the sunlight fast enough. And there, we would quarrel over something meaningless, which would cause my mother to wonder what good confession had done us.

ॐ

At seventeen, I was graduated from high school.

For years I had known that the next step would be a "good" college. It would be coeducational, or, if not, it would be affiliated with, or in proximity to, a boys' college.

The time had come for me to begin making choices of my own.

2

Slumming

St. Mary's was not my first choice for a college. I had applied to Duke, but there were too many applicants, and my name was placed on a waiting list.

After graduation from Miss Harris' in June, our entire family took a trip across country, considering the merits of various colleges. We stopped at Duke, where we kept an appointment with the dean of admissions, hoping to expedite my entrance.

In the midst of the interview the dean was called away for a few minutes. I got up and walked to the window to look out over the campus. As I returned to my chair I passed her desk on which a manila envelope containing my records had been placed, and I could scarcely believe what I saw!

Written across the envelope in large letters was the word "Catholic."

Trembling, I returned to my seat beside my parents.

The dean returned and the interview continued pleasantly, though I scarcely heard it. I saw only the word "Catholic" written in a bold hand. I, Shirley Dyckes, was on the outside. A gate had been slammed across my path because of my religion.

When I returned to the car, I broke into tears. For a time, my parents were as puzzled and heartbroken as I. Only later did we realize that the religious designation on my file had not meant to discriminate against me personally, but was to remind a clerk who maintained the files that since Duke was a university associated with the United Methodist Church, qualifying applicants from this denomination must be given first priority. And indeed, on my return to Miami, I found my acceptance letter from Duke. But to a seventeen-year-old girl crying in the back seat of a car for most of the long drive to Washington, D.C., it was an overwhelming lesson on being on the wrong side of discrimination.

In Washington we considered Trinity College, which is across the street from Catholic University (a coed campus). A nun escorted us about, answering our questions. When we came to the social life of the Trinity girls, she pointed out that many parties were held at all-male Georgetown University, across town. She enthusiastically described some of these outings—the girls riding off to dances in the college buses, the boys following in their cars.

I lost interest in Trinity College.

Our next stop was St. Mary's, which borders the campus of Notre Dame in South Bend, Indiana. The entire family fell in love with the space, the foliage, the opportunities for study, and the apparently never-ending supply of men. Plus, my father loved to watch football. With a daughter at St. Mary's, he would have easy access to the Notre Dame games.

One of those decisions in life which one makes, not totally aware of their significance at the time, was made. I enrolled at St. Mary's, thus choosing an avenue which would lead me to different personalities, opportunities, and happenings than if I had turned at that time in another direction. My mother, in the future, was many times to regret my choice of St. Mary's, but I was blissfully happy there. My experiences at college led me to the convent, and my years in the convent, joyous in themselves, also played a significant part in my preparation to become Mrs. Clarence Kelley.

It was summer. I had never experienced winter. Indeed, I had experienced little of life. My parents had not lived it for me, but they had cotton-padded, cautioned, cared for me, and would have abraded any rough spots, if any had occurred. On campus I would be away from them for the first time. I would be away from Joyce. I would be on my own. To me this looked like a marvelous adventure. Freedom! Not from my parents, but from suburbia. An entire new world lay before me. I could scarcely wait to explore it.

In September I settled into life at St. Mary's. I loved everything about the college except the adjoining convent. The convent seemed to be a little world of its own within the reaches of my new one. There was mystery about it, not an attractive mystery. It was a complex of dormitories and study halls, an infirmary for aging nuns, a priest's house, and administrative offices. A working farm which contributed to the nuns' meals was also a part of it. One thing that disturbed me about the convent was its silence. It seemed abnormal to have young people ensconced in such an atmosphere. Our section of the campus was active with brightly clad figures moving swiftly about, noisy and vivacious with life. By contrast, the convent was inhabited with soundlessly moving, mute beings clothed in black and white. The whole idea of the convent turned me off. The idea of living amid those nuns seemed the end of the world.

All freshmen at St. Mary's were required to take a course in theology. My teacher was a dynamic woman of about thirty, Sister Charles Borromeo. I had not expected to like this course, but soon found its study to be an exhilarating, freeing experience. All my life I had had questions in my mind about the meaning of life and death, and in my studies I began to find the answers.

Once, when I was ill, as a child of perhaps eight or nine years of age, my mother had bought me an encyclopedia for children. In it I saw a picture of the world floating in space. The thought of the world all alone in a terrible void terrified me. For some reason I had not previously realized that the world was round and that it was not solidly anchored down. I read the description of the universe, and the entire concept impressed me as frighteningly awesome. I felt helpless of wresting myself from this undependable world, or situation. It did not occur to me to seek within my church or religious classes a possible source of explanation of the phenomenon of life. In theology class I was relieved to find, at last, some answers to my innumerable questions. Religion filled the empty spaces in my heart and mind, and I began to feel a reason for living. For the first time I was made to feel that every waking minute of one's day could contribute to a better future, both here and hereafter.

Sister Madaleva, the president of St. Mary's, herself a Chaucer scholar, invited several guest speakers from about the world to address us. Baroness Stauffenberg lectured to us on Christianity under Nazi Hitler, and Sir Shane Leslie addressed us on British royal history. Dr. Charles DeKonick, of Canada, spoke on the philosophy of dress.

To my mind one of the most memorable speakers was Sister Olivette, a Holy Cross nun who had been in Manila when the Japanese had captured it. She had been interned at Los Baños for several years. Seasons came and went, banana trees blossomed and bore fruit before the starving prisoners' eyes, but even when they fell rotting to the ground, they were not allowed to eat them.

Sister Olivette told of a smartly dressed Japanese officer who every morning would force the ragged prisoners to line up for inspection. As he reviewed their lines, he would place his pistol at the temple of a tortured body and would pull the trigger. Sometimes it fell on an empty chamber. Sometimes the body slumped dead to the ground. He did this twice to Sister Olivette, each time over an empty chamber. The second time she looked him resolutely in the eye.

"Don't you ever do that again," she said.

He never did.

It became clear to me that life was fleeting, and that while I had been playing and wasting my years, many people were doing constructive things. I began to feel a need to make a positive contribution to the world.

There is a prayer that says: "Come Holy Spirit, fill the hearts of thy faithful and kindle within them the fire of thy love . . . so that they shall renew the face of the earth."

I began to understand the idea that a Christian working with Christ could make a better world. In line with this, I received a first understanding of the work of the nuns in the convent that had been so unattractive to me.

There are many orders of nuns in the Catholic Church. At St. Mary's the order was the Congregation of the Holy Cross, whose members held as their model the Mother of God sorrowing at the cross.

This was not to remind one that suffering was good, but that by absorbing some of the suffering of the world, by carrying a cross of present-day problems, one could reduce the suffering of the world and make it a better place. The Sisters of the Holy Cross lived very much a here-today life while at the same time preparing their souls for the next world.

I began to appreciate their work. But to join them? I never considered it! A few of my friends from the theology class thought the nun's long black habits picturesque. Not I!

Sister Charles Borromeo made a deep impression on my young life, opening to me the doors of intellectualism which I had not even suspected were there. Afternoons, after classes, Sister would invite four or five girls to walk about the farm on St. Mary's campus with her. As we walked the lanes, one of the girls would read poetry aloud. For the first time in my life, I was thrown into an intellectual atmosphere, and I found it heady stuff, endlessly fascinating in its depth and beauty. It was like throwing myself into ocean surf after having spent a lifetime splashing about in a wading pool.

Besides my studies, I became fully immersed in college life. I was elected secretary of my class and began meeting and sharing the personalities of my 149 classmates; and I enjoyed my share of the ten-to-one ratio of Notre Dame boys. We had marvelous parties and balls. But before I could attend the first of these, I had a brief run-in with Sister Samantha. She told me that St. Mary's girls did not wear strapless evening dresses! Before I was allowed to leave the dormitory, I had to have some absolutely worthless, but fairly innocuous ribbons sewn into my gown!

Other items in my wardrobe caused comment. Some of my convent-educated classmates offered advice. My darling black lace pumps might be considered inappropriate, and a gorgeous red dress with a black velvet collar might be a problem. I had never heard that "ladies don't wear red dresses." In spite of this disapproval, I continued to wear the dress. Sometimes I even wore it with my black patent-leather pumps! Until I attended St. Mary's, I had not heard that these, too, were considered unladylike—that there was a possibility that if they were polished to a high shine, they might reflect the upper leg to a careful observer.

Slumming

ॐ

In October our house held its annual Halloween party, and a girl from Alabama and I were chosen to gather cornstalks from a field about a mile or so distant to use as decorations. It is difficult for me now to believe our naïveté. When Cindy and I set out on "our walk," it was snowing. Such delightful stuff, snow! Neither of us had ever seen it before. It fell about us like drifting, dazzling stars, and was so soft and quiet underfoot. We danced and played in it!

A slippery, slidy, frigid hour or so later, two half-frozen southern girls had become acquainted with winter in the north. Our fingers and cheeks were frostbitten, and our thin coats and shoes soaked through. But triumphantly, we brought home the cornstalks.

ॐ

In the spring of my freshman year I had an experience that began to set my course for the choice of a vocation.

One of my friends, Bridget Mallory, whom I was coming to enjoy more and more, told me she was going to the Chicago Commons with several girls and the assistant dean of upperclass women.

I wanted to go. Not only would I have an overnight visit in Chicago, but I would be permitted to skip Friday's classes. St. Mary's was run on a strict go-or-go-home basis. Students were there to be educated. Skipping classes, unless one was ill, was absolutely not countenanced. I was delighted when room was found for me to join the group, *if* I had my parents' permission.

I made one of my more famous collect calls to Miami.

My father answered the phone and I told him I wanted to go to the slums of Chicago on a field trip where I would stay at a social-work house with a supervisor and some of the girls.

"What's that?" he demanded to know. "A *work* house?" He was almost stuttering. "A house of . . . ill repute?

"No, a social-work house."

I barely finished my sentence before he interrupted. "I work hard so you don't have to live in a slum, and you want to *visit* one! I pay money to send you to one of the finest colleges in the country, to get an education, and the next thing I know, you want to spend the night in Chicago. A dangerous place at best! And you want to sleep in its slums!"

I did everything but cry.

And, of course, eventually, I won.

Amid the countless blocks of dingy tenement housing, the Chicago Commons was a glimmer of hope for the poor. Our group from St. Mary's was given a small apartment on an upper floor which, it was explained to us, was kept for the temporary use of people evicted from their homes.

We toured the establishment and studied its programs for the poor and the elderly. There was a sewing room, game room, crafts room, and health facilities. But through every window the gray light of Chicago sloped in, and through them I saw the dark caverns of streets between crowded buildings. The people seemed gray too—somber, heads down, shuffling. Gray in dress and mood.

At dinner we met the staff, which included college students from Wellesley and Antioch. The dining room was handsomely appointed with heavy carved chairs and a beautiful table. (Here, as in many convents, fine furniture is often willed by an interested donor.) Our dinner was excellent. I could see that the sociology majors working there were not uncomfortable. They were not making any sacrifices. They were being paid for their work. What I am trying to say is, they were *at* the scene, but *not a part of it*. I felt comfortable with them. We were not there to work, but to observe, and to be educated to the fact that certain situations existed. There was no thought of our becoming personally involved.

But on my return to St. Mary's I found myself awake to a whole new dimension of the world. Again I was brought to realize that people did important, unselfish things with their lives.

I returned to my sociology classes aware that I was studying "sociology between book covers," not real-life sociological problems which I could see and smell.

During spring vacation at home I was pleased when my father asked me about my slum trip. It provided an opening to discuss an angle of the topic which had deeply disturbed me and about which I had given much thought. I described my visit to him, and the people I had met. Then I told him that in discussing the conditions in Chicago with a sister at St. Mary's, she had told me that some of the sons and daughters of the slum lords who owned those degrading tenements were educated at St. Mary's and Notre Dame. She had countered that by adding that sometimes those same young people, upon graduation from college, entered the slums in social roles, determined to compensate for the injustices perpetrated by their parents.

Frankly, as I told my father this, I was in considerable torment. Until I had talked with the sister I had never given a thought to what my father's investments might be.

"It must be a terrible thing," he said, "for a man to know that his comfort is provided at the cost of suffering to others." His eyes met mine. "How good it is to be able to go to bed at night with a clear conscience, having honestly earned my money."

"How good it is," I thought with relief, "to be your daughter."

Summer arrived, and ahead lay weeks of a carefree life of swimming pools, tennis courts, boating, and dinner dances. But! I had brought home a failing mark in French. I understood French. My poor grade resulted from preferring to study theology and Chaucer!

I enrolled in the summer school progam at Barry (Catholic) College for a course in French literature, and while I was there signed up for ethics. Joyce, who would enter St. Mary's in September, drove me to my classes and took a course in typing.

Can you imagine our surprise when we arrived on campus the first day to find that except for possibly twenty-five of us, all the other students were nuns! For the first time in my life I was in daily contact with nuns on a peer level. I discovered them to be enjoyable people with great senses of humor, not the strange creatures they had seemed as I saw them from afar across the campus at St. Mary's.

There was a beautiful little chapel at Barry, and I frequently dropped in to pray. Meditation, I had learned at college, added a richness to my life which I found in no other source.

My afternoons were crowded with seeing former friends and the old routine of boating with Clark, tennis, swimming, and relaxing. I had a lot of time to think. More often than I liked, I would find myself thinking of those with lives less favored than mine. I imagined what a hot summer meant to those lonely poor people in Chicago. Such thoughts left me less than satisfied with life in Miami as I knew it.

At the end of summer I told my parents that I had decided on my major. It would be theology.

There were shocked by this.

"Why don't you take up home economics?" my mother asked.

"I think you might find an excellent future in commerce," my father stated.

"Theology fascinates me," I said staunchly.

"What future can there be for a woman in theology?" my father wondered.

My mother quizzed me closely. "Is it the sisters?" she asked. "Are they pressuring you?"

I assured her they were not. We had several "discussions" on my choice.

In the fall I returned to St. Mary's almost with a sigh of relief. I felt as though I had been treading water all summer, and that now I could stroke out and swim for the shore. I did not know what was on that shore, but I was pretty sure it was not the city of Miami!

ॐ

In November of my sophomore year Bridget suggested that we should do some further study of the slums of Chicago, but, she felt, we would never be able to observe true conditions if we arrived heralded as a study group. Just the two of us should do some exploring on our own.

I was all for that, but I knew my parents had been less than enthusiastic about my well-supervised trip of the previous spring. They were not likely to back me in an adventure accompanied only by a classmate. We would have to circumvent the authority of both the dean of women and our parents.

The following weekend a group was signing up for a tour of the Art Institute of Chicago. We placed our names on the list, figuring we would play the rest of the project by ear.

Many times in our theology class we had heard Sister Charles Borromeo mention the St. Martin de Porres House in the Black Belt of Chicago. That seemed a likely place for our study.

St. Martin de Porres was a black Dominican brother from Lima, Peru. He was one of the first two canonized saints of the Western Hemisphere. Since he was a poor black in Peru, he was qualified to enter a religious order as a lay brother. (To the uninformed in the stratifications of the Catholic Church hierarchy, I should explain that

21

lay sisters and brothers in orders do the maintenance work, as compared to educated priests and sisters who teach and work in professional pursuits.) St. Martin became a saint admired by many, especially by black Americans. In the fifties there was a notable lack of blacks in the Catholic Church, although in the past ten years there has been an influx of converts.

Before starting out on our venture, Bridget and I carefully considered our wardrobes. We realized it was necessary to dress as well as the rest of the girls so that they wouldn't wonder about us, but still, we wished to wear the most plain and serviceable clothes we owned, the better to fit into the landscape of Chicago's slums.

After lunch in Chicago, we "lost" the art group and found the bus that would take us to the Black Belt. Bridget and I were the only two white people on the bus. We were also the only females. Our attempt at down-playing our clothes was a failure. We stood out like two manicured thumbs on a workman's hands. We could feel all eyes upon us. All conversation ceased.

In later years, under circumstances like that, the habit of the Congregation of the Holy Cross would be a great comfort to me. When I met the poor, they identified with me, and I belonged to them. How different it was when a person from a different stratum of society visited the slums! The eyes upon us were suspicious and questioning. We wished only to show goodwill to these people, but there was a gulf between us. Our clothes, our carriage, our countenances, separated us.

We could not have missed the Social House. It announced itself with an enormous plaster statue of St. Martin in his white and black habit from the window of the storefront building.

The door was unlocked, and we entered into a large room, about the size of a neighborhood store, which it was apparent the room had once been. A white woman, in her late thirties, looked up from her writing as we entered and asked what she could do for us. We explained that we were friends of Sister Charles Borromeo and had come to see how the house functioned and what their programs were.

The lady introduced herself as Elvira and offered to show us about her quarters. We went up two steps to a room which was obviously for dining. Behind it was a large room with a linoleum floor, a kitchen table which would seat six, and a counter for working. On this level there was also a bathroom, and upstairs a bedroom or two.

As we toured, we met the rest of the staff—Mrs. Murphy, a kind-faced lady of about sixty who acted as housekeeper, Ralph, in his thirties, who was holding a broken chair and spoke of repairing it, and Al, a clean-cut, gentle-eyed, athletic black man, who was in his twenties. Al provided a constructive recreation program for the local kids, and gave them guidance, as did Ralph.

The most striking thing about this place was that it was so obviously poor. There was no private area for the staff, and none of the finer accommodations as at Chicago Commons. There was also something else. Radiating from the faces of these four people seemed overwhelming kindness, an outgoing love for their involvement with work and people. They weren't people from college taking a course in practical sociology. There was no discussion of sociological tendencies, of programs being implemented, of seminars and workshops attended. These people blended with the people with whom they worked. The only thing that marked them as different from the rest of the people in that bleak neighborhood was their radiant faces. They spent the afternoon explaining their work to us, which was to bring Christ to the slums, to help all those in need, and to give guidance.

Ralph pointed out to us the decrepit building next door where a woman was living with five children. Her husband had left her, he told us. The basement she was renting had a partially dirt floor. Its lights were hanging bulbs. There was a minimum of plumbing. For this she paid about $135 a month. After she paid her rent, she had almost nothing left. When we asked why she did not leave, he said she had no other place to go. The woman was ignorant. She had no idea how to get out of her situation.

This case horrified me. For the first time in my life I was sincerely outraged. I had heard about slumlords. Now I knew they were real.

About five o'clock Mrs. Murphy invited us to share their supper. Bridget and I glanced at each other and knew we could not refuse. While we sat at the kitchen table Mrs. Murphy brought out two cans of soup, tomato and celery. She dumped these together in a saucepan. While the soup heated she cleaned some half-rotten tomatoes, carefully cutting away the spoiled sections. She added scraps of lettuce to this for a salad. She brought out bread and a jar of peanut butter, and made a pot of tea, and placed all this before us on the linoleum-topped table. That was our dinner. I was impressed that these dear people happily shared what they had had for four, and stretched it to feed six.

Immediately after dinner Al excused himself to go gather up some young people for a basketball game.

Bridget and I looked out the window. It was dark! We had not realized how late it was. It was almost our curfew hour. We would never be able to make it back to campus in time.

As quickly as possible we said good-bye and hurried out into the poorly lit streets. Somewhere we must find the Elevated that would take us to the Southshore Station where we would get the train for the hour-and-a-half ride back to South Bend.

Bridget fussed at every step. Did I hear anyone following? Was this the right turn to the El? Why hadn't we watched the time?

Was I worried?

No, I was in a state of euphoria. I had never known such Christian people. I was immeasurably impressed by what I had seen. Those people each had an inner quality, Elvira, Mrs. Murphy, Ralph, and Al, that was truly inspired. To me, they were like candles radiating through the darkness of despair on that street.

I talked on and on about them.

We found the stairs to the El, and climbed them, Bridget grumbling on every step.

"Get off your cloud, Shirley. We're in trouble. Why did we ever stay for supper? It's already past curfew."

I was unconcerned. I could think only of those four sincere people.

"The art group will be home," Bridget fretted. "They will know we aren't with them."

Still, I did not join her worrying.

"Perhaps," she said, "you might start considering how we are going to face the obvious fact that we have been down in the slums all day, by ourselves, without permission from school or home."

I paid no attention to her.

She grabbed me. "Shirley," she said forcibly, "will you just look around this platform and see what kind of characters there are?"

I looked.

They were not savory. They were the same type of people we had seen on the bus in the early afternoon, but they were more worn, more dirty, and many of them were tipsy from drink. They were also staring at us. As I came out of my reverie I felt the cold, and saw the dark, and recognized our precarious position. We were two young white girls, unescorted, obviously defenseless, probably with money in our pockets, quite all alone. I began to see that Bridget had a point. But we had no choice except to wait for the El.

Having once accepted that, I immediately returned to the intellectual enjoyment and the emotional ecstasy I had gathered within myself from having peeked into the lives of four people who were spending their lives radiating such Christlike hope and confidence in such a desolate setting.

ॐ

God must have had something better for me than being murdered on a Chicago elevated platform. The train arrived and we made it back to school. And more than that! Fortune of good fortune, our beloved and understanding Sister Charles Borromeo was at the reception desk. She unlocked the door and let us in and promised to keep our story to herself. Of course she had a few sobering thoughts for us. She reminded us that violations of school rules should not be taken lightly. Even with good works as a motivation, she said, we might find ourselves expelled. But she enjoyed hearing of our day.

I went to bed still in an ethereal state—removed from myself, yet closer to myself than ever before in my life. In my mind I did not see the squalor of the day. I saw those four plain people who were giving their lives toward the healing of incurable social ills, and they were beautiful. Those four would have been the last to indicate that their efforts were, in any form, a sacrifice. They believed in what they were doing, and that their cause would succeed. Against the wretchedness of the poverty I had seen, their faces were indeed beacons sending their lights afar. They had discovered their purpose in life, and were living it. My frivolous, securely protected station in life seemed impoverished by comparison to the gift of spirit these four had received.

As I silently repeated my prayers there began to grow in me a sense of arrival. At last I knew my destination. I would declare for the religious life.

3

In or Out?

When I have made major decisions in my life it has been without histrionics. I did not ask my parents "if" I should enter religious life. I did not sit around the dormitory endlessly discussing my thoughts with friends, as they, in easy chatter, examined the personalities of their boyfriends, their home lives, and their futures. I was not silent, of course, but I did not lay out my personal concerns like linen stretched at a quilting bee for all my friends to work upon.

My sister, Joyce, was enrolled on the same campus. I saw her frequently, but I did not take her into my confidence about what I was considering. A decision as serious to me as deciding to enter religious life could not be determined by a committee. Dedication of purpose in life, love, or duty was, to me, a personal responsibility, something which I alone could decide and perform.

There were three times a year when one might enter the convent, January 1, and the first of August and September. I wrote to the mother general declaring my intention, and asked to enter on the first of August of the following year. I had no doubt that I would be accepted. It would be unnecessary for me to take intelligence tests, as I was already enrolled at St. Mary's, and my health records were also a part of their files. As far as qualifying in character—well, I *had* asserted myself rather visibly in wearing that red dress, but I knew Sister Charles Borromeo would attest to my sincerity!

I suppose the idea of a girl entering a convent gives rise to many reactions, but to me, at nineteen, it struck me as a good and great adventure. Having written the letter, I began to grow more and more enthusiastic about my decision. It was *right*. Knowing one is heading in the right direction is an exhilarating experience.

୫ତ

One day I heard that Bridget was ill and confined to bed. I went to her room and found her propped up on pillows, looking far from her usual carefree self, surrounded by books and Kleenex.

"Don't come close," she said. "I've got a horrible cold."

I assured her I wouldn't.

"You look like a cat who swallowed a whole tank of goldfish," she said. "What's so great about the world?"

I really hadn't meant to share my news with anyone yet, but after all, Bridget had been most active in opening the door for my decision to walk through. I told her of my decision to enter religious life.

Her reaction was astonishing. She was furious with me!

"Some great thing!" she stormed. "Shirley Dyckes has her life all figured out—no doubts, no decisions, no problems! You come waltzing in here and tell me your decision is all made!"

I was taken aback. Here was the friend who had thought working for the poor was such a great idea. She had braved the dangers of the slums with me. . . .

Then the truth came out.

"I've been thinking about it myself," Bridget said gloomily. "I don't know what *else* I can do. I *hate* the thought of the convent. I hate it! But . . . I feel an obligation."

She looked at me as though seeking reassurance, or guidance. I knew I should give her none. The decision to enter religious life, if it came, must come from within herself.

Personally, I was amazed at her statement. I could scarcely think of a more unlikely candidate for the convent than unregimentable Bridget Mallory. I knew that she was interested in the Apostolate, but I had never given a thought to her becoming a religious. I should define

Apostolate, which differentiates the Christian who attends church and prays on his knees from the Christian who goes out to carry Christianity into the lives of others. The Apostolate is the latter.

Bridget continued to study me hopefully.

"I know that once I get *in*," she said, "once I make the decision, I will be happy. But I just hate it!"

This philosophy is one which I would never have understood before going to St. Mary's, but it is beautifully simple. Everyone in the world wants to be happy. In Catholicism we were taught that one will find true happiness when one lives one's vocation. In my own life, I certainly found this to be true. Once the decision had been made, and the sacrifice of going into the convent had taken place, I was truly happy.

Bridget continued to waver.

"I suppose I could take a shot at it," she said rather irreverently. Then she looked off into space. "But I think I will go to Europe . . . first."

১৯

A few days later Joyce came into my room.

She said, "You are going to enter the convent, aren't you?"

"Yes, I am," I replied.

Darling Joyce burst into tears, words tumbling out between sobs. I finally made out what she was saying.

"Now . . . you won't . . . be able . . . to be . . . in my wedding."

"But Joyce, you aren't even in love yet."

"But I will be," she sobbed, "and I'll get engaged and be married, and it will be a beautiful wedding, and I want you to be in it."

It took explaining to tell Joyce why I felt my life must go the way I had chosen. Then her eyes widened. "Shirley," she said, "what will Mother and Daddy say?"

Actually, I was so totally convinced of my decision that I had not given much thought to how my years within the convent, with only rare visits home, would affect those who loved me most. I had no desire to hurt my parents, even fleetingly, but my decision was irreversible.

Joyce came to my aid. Suddenly she was all business.

"Let's not let this ruin Christmas vacation. The first night we are home we'll sit down with Mother and Daddy and get it over with, and I'll be on your side."

I was to remember her staunch alliance years later when Joyce had a confrontation of her own.

The problem at hand, of course, involved more than two teen-aged girls standing together to assert the right of the older to test her wings. I was declaring my life to the convent, consecrating my mind and body to the Church, thus totally removing myself for long periods of time from my parents' sight. From the moment of entering the convent I would release myself forever from their guidance. That would not be my parents' choice for me. For nineteen years they had enjoyed every stage of my development, and they had expected that that would continue for as long as they lived. They would share me, and enjoy the ongoing family life that they anticipated through me, and a marriage, and children, and grandchildren, toward which they had spent their lives preparing me. Yes, I realized, my news would not make them happy.

But it was impossible to keep joy out of my voice as I told them my decision on the first evening of vacation that we were home. I felt like a Christmas bell ringing.

I watched the faces before me, hoping they would share my happiness, and saw them undergo swift changes as they realized what I was saying. Tears came to my mother's eyes, and then anger. She did not focus it on me, but on the Church.

"We were a happy family," she lamented, "with no problems until Catholic schools entered our lives. Now where are we? Shirley, it was better when you did not know so much about religion. Oh, why did I ever let you enroll at St. Mary's? For two years we have had nothing but trouble over religion."

My father found his voice.

"Here you are," he said, "a young lady exposed to the finest education the city of Miami offered. Since kindergarten we have given you the best schooling. Then at three thousand dollars a year tuition you had to go down into the slums. We always avoided the poor sections of Miami, but for thousands of dollars a year you had to go traipsing off to visit the slums of Chicago!"

"It was the nuns!" my mother said. "They talked you into this, didn't they, Shirley? You could not have come to this decision—to leave us—by yourself." By then she was weeping.

"I should have known when you chose theology as your major," my father said, "that the next step would be the convent. When you go a way, Shirley," he said, looking downcast, "you go *all* the way."

It was a sad evening. My mother seemed to feel, not that I was

29

dying, but that I was relinquishing most of my life. To her, a good life meant a husband, daughters, a comfortable home, and a pleasant social life. I would have none of those. For me to forsake all the accouterments which she knew to contribute to her happiness and well-being for the poverty and singleness of the convent was a drastic reversal in her plans for me.

On Christmas morning my father decided our period of mourning had continued long enough.

"Lillian," he said to my mother, "no more crying. It is obvious Shirley has made up her mind. Let's have a good time for as long as she is with us."

I returned to St. Mary's eager to do especially well in my classes and to begin to prepare myself for the life which would start in August. Of course I was dating, attending Notre Dame games, and movies and dances, having a marvelous time. I dated several boys, not concentrating on any one. Usually they were rather serious-minded. Our encounters were more fun and discussion than flirting engagements. August seemed a long way off, and I did not mention that my future would be in the convent. I did not want to have to face the query of *why?* I did not want my decision to be taken lightly, or to be the butt of frivolous argument.

One day Bridget reminded me that after August 1 there would be no more strolling around campus hand in hand with *any* boy, ever again. Thinking about that, I decided to give up boys for Lent. I cannot report that it was the best time of my life—six weeks was a long time. But I did it, and lost some friends. One boy seemed to feel that my no-dating vow was an affront to the entire male population. Another told me the idea was so silly he would scratch my name off his list.

Scott did something else. He wrote to me.

I had met him in December when I attended the wedding of a friend who married a man from Notre Dame. At the wedding breakfast a tall, blue-eyed boy was seated by my side. It was Scott, who was a senior at Notre Dame. He was delighted to discover that I attended St. Mary's.

When we began talking, almost his first words were that he had worked in the slums of Chicago! He told me that in his curiosity to know true conditions in the slums, he had taken a job with an ice company and had spent the hot summer delivering ice in some of the worst parts of the city. He had carried cakes of ice up four or five flights of stairs only to discover when he reached the top that the people had no money to pay for it. Time and time again, he gave them the ice, making up the amount to the ice distributor out of his paycheck.

The coincidence of our interest in the slums seemed very special to us. When I left the reception, Scott escorted me to my taxi, and as it drove away, pelted me with rice, which he had not thrown at the bride.

I had had several dates with him. When Lent arrived and I told him of my no-date sacrifice, he looked very thoughtful. Then he smiled and said,

"I'll write to you, Shirley."

It seemed a crazy thing, to be right next door, and mail letters, but he insisted.

"I'm going to be a lawyer," he said. "I have a case to state. I will write."

"But I don't think I should answer," I said doubtfully. "It would be contacting you."

He truly had a great smile, a wide mouth with strong white teeth and curling lips.

"I'll wait," he said.

His letters, all through Lent, arrived with surprising frequency. They told me a great deal about him.

My first day back from Easter vacation, my phone rang.

It was Scott. He was downtown, he said, and would like to come out for the afternoon.

"There's just one thing," he warned. "I came off in just a sweater. No coat."

There was a strict rule in regard to young gentlemen visiting the campus. They must be attired in a coat and wear a necktie. I reminded Scott of this.

"But I am only wearing a sweater. It's a nice sweater." He laughed. "It even has all its buttons."

I could just imagine him in that phone booth, big fellow that he was, peering down, counting his buttons. My heart pounded. How I wanted to see him! But I didn't want to get into any trouble.

Again I reviewed with him the rules and regulations of St. Mary's.

He responded immediately. "I know the rules and regulations, and I have on a blue sweater. May I come anyway?"

I said yes.

In or Out?

When he arrived I was at the door, ready to whisk him out of sight before anyone saw him and ordered him off campus. I had never seen anyone more handsome in a sweater. The blue matched his eyes, and when he smiled at me I felt as though both my feet were off the ground.

If we remained on campus, we were sure to come within the range of vision of some of the nuns. We headed for the dirt road I had walked many times with Sister Charles Borromeo while we read poetry and discussed theology. Scott and I hurried along it to a more remote lane which was off limits to both Notre Dame boys and St. Mary's girls. Beyond was a woods and a glen.

It was a magic afternoon. I loved hearing his crisp male voice. His strong fingers linked through mine were like an electric conduit. He was a most exciting person. Everything he said seemed wise and bright and meaningful to me. I was utterly happy to be with him.

Scott would be graduating in June, and in the fall would enter law school at Notre Dame. How great it would be that we would continue to be near each other, he said. He intended to use his degree to work for just housing in the slums of Chicago. Someday he would be a lawyer for the poor. He would give away his services.

I laughed. "Like the ice."

"Like the ice. Whatever I can do, wherever I can do it, I want to serve."

He repeated some of the things he had said in his letters. He had found a girl to whom he could pour out his dreams, a girl who had the same compassion for humanity that he had, the same need within her to help the struggling poor. We walked through the quiet woodland, under the leaves. I felt I could have walked on and on, my hand in his.

I loved him. With every step and every word, I knew I loved him. I had been in love with him all spring. With the arrival of every letter, I had known and loved him more. I had not permitted myself to recognize or acknowledge it, but, for the first time in my life, I was in love.

At the edge of the woods he took me in his arms to kiss me. It was the moment I had been anticipating almost since our first meeting, when we had first spoken together. Since then I had come to know him. I felt he was all I had ever hoped a man might be.

I stood close against him, within the circle of his arms, not daring to look up. I was afraid to lift my face. If he kissed me . . . if I let him kiss me . . .

My life was so neatly planned. It was all precisely arranged in my

32

mind, each detail fitting into the next like a nearly completed jigsaw puzzle of an arrow pointing toward August 1.

"Scott," I said, ". . . wait . . ."

I stepped back from him and studied his face. There was such love and understanding there, such maturity and wisdom, that I almost fled back into his embrace.

Just beyond where we were standing was a small chapel of Loretto—a place where boys and girls from the colleges often came to make private prayers. I took Scott's hand, and together we went into the chapel and knelt on adjoining prie-dieus before the tiny altar.

As I closed my eyes, all I could see was his face.

"Dear God," I prayed. "I could be happy with him." My prayers stopped there. I could not think beyond. Where did I go from there? Where did I go? "I love him, God," I prayed. "Help me to see the way."

We left the chapel hand in hand. Just beyond was a little ravine. We walked to its edge without speaking.

My future seemed at the brink. I had firmly made my decision to enter the convent, yet if I loved Scott, my declaration would go tumbling into oblivion. I loved this tall blue-eyed young man, and yearned to submit my will to his. But I was equally certain that my life's work could only be pursued through the convent.

We returned quietly to my dormitory in the almost-twilight, both of us filled with searching thoughts. I found myself loving him beyond all else for his patience with me, for understanding my need to think.

We said good-bye, and I watched his jaunty but illegal sweater swing out of sight under the trees toward Notre Dame.

We had spent the whole afternoon together, he in the wrong attire, and both of us in a forbidden area, without being found out.

Back in my room I faced the alternatives before me. I could never see Scott again, or I could see him, give up the convent, become engaged and married to him, and help him in his work in Chicago. I was drawn to the second choice. But my thoughts carried beyond.

For a Catholic woman, marriage was not complete without children, and sometimes God gave them with astonishing regularity. I was willing to take a vow of poverty for myself, but I could not see myself married to an idealist who was willing to accept radical destitution. If I were to have children, I could not willfully raise them in a state of privation.

Scott had the right to dedicate his life to free service to the poor. But was it right for a woman, with the burdens of marriage, to join him?

For the next several weeks I thought almost constantly of Scott and the dilemma of loving him. I prayed to God to take my vocation from me, to free me. I prayed to be shown the way to turn to this understanding, loving man. My thought of life with him far outranked my thoughts of the Apostolate those spring days. Sometimes I was so drawn to him I thought I would throw in my lot with him no matter what the consequences. I dearly loved him. If he kissed me, I would give myself to him. I was as eager for him as all the other creatures of nature which were sending forth their messages of acceptance. I dared not see him.

When he phoned, I had my roommate answer and say I was unavailable. I knew if I saw him, I would be able to refuse him nothing.

It was in such a moment, when I yearned to see him, to touch his hand and walk beside him, listening to his voice, that within my mind I had a vision.

I was thinking of Scott and felt myself surrounded by his kindness and confidence. Suddenly, his face within my mind changed. I saw an older Scott standing before me, gray at the temples, his face worn. In this vision I saw myself as about forty years old. Behind me were numerous children. On my beloved's face I saw forbearance. He was no longer looking at me with loving eyes. I had weighed him down. He was tied into marriage and burdened with our children. He was no longer free to do the things in life he had sincerely wished to accomplish.

I believed what I saw in my mind's eye. It was not the answer to my prayers for which I had beseeched God. But it was God's will.

I would enter the convent.

One day my roommate, Carol, told me that Scott had called and had asked her if it was true that I was going to enter the convent. She had told him yes. She studied me thoughtfully before saying, "What a wonderful Catholic couple you two would have made."

I suffered. It was not easy to stop loving him. It was agony to realize I was causing anquish to him.

Scott had his dedication. I had mine. I would accomplish mine through the convent, where, when I took the required vow, I, too, would know poverty, though the basic necessities of life would be retained. I would live in an atmosphere of dignity and niceness denied the poor.

In 1953 the must-marry theory was still prevalent. It would be some years before it was more widely recognized that in many careers, marriage did not fit. Marriage is a responsibility to another person, or persons if it includes children. In the careers of many dedicated people there simply is not time to do a competent job in both fields. To me at nineteen, that was heartbreakingly apparent. I relinquished the thought of marriage to uphold my choice.

In many little ways I had begun preparing for my life ahead. I had long been aware that nuns were early risers. Bridget, who was still thinking of entering the convent, after she returned from Europe, and I decided to see if we would be able to get used to getting up before sunrise. We began playing tennis at 5:30 A.M., the same hour the litany services began in the chapel for the nuns. I found early rising not to be difficult, and actually enjoyed being up and active in the early morning freshness. However, we had only played two or three mornings when we were asked to please refrain until a later hour. Our voices, gaily calling out our scores, and the ping of our balls against our rackets were disturbing the nuns at prayer in the chapel with its open windows just above the courts!

For a few mornings after that we quietly joined the nuns at their litanies, but this soon wore off. Again we became sleepyheads like the rest of the girls at St. Mary's.

During Easter vacation at home I had begun sorting out my possessions to give away. The vow of poverty is absolute. Nothing that was mine could remain mine after August 1. It was easy to go through my winter clothes, to think of the pleasure and warmth they would give the people at St. Martin de Porres in Chicago. I wanted to give them everything I owned except what I would use during the summer months.

My mother, however, thought my beautiful muskrat coat would find a better home in the closet of a needy lady of whom she had heard in Miami. She herself decided to keep my 14k gold charm bracelet along with a set of exquisitely embroidered satin lingerie envelopes. To Joyce I gave my cashmere sweater sets. A dear friend admired my black lace evening pumps, and they fit her, so she acquired them.

It must have been painful for my mother to watch me blithely disposing of my worldly goods. I shipped a trunk and two large cartons of clothes, including six fluffy, strapless evening dresses, to St. Martin de Porres. We were able to laugh together over that, wondering who would next be wearing them, and to what kind of a party.

Giving away all the familiar things I had ever owned—my stuffed animals, childhood dolls, trinkets, books, costume jewelry, the few good pieces that I had—all seemed very matter-of-fact. It was a step which I was taking so that I might then take the next step, a step I most sincerely wanted to take. I never once thought as I gave those things away that I would ever see them again. It didn't occur to me that I would leave the convent, once I had entered. This is not true with all girls who become postulants. Many are not sure they will stay, and enter with the thought in mind that they are "just trying it out." Not me! I was sure! Before I departed for South Bend for the last time before entering the convent, I had given away every single thing that I owned except the summer clothes upon my back.

ễ

My decision to enter the convent had brought mixed reactions from many people. My high school sorority sisters decided I was crazy. Karen Wylie was the most vehement among them. She was appalled at my choice.

When I saw dear Dr. James, he wished me well, but I felt a note of sadness in his voice. He covered it by smiling broadly at me, touching my blond hair.

"I hate to see that beautiful head all covered up in bandages," he said.

At the end of July my parents gave a catered dinner party for me, with about twenty-five people present.

Grandmother Dyckes, devout Catholic that she was, was subdued in her congratulations to me. "It is good," she said. "I am proud of you." Then she seemed to feel the need to say something further. "For myself," she said, "I could never bear convent life. I am too independent to stand a life of constant obedience."

I smiled at that dear, wise lady, and wondered if she was trying to tell me something.

I would soon find out!

4

Acquiring
a Habit

"Good Lord, lady," the salesman said, "what are you doing in those god-awful shoes?"

I laughed, looking down at the stout, black, laced, and tied shoes I was trying on. They did not coordinate at all with the mint-green linen short-sleeved dress I was wearing, with its dainty fringe of Irish lace outlining the front panels and edging its Peter Pan collar.

"I need them," I said. "I'm entering the convent tomorrow."

He looked me over in a way I was not to experience again for many years. Then he shook his head. "What a waste," he groaned. "What a waste."

Tomorrow would be August 1, and at last I would begin on my life's work.

I had arrived at South Bend on a noon plane from Miami via Chicago, carrying one small suitcase containing my toilet articles, six granny-style nightgowns—three long-sleeved, high-necked gowns of summer weight and three for winter. We also supplied our own bras-

sieres and girdles or garter belts—things which required too personal a fit
to be supplied by the convent. During the summer I had been in
correspondence with St. Mary's and had been advised to bring "modest
one-piece gowns." No "baby-dolls" or pajamas—two pieces would have
required extra handling in the convent laundry! I was also to bring with
me comfortable shoes. Shoes for nuns were required to be both durable
and supportive to enable her to perform her tasks effectively. The entire
habit was purposeful in design. It was not fashioned for penance, as was
sometimes presumed, but to be practical, efficient, and ladylike.

I stopped in South Bend for my final purchases.

After testing the heavy shoes, I removed them and put on my own
white, sling-heeled, open-toed pumps.

The young salesman returned.

"Good," he said, "I hoped you would change your mind."

I smiled happily. "I'll take three pairs," I said.

With the shoes in a bag, I stopped for my last purchases at a
bookstore. I chose religious books and had them mailed to friends and
family members to encourage them in their thoughts and prayers for
me. Then I took a cab to St. Mary's College, where I would spend the
night.

I think here I might detail, since it has been asked of me many
times, how I might describe a "typical nun"—or a young woman who
might choose to become a nun. She is not the docile, apathetic, or
mooning-over-a-lost-love type of girl one sometimes finds portrayed in
fiction or films. To qualify for a convent, she should be a professional
person of good character, with an outgoing personality, one who is
interested in people—not in *one* person, but in *all* people. The happiest
nun is outgoing, gregarious, and creative.

The Congregation of the Holy Cross, which I was joining, had an
Apostolate which had many freedoms. It received its name in transla-
tion from the Latin *Congregatio Sanctae Crucis*. This Latin form
indicated that it was a papal community, which placed it directly under
the Pope, rather than a diocesan community; it was not answerable to
any one bishop. The nuns of the Holy Cross were generally well
educated, and many were well-traveled women who had entered the
convent after college. In some of the orders, which number about two
hundred in the United States, women enter directly from high school.
They are not necessarily as interested in furthering their educations, and
serve their communities in other ways, rarely traveling much farther

than within the county in which their convent is located. Sisters of the Holy Cross traveled widely throughout the United States.

Arriving at St. Mary's, I presented myself to Sister Sophia, the dean of women, who escorted me to a guest room where I would remain overnight. She showed me my regulation trunk and its contents.

Before entering the convent, each girl is presented with a list of essentials she must have. She is required to have these and no others when she arrives. She may either purchase them independently, or, if she is already known at the convent, the sisters may assemble her things for her with the bill sent to her parents. Since this list is self-descriptive, except, perhaps, for the next to last item, here it is, complete with 1953 prices.

SAINT MARY'S COLLEGE
NOTRE DAME, INDIANA

1		Trunk	31.50 -tax 20%	37.50*
15 yds.		Serge	4.50	67.50
25 "		Muslin	.32	8.00
1¼ "		Batiste	.50	75
1 pr.		Gloves		1.65
1		Robe		11.75
1		Kimona		5.99 99
4		Sheets		6.82
4		Pillow Cases		1.85
1		Umbrella		5.25
1		Spread		5.75
8 pr.		Hose	.85	6.80
3		Aprons		5.73
3		Underskirts		4.62
3		Blk. "		5.73
8		T-shirts		9.20
8		Otis panties		6.00
3		Blouses		4.80
1		Shawl		15.00
1		Liber		6.50
				$207.19

12   *handkerchiefs*   5.75

212.94

Make out check to:
Saint Mary's College, attention — Sister M. Clarice
c.s.c.

---

*Sic.

The "Liber" is a black-bound book with pages edged in red containing the Gregorian chants said by the nuns.

One after another Sister Sophia removed precisely folded items from my trunk, opening them for my inspection while she explained the wearing and the purpose of each garment. There I stood, in my cool linen and my barefoot sandals, the temperature outside registering 98° in the shade, not a leaf wiggling along the treelined drive between St. Mary's campus and Dixie Highway, while Sister showed me, not one, but two, ankle-length cotton petticoats, both to be worn at once, plus a voluminous black woolen serge skirt I would soon be wearing. It looked like a lot of clothes to carry around.

That very morning, only a few hours earlier, I had showered and dressed in Miami, admiring my all but all-over suntan, and had traveled to Chicago dressed in the minimum clothes publicly allowable, and before me looked like about twenty pounds of garments with which I would soon and forever swath myself! I had one bright flash of myself leaping about the tennis courts at home in sleeveless vest and gleaming white shorts, of bathing suits and sundresses, and then I tucked those thoughts away. This was my choice.

Late that afternoon Lettie Miller arrived. I had known her as a freshman at St. Mary's, though she had then been a senior. She was a bright, clever, active young woman. During the year since her graduation from St. Mary's, she had biked through Great Britain, spending her nights at youth hostels. She had also had some adventures on the Mississippi River, where she had traveled for long distances in a canoe. Her exploits when we had been together at St. Mary's had always kept me breathless. I had been delighted when I had heard she would be entering the convent on August 1.

She came into the guest room at St. Mary's where I was sitting alone, awaiting the bell which would assemble us for dinner. This was not the joyous, enthusiastic Lettie I remembered. She was wearing a wrinkled blue cotton denim dress and tennis shoes with no stockings and no makeup. She was hot, and her hair looked as though she had combed it with a wide-toothed rake.

I greeted her, and she was pleased to see me.

"What am I doing here?" she exclaimed. "How did I ever get myself into this?" She paced about the room, stopping at the window where she could gaze across the lawns toward the convent buildings.

"Shirley," she said, "do you *realize* we are going to be limited to that one building over there for two years? Imprisoned—captive . . ." She looked about wildly. "Let's get out of here!"

I had heard of changes of heart by people before taking an irrevocable step, but I was shocked to see this reaction in a person as worldly as Lettie.

I laughed. "Are you a little nervous, Lettie?"

"I resisted," she said. "I fought it all the way. Nobody yearns to be free more than I. But "—and she looked ready to weep—"I kept hearing this call to religious life."

Fortunately, at that point, the bell for dinner rang.

"Let's eat—we'll both feel better," I suggested, and started for the hallway.

She sighed, and turned to follow me.

For the first time she became aware of her appearance and made a quick retreat to the bathroom.

I waited for her, and we moved together down the stairs to the entrance corridor below.

To feel the impact of what I saw there, you must realize that I had never been at St. Mary's during a summer session. Always before, the buildings and walks had been busy with talking, laughing college students. That August, about 150 nuns were using the college buildings. They were making their retreat—in silence.

As Lettie and I entered the long arched hallway, we were astonished to see what seemed to be hundreds of people, each in black and white, from head to toe, all walking toward the dining room and *not saying a word*. There was not the shuffle of one shoe. There was no hint of sound rippling the silence, not even the chink of one rosary bead glancing against another. Before us there was a tremendous, noiseless, forward motion of similarly garbed human beings moving, with neither its beginning nor its end visible to our eyes, a vast army pressing silently onward.

A fact about this scene was that though it then seemed so foreign to me, once I was in the habit, and part of that group, I was never again aware of it. If it had not been for this initial shock of being exposed to all those nuns at once, I would never have understood the awesomeness of the spectacle to the outside world. This vast group was a force. Not a silently moving tide, but a force. A tide is a mindless thing. Nuns are not puppets. In all the years that I lived in the convent, I was never to feel that I had abandoned my decision-making ability for my actions to my superiors. Decisions were made for me as to time and place and duties and meals, but these are not the core of human consciousness or responsibility. I found the Catholic Church, through its convents, to be a great advocate of freedom. I found, through my studies, that indeed, "the truth shall make you free." The essence of man's freedom is in his mind.

Lettie and I tagged along at the end of the column of nuns. She seemed to be almost physically ill. She was unable to eat her dinner, excused herself, and returned upstairs to lie down.

In the morning, she was little better, and spent her breakfast mangling a fresh peach, repeatedly sticking it with a fingernail.

When it was time to leave for the convent, I stopped by her room. Instead of finding a neatly prepared candidate, I found Lettie stretched out on her bed in a rumpled heap, her face a map of swamps and ridges.

"Are you going, or not?" I asked her.

She grunted and slowly sat up. As though she was agreeing to walk the last mile, she said, "Well, I might as well."

We walked toward the novitiate and were joined by Sisters Sophia and Charles Borromeo. The latter was especially sympathetic to Lettie. She revealed that on her own first day at the convent, she had had similar doubts. That seemed to hearten Lettie. By the time we rang the doorbell, she seemed more like herself.

Besides the convent facilities I have previously mentioned there were reception and recreational rooms, a kitchen and dining room, and guest bedrooms for visitors. There was also a room equipped with a dental chair and an examining room for medical needs, where doctors and dentists made charitable contributions of their time and skills to the convent.

As each nun entered the convent, she presented a detailed report of her physical condition. While they were young, medical problems among nuns were rare. In fact, poor health, other than colds, was usually a sign that a sister, either emotionally or physically, should not continue in religious life.

No nun was ever restrained from leaving the convent for any reason. It was felt that an unhappy nun was worse than none at all. If a sister stated her desire to leave, she left quietly, unobtrusively. The next morning she simply was not there.

The novitiate door was opened to us by a smiling novice who knew the sisters and introduced us to Sister Paschal, the substitute mistress of postulants.

In the novitiate at that time, one hundred women were living, but there was not a sound. All the floors were bare, uncarpeted wood, but not one heel clicked. The unadorned walls echoed no sound of people passing, no whisper of human voice. The vast building included dining and service rooms, but there was no clink of utensils, no motors whirred. We seemed to be part of a silent movie.

In the face of this silence, Lettie began to giggle.

For years we had seen the novitiate across the campus, but observing it from a noisy group and becoming part of it was a different experience. It was awesome.

We were sent to a side room to dress in our postulant habits. The little parlor we entered had a window, but no mirror. Sister Sophia seated herself on the windowsill and Sister Charles Borromeo offered to help me with my back zipper. Lettie was on the verge of falling apart.

"Somebody should drop a shoe," she said in a stage whisper.

Sister Sophia shook her head. "Shhh, Lettie."

I stepped out of my dress and my lace-edged slip and hung them over a chair. These clothes would be stored in our trunks and kept on hand in case there should be a decision to leave the convent. One might have thought they would have been sent home as a means of discouraging a postulant from changing her mind. This was never done. The idea always presented was that the sisters needed the convent, not that the convent needed them.

Sister Charles Borromeo held something out to me. It was an item I had only previously seen in a classic issue of Sears Roebuck's catalog—a white, woven, two-legged, knee-length garment with an elasticized waist. These were Jamisons' convent order underpants. Jamisons was one of the few companies in America who catered to this trade. When the contemporary habit was adopted, they lost many of their customers.

I drew it on, not daring to glance at Lettie, or we would both have burst out laughing.

Next I was handed a convent-issue undershirt of woven cotton, high-necked, with long sleeves. Long black cotton stockings followed. Lettie pulled hers on quickly. I struggled with mine and fastened them up with garters. In this, we had been allowed freedom of choice, either a garter belt, garters, or a girdle. Girdles were encouraged, as it was thought they gave support to muscles which might be strained by heavy lifting.

I straightened up in old-fashioned underwear and hip-high black cotton stockings. As with one mind, Lettie and I laced arms and began lifting first one leg and then the other in a cancan. In spite of the sisters' efforts to stop us, we completed several dance steps and merrily bumped our hips together. By then we were pealing with laughter! The sisters were laughing too, but they laughed silently, not from their stomachs as we were. *They* had learned how to laugh.

When we had settled down we were handed plain blue cotton petticoats to put on over our drawers, which we then covered with a black cotton petticoat. This skirt was full, gathered at the waistline, and had two pockets. In them we were to carry everything that we needed, since we would not be carrying handbags. Small pincushions, already equipped with pins, which hung from ribbons, were given to us to attach to a pocket. Next we put on heavy black woolen serge skirts. They were hot and scratchy. On both sides there were openings for our hands to reach through into the pockets of our petticoats. The purpose of all these skirts was for insulation from both heat and cold. The blue petticoat protected the outer skirt from underneath. The black serge skirt could be shaken, and most dirt would fall off. I would find that it stayed amazingly clean.

Over the undershirt went a black cotton collarless blouse with long sleeves. This was topped with a black wool serge cape which came down to the waist.

Through all this dressing Lettie and I continued to joke and laugh, making fun of the clothes, which, to our eyes, looked formidably old-fashioned.

The sisters picked up our high, white, plastic-coated collars. These, we were told, could be scrubbed clean with a brush and soap, and must at all times be spotless. They placed them around our necks, flipping the fastening elastic tightly around its button.

My laughter was choked off.

I looked at Lettie.

Her eyes were wide with surprise. She had stopped laughing too.

How I wished there was a mirror! I had waited over half a year for this moment. But there was no mirror. Even the reception rooms of the convent were without mirrors—henceforth, only the beauty of one's soul was to bear reflection.

Sister Paschal showed us upstairs to a space partitioned into six cells by white seersucker curtains pulled around groupings of bed, desk, chair, chest of drawers, and trunk. There was a coat hanger on the end of each bed on which to hang a habit. My cell was in the center of three. Across a passageway, in a corner of the same room, Lettie was settled.

The furniture was painted white, or made of white fabric. It was comfortable, but institutional. In the winter my cell was very cold. The heat was turned off at night, and some fresh-air freak occupying the cell near the window would open it wide. I was to suffer some super colds during the two years that this space was my home. I always wished I could have a window so that I could keep it shut all night, but it never happened that way.

Before lunch Sister Paschal met with the thirteen new postulants in the recreation room. This room could seat about fifty people. Without the extra chairs brought in for large meetings, it was like a sparsely furnished living room. About its sides were cabinets in which each girl was assigned a drawer to keep her writing and sewing material.

At that hour, every day, Sister Paschal told us, certain prayers were said. Since we did not yet know them, we were to kneel and listen. Later, we joined the nuns who were in retreat in the convent for lunch.

A retreat was a period for meditation, prayer, and reflection, taken by most nuns at least once a year. It lasted one or two weeks and was held in silence. This was a time for reassessing values, thoughts on life, and what had been gained in relationship with God, the Holy Mother, and within. Since this was a time for personal accounting, it was interfered with as little as possible. The nuns must eat, but this hour was also a part of their spiritual growth. No conversation took place. The voice was used only for prayer.

We thirteen postulants silently followed the nuns into the dining room which held clean, linoleum-topped tables, each set for ten with a china plate, cup and saucer, a glass, and a cloth napkin wrapped around the necessary flatware at each place.

I found myself across the table from Lettie.

Standing behind our chairs, we faced the end of the room, where a large crucifix hung on the wall. Before it stood the mistress of novices, who led us in prayers.

At the final "Amen," everyone was seated.

I was hungry and could scarcely wait for lunch to be served, but nobody moved. All eyes, I saw, were fastened on the end of the room, where, on a high seat behind a lectern, sat a sister with a book in her hands. As we continued to sit, with no food in sight, our hands cupped together in our laps, she began to read to us from the Book of Obituary for the Sisters of the Holy Cross, listing the names of all who had died within the congregation on the anniversary of the following day. This, we were instructed, was to remind us to remember them in our prayers.

Still unserved, Sister read to us from the book of Roman martyrology, listing, and making note of the deaths of all saints through the centuries who had died on the current date, going into details and description of the way of their death, if it was unusual.

I do not now recall in particular a saint who died on August 1, but as an example of such a reading, I will mention a martyr's death I well remember. This was only one of perhaps five to fifteen such reports we might hear at any lunchtime, depending on how busy a day for martyr-dying that date had been. It would read something like this. "St. Lawrence of Rome gave up the Ghost gloriously to our Lord [date], after being cruelly burned alive by his tormentors. While roasting on the grill, St. Lawrence, a kind and good spirited man, known for his humor, witnessed to Christ before his torturers by saying, 'Gentlemen, I find I am well done on this side, please turn me over. . . .' "

As I first heard these accounts I was both shocked and amused. I dared not meet Lettie's eyes across the table. Through that solemn hall, Lettie Miller's laugh would have thundered like cannon shot. As time went by, I began to feel the weight, by sheer numbers, of the countless devoted people who had sacrificed their lives, many to the most cruel tortures: burial while still alive, being fed to wild animals, or even drawn and quartered. Their accounts, while not adding to my appetite for food, certainly gave me much to think about in the history of the Church and its survival through ages of persecution.

Finally, we were fed. Sisters with habits covered by enormous white aprons arrived carrying family-sized platters and bowls of steaming food. During the entire meal, we maintained silence. The sister on the high stool continued to read aloud to us from a book concerning the life of a saint. This part of our daily program I found most interesting. Not having studied much about Catholicism as a child, the lives of most of the saints were new to me, and learning about them was an excellent use of the time while we ate. I found it a relief from having to talk, day after day, for two years, to the same group of women about nonessentials.

At the end of that first meal, after we sipped our last drop of coffee, the sister on the high stool closed her book. The sisters who had served reappeared in their abundant aprons, each carrying a small pan and a spatula which they placed at the head of each table. This pan was passed from sister to sister. Each lifted her plate and with the spatula scraped her leftovers into the pan. If there were dregs of coffee or milk in her cup, or water in her glass, she added this to the gathering mixture. She passed it on to the next sister, who scraped with the spatula, added the leftover contents of her dishes, and passed the mess on.

The apron-clad sisters next brought to each table two large dish-pans filled with hot, sudsy water, two dishmops, and two towels. They placed a set at either end of each table. The sisters seated about the table sent their drinking glasses to the sister in front of whom sat the dishpan. Solemnly, she washed each glass, dried it on the towel, and returned it to its owner. When each glass had been relocated in its place, she washed her own plate, cleaning it with the dishmop. When it was clean, she placed the dishmop on the opposite side of the dishpan toward the sister seated to her left. While she dried her plate on the towel, the sister seated to her left mopped and washed *her* plate, and decorously returned the dishmop to the first sister. The first sister then mopped her dessert plate, returned the mop to the sister, and dried her dish. All around the room, like a well-functioning machine, this procedure was being carried out. None smiled or looked askance. I didn't know whether to be horrified or to laugh. I could only think of my mother reminding me of keeping my elbows off the table, not talking with my mouth full—but none of these admonitions seemed to fit what was happening! With utter decorum, as though they were taking tea with the Queen of England, these ladies, dressed in their splendid headdresses, starch-collared, without qualm or quiver, took turns washing and drying each of the items in their place setting, and then passed on the pan, with its water becoming increasingly gray, and the towel, limp and damp, to the next sister.

When the process was completed, and we pushed back our chairs, I looked around. The tables were as neatly set as when we had entered the room. Each napkin rolled around its silverware, each cup on its saucer. All the clearing and carrying and sorting had been done for the next meal. Quite a labor-saving device! But it took me a while to get used to it.

We were allowed a brief period of relaxation before being summoned by handbell to assemble while a sister demonstrated to us how to put on our long white muslin veils. These hung down our backs and reached to our fingertips. In them, we attended chapel to hear a conference headed by the retreat master.

Unused to the abundance of our clothing, we were sweltering. It was so hot that when a new postulant, sitting beside me, leaned back hard in her pew, her veiling stuck to the varnish, which, in the heat, had melted. When she tried to release herself from it, her veil tore. Many of us, when we stood up, discovered that we had brown marks from melted varnish on our new white veils.

We returned to the study hall and heard a lecture by Sister Paschal on some of the rules and regulations of the convent. She introduced us to the first rule—no needless conversation, particularly in our cells. This meant there was to be no talking. For the life of prayer and study and concentration which lay ahead for us, this rule would be a most basic necessity. It was one I came to appreciate.

Sister Paschal assigned us each to a household duty.

My job was to sweep a long enclosed walkway which extended between two buildings of the convent. It was used only in bad weather, and its planks were old and splintery.

First, I must learn how to hitch up my black serge skirt. The approved way, Sister showed me, was to swoop its ends up to my sides and fasten it, front and back, with the pins from my pincushion. I was then wrapped in an ankle-length apron of small blue checks. Thus swathed in four voluminous skirts, I was given the remnants of an old broom, which had been worn down almost to its handle, and told to sweep.

The boards were rough and knotty. The straws in the broom caught in the crevices and stayed. I had to lean over in all my skirts and yank them out. It was hot. My hands perspired, and little blisters developed between my fingers and broke. I did not think I would ever reach the end of that corridor. But I did! I must have accomplished my task to satisfaction, because I was assigned to cleaning that hallway for weeks. Day after day, whether there was dirt or not, it was my job to sweep.

After a short rest we returned to chapel for an hour of prayer which I particularly came to anticipate. The Rosary and prayers from a prayer book were said. As the outdoor shadows lengthened, we sat within the stillness of the church in silence reading from our prayer books. Then our voices joined together in community prayers and the lovely recitation of the Angelus. Peace and blessedness seemed to surround us.

Dinner was a lighter meal than lunch, but the cleanup performance was the same. Then we were allowed another brief recreation period, during which we might talk together, before returning to the chapel for half an hour of evening prayer.

It was dark when we walked back to the dormitory toward the end of that first full day. Before us stretched two hours until lights-out, during which we might do as we pleased—read, write, study, go to the library, or go to bed.

I removed my habit and hung it for the first time on the hanger at the end of my bed. For the rest of my life, I supposed, it, or one of its two facsimiles, would always hang by my head. I showered, donned a summer-weight granny gown, and slid between the sheets.

It was a hot night. Any air which might have stirred was blocked out by the pulled curtains of my cell.

I lay awake a long time. My mattress was a miserable combination of lumps and hollows. Never before in my life had I slept on such an uncomfortable mattress. When Sister Paschal had brought us to our cells, she apologized for our beds. They were temporary, she promised. There were so many extra nuns at the convent making their retreats that extra beds had had to be hunted up.

The convent had been built in the mid-nineteenth century, and I was sure my bed must have belonged to a founding father (mother?).

It seemed as though I had barely been able to fall asleep when the big bell in the tower, in doleful tone, tolled 5:00 A.M.

Another day was beginning.

5

Poker
With a Bishop

We had lived in the convent less than a week, when surprise! We learned we were to have a holiday! A ten-day vacation. This news was almost a shock in reverse. We were not quite ready for it. After all, we had had only four days of penance and suffering, and now we would have more than twice that for relaxing! We felt almost abused; after just having given up luxury for a life of hardship, now we would be all softened up again.

We had spent the first days of August in gradual orientation. We prayed, ate, exercised, and I swept that impossible corridor.

While the nonspeaking nuns in retreat silently pursued their courses, we postulants took walks down the lanes of the farm. To save our black serge habits from the dust of the roads, we always took these hikes swathed in aprons, our black skirts folded up. Our heads were unbound, as we wore our white veils only in church, and the black veil with the white band around our faces would only be worn when we left the convent for classes or duties. There was a lovely sense of freedom in having our hair out. As I viewed my sister postulants walking about the farm in their black shoes and stockings, our waltz-length petticoats showing, our costumes reminded me of scenes of groups of Mennonite or Amish girls, or possibly French peasants.

There had already been some radical outward and visible changes for us thirteen, who previously had been so lightly and colorfully dressed. With every passing day, through study and prayer, inward and invisible changes were likewise taking place. I think if the weather had been cool, these spiritual changes might have occurred more rapidly. But it continued unbearably hot.

Actually, we were being sent away from St. Mary's because there was no place on the program at that time for thirteen postulants. There were, that August, besides the 150 nuns in retreat at the convent, another 100, all of whom were to go into retreat from August 5 to 15. Every single person on the campus and in the convent would be on retreat. There simply wasn't any place for *us*.

The mistress of novices, Mother Regina, was to accompany us on our trip. She was tall and slender and carried herself erectly. Her mannerisms were Victorian. Her spine never touched the back of her chair, her ankles never crossed while sitting. Her face in the setting of her elaborate headdress was saintly. She appeared truly angelic, one of those rare religious that impress one as not being totally of this earth.

Limousines would arrive early next morning, and when we returned to our cells, we found that our suitcases had already been pulled out of storage. We had not been told where we were going or what resort facilities we might expect, but that did not create a packing problem. Our choice of clothing was none at all—it was only *change*—habit or habit.

Next morning the thirteen of us and Mother Regina gathered between the enormous white pillars of the porch of the novitiate. A shiny blue convent limousine, followed closely by the bishop's black one, and two other large automobiles lined up before the house. An enormous quantity of food was loaded into the two cars along with our luggage.

We piled into the limousines, two postulants in front with the driver, two more on the jump seats, and I was lucky to be seated in the back beside Mother Regina, with another postulant beyond.

The two limousines pulled away from the convent followed by our entourage carrying our food and clothing.

51

Poker With a Bishop

We had not gone very far when the combination of the warm day and seven bodies dressed in habits, plus the driver, began to be uncomfortable. We opened the windows to let the fresh air blow through.

In the front seat sat two girls from Boston, definitely younger and less worldly-wise than we girls who had attended college. Shortly it became obvious to us that they had with them a supply of caramel candies, which they were unwrapping and devouring. Each time they unwrapped another sweet, they tossed the paper to the breeze, which caught it and blew it back into the car through the rear window. The first one landed in the lap of Mother Regina. Did she complain? No. Except for the slight motion of crumpling it in her hand, one would have thought one imagined the incident. Then another sticky wrapper flew back, landing squarely against the mother's cheek! Surely, I thought, she will stop the car and toss the culprits out. She will make them walk back to the convent—possibly even expel them!

Did that happen? No indeed. Mother wordlessly removed the paper from her face and placed it in the ashtray before her. Ahead of us the jaws continued to chew until the entire sack of candy was depleted, but no word was said. Most astonishing to me was that the girls *had* the candy. After all, on entrance, we had supposedly relinquished all our "worldly goods." Perhaps the candy was heavenly? It smelled delicious.

We had ridden for about two hours when the drivers brought the cars to a halt beside a lake. Small boats with outboard motors and pilots were waiting for us. About a half mile out from shore we could see an island with a pier jutting out into the water. Through the trees we could make out the shape of a huge Victorian house. It was Bishop's Island. The waiting men loaded our food and suitcases, and the fourteen of us, into the six boats, and we put-putted off to an island with no telephone, no roads, and only the bare necessities provided by electricity.

The island belonged to Bishop Noll, a man well known among American Catholics for a newspaper he had instituted, *My Sunday Visitor,* an insert in many diocesan papers.

When we arrived at the dock, the men unloaded the food into the kitchen. Mother proceeded to the house, where she had a room with a private bath on the second floor. Carrying our suitcases, we also climbed the wide stairway to our second floor quarters. Three rooms had been given over for our accommodation. In the one to which I was assigned, five cots had been lined up so close together that it was necessary to step on one to reach the next. Down the hall was a bathroom with a toilet and sink for our use. It contained neither shower nor tub.

We viewed our accommodations and then each other. There we were, packed closely together. But it was a lark! The island was beautiful, with deep forests, many boulders, and colorful splotches of wild flowers. At the dock there had been a rowboat and a canoe. We could lap up the sunshine, and maybe even get in some swimming, though none of us had brought bathing suits.

When we had put away our clothes, Mother Regina's voice called from the stairway. We were to go down to meet Bishop Noll.

He had twinkly blue eyes and thinning reddish hair—a grandfather type whom it would be easy to love. He welcomed us warmly.

Mother Regina showed us through the house. When we came to the kitchen, she announced, "I have here a list of menus. We will tack it on this board. Alongside it will be this chart of your duties. If you will look after your names, you will find your assignments for each day. Dinner will be at noon." She pressed thumbtacks into the sheets of paper and departed, leaving thirteen postulants staring at one another.

We were the hired help!

We had been brought to that wilderness to scrub the floors, and dust the furniture, and prepare three meals a day.

My first job was to make dessert for lunch.

Mary Miller, a girl from Washington, was to roast the beef.

"We're both on lunch shift," I said.

She began laughing. Suddenly we were all laughing. It was just another long corridor to sweep! It was the bishop's custom to invite different groups of nuns in his diocese to enjoy a week on the island. In this way he came to know more of his people, and he was always fed, and his house kept clean.

When Sister assigned me to preparing dessert, she had no way of knowing that I knew nothing whatever of food preparation. The dessert was to be a tapioca pudding. It had always looked simple when I had seen my mother prepare it. All one had to do was read the amounts on the side of the box, put them together, and stir. Of course, for fifteen people, one needed a large pot and a lot of tapioca.

I assembled the ingredients and started cooking the pudding. As I stirred, I chatted with the other girls bustling about. I also watched the pot. After a while I began to wonder, "Is this tapioca?" Little brown spots had started floating to the top. Maybe, I thought, it was chocolate tapioca. Everyone around me was busy with her own duties. I kept stirring and the brown spots kept multiplying.

Finally Mary Miller happened to glance into the pot.

"I think it's chocolate," I said.

"Chocolate?" she repeated. "That's not chocolate, Shirley. It's burning! That's burned tapioca coming up from the bottom."

Burning? Why hadn't I thought of that? There I was, about to top the first meal of the season for the bishop, the *first* bishop I had ever met, with a tempting dessert, and it was burned.

I had emptied the entire box of tapioca into the pot. There was no more.

"We'll never even notice it," Lettie said blithely. "The rest of the meal will more than make up for it. Mary is a whizz with meat."

With that reassurance in my ears, I heard dinner announced.

We were seated along picnic benches on either side of a long table, the bishop in an armchair at one end and Mother Regina opposite him.

After a lengthy grace, we raised our heads and unfolded our napkins. Mary marched in with a platter bearing her splendid roast of beef, followed by two postulants carrying bowls of carrots and potatoes and plates of bread and butter. Another postulant brought a tray with glasses and a tall pitcher of milk.

When the succulent browned roast in a pool of red-brown juice was set before Mother she looked up at Mary.

"My dear Miss Miller," she stated in her soft voice, "this meat is not cooked." And for good reason! Mary happened to prefer her meat rare. While we had been working together in the kitchen, she had taken a poll among us, and discovered a consensus for rare-to-medium beef. With only the faulty country stove to work with, we felt she had done an outstanding job. She had produced a gorgeous roast, brown on the outside and bloody pink in the middle.

As Mother's words hung in the air, we gently offered support.

"It looks delicious to me!"

"That's just the way I like it."

"It's gorgeous!"

Mother would have none of it. Never losing her composure, she said gently to Mary, "Sister, we cannot serve it this way. Remove it."

The meat was carried from the room before our hungry eyes. Mary returned to the table empty-handed.

Meekly we passed the potatoes and carrots, the bread and butter, and ate them enthusiastically.

Then the moment I had dreaded arrived. I excused myself from the table and went to the kitchen and brought in the polka-dotted dessert.

When Mother inspected hers, she said, "My dear Miss Dyckes, what is this in the tapioca?"

I responded promptly. "I don't know, Mother. It must have been in the package."

Mother did not contradict me, but the rest of the dinner guests could scarcely contain their smiles. They began making halfhearted attempts to eat my awful concoction. At his end of the table, the bishop ate what had been placed before him.

Mother pushed her bowl delicately away.

"Well, Sisters," she said pleasantly, with an obvious effort to cheer us. "In the light of this meal that has been served, I suggest that we now serve the candy."

Thirteen young ladies sucked in their breaths. Thirteen faces paled.

At last Mary Miller broke the silence. "But, Mother," she said, "we can't serve the candy."

"You can't serve the candy?"

"No, Mother. It is gone."

"The box of candy is gone?"

"Yes, Mother. We ate it—for snacks."

Still disbelieving, but exceedingly polite and prim, her voice not rising in register, Mother Regina asked, "You mean the five-pound box?"

"Oh, Mother," Mary said innocently, "was that five pounds?"

"Yes, Sister," Mother replied, her voice beginning to show an edge of irritation.

Throughout this the bishop had sat not saying a word. Now he pulled out a cigar and began preparing to light it.

"Mother," he said, in a noble effort to keep peace, "why don't you and I go sit on the swing and enjoy the view? The girls will clean up the kitchen."

That was exactly what we wanted to hear! In the kitchen was Mary's roast, which she had not returned to the oven for further cooking. It was still warm and rare and waiting for us.

In spite of the fact that between us, as we had prepared the meal, we had consumed five pounds of candy, we ate every scrap of the meat down to the bones, and it was delicious!

Our days were spent cleaning the floors, scouring the kitchen equipment, tidying the bathrooms, and always, there was another meal to prepare and clean up after. In the afternoons there was time to fish off the dock and boat a bit in the canoe and rowboat.

One particularly hot day Lettie discovered some bathing suits in a previously unexplored closet. They weren't much for style, but they would be better than nothing. With great glee we began figuring who would wear which.

We were interrupted by Mother, who reviewed us with disapproving eyes. "Just what do you think you are doing?" she asked.

"We're going swimming, Mother."

"There will be no swimming on this vacation," she stated.

"But, Mother," Lettie reasoned, "other nuns left the bathing suits here."

Mother was firm. Completely dashed, we remained in the layers of our habits, which after the brief dream of freedom, seemed more oppressive than ever.

I would soon grow used to my habit. I came to recognize its function and learned to hold it with great respect, to love it and find it beautiful. But those hot weeks in August were a period of difficulty for me in accepting my new wardrobe.

Later that afternoon, while we were boating, fully robed in our habits, enjoying the fresh breeze that flirted over the lake, Lettie, Mary, and I decided to change places in the little boat. Lettie had been rowing for some time, and thought someone else should have a turn. We three had hardly stood up in the boat when a terrible clanging from the porch reached us across the water.

We could see Mother Regina's figure, resplendent in her headdress, furiously banging on the side of the iron glider with something heavy and metallic.

Something terrible must have happened to cause her to create such a racket.

We rowed furiously toward shore, where we found a less-than-composed Mother.

"Foolish women!" she chided us. "Standing in the boat. You might have capsized and all have drowned."

"We were careful, Mother."

"It was a reckless thing to do!"

"But we were only changing positions, Mother."

"You could all drown," she repeated, "cavorting around in full habits in a rowboat."

"Mother," I said a bit condescendingly, "Lettie is an experienced water-woman. She paddled a small canoe down the Mississippi River. Mary's father was a captain of the annual Washington ship regatta, with Mary at his side. Even this summer, I have been driving speedboats all over Biscayne Bay. We are sure we can handle ourselves in water."

Mother was not to be persuaded. "I would like you to remember," she said stiffly, "that in the days you were cutting such impressive figures, you were not dressed from head to foot in fifteen pounds of clothing. The subject of boating is closed. There will be no more."

It was a bitter pill to swallow, to realize that by our foolhardiness we had spoiled boating for all the postulants. From then on, we were confined to the island.

ॐ

Our first evening at Bishop's Island, Mother told us that we could amuse ourselves by reading or watching television.

"Or," the bishop said, his blue eyes twinkling, "would any of you like to play Polish poker with me? Perhaps you would like to play also?" the bishop invited Mother Regina.

"No thank you," she replied coolly.

No signal of displeasure ever seemed to sway the bishop from his chosen path. He was soon dealing and teaching us the fascinating game of Polish poker. We played until eleven o'clock, while Mother read in another room.

At that time, she returned. "Your Excellency," she said, "don't you think the postulants should go to bed?"

The bishop had just reached a most strategically important stage of his game. "Oh, Mother," he said, removing his cigar from his mouth and waving it airily, "you must be tired. Why don't you go to bed? The girls will go up in a minute."

With a sigh, Mother Regina retired, but we didn't.

The bishop was an inveterate player, and night after night, we played until the wee hours.

When the game finally broke up the first night, the bishop announced, "Now in the morning, when it is time to get up, I will stand at the bottom of the stairs and I will sing *Benedicamus Domino* (Let us bless the Lord), and you will answer *Deo Gracias* (Thanks be to God)."*

We stumbled upstairs and climbed over one another until we were all tucked into our proper cots. I fell asleep wondering how I was ever going to be able to sing in response to the bishop.

It didn't seem any time at all until the sun was streaming in the windows, and from below his cheery male voice sang out the prescribed salutation to God.

I sat up in bed and tried to sing. Only a squeak emerged, and off-key at that. The others were in no better voice. But it seemed a happy way to start the morning.

At the end of our "vacation," we returned to the novitiate. For ten days we had been unable to bathe and had only been able to sponge ourselves. There had been no place or means to wash our hair. We must have been a sorry-looking collection of sisters who arrived home just in time for vespers. We were told to enter the chapel by a side door, instead of making our usual long procession down the center aisle.

It had been a surprising, but pleasant, trip for us. We were shocked to hear from Sister Paschal that Mother Regina had reported that it had been the most mortifying ten days of her life!

---

*From the Gregorian chant.

6

Becoming a Nun

I suspect that my most lasting contribution to the convent of St. Mary's may well be the ghastly scar in the shape of a large ring which I created on the library floor. Stripping, resealing, and varnishing the oak floors of two rooms of that huge building was the assigned task I drew with another nun, Betty, during my postulant year. If it was meant to be humbling, I certainly discovered that I had knees.

My years in the convent consisted of days filled from dawn until nearly midnight with spiritual, mental, and physical development. I had expected the first two, but I had never given even the smallest thought to the hard manual labor which was expected of nuns.

Each morning a great bell in the tower awakened us at five o'clock. We were allowed a half hour to dress, make our beds, and arrive at chapel for prayer. Thirty minutes were spent in total silence, meditating, followed by the chanting of the Little Office, first by one side of the church, and then answered by the other. It was quite lovely to hear, and I always enjoyed both the listening and the responding of this antiphonal prayer. The Mass followed and was completed in time for us to arrive at our places at the breakfast table at 7:30. Quite a start of the day for a girl who had considered sleeping until 7:30 one of the basic requirements of life!

Perhaps an outsider might wonder what nuns might find to meditate about for half an hour beyond their many prayers. I found that the more years I continued this practice, the shorter the period seemed. The vast tract of the soul is largely unexplored, as compared to the inroads of investigation the average person makes into his mind in a lifetime. Within the soul there are endless avenues reaching into unseeable space, which one may take as a means of seeking perfect grace. The more one searches for this goal, the more one becomes aware of the possibilities in the spiritual world.

When the regular school session began in September, there were about fifty* postulants in my class. Ten or twelve had already had some college training, and we continued our studies at St. Mary's campus, taking subjects which required our attendance all over campus. We were almost always alone as we pursued our individual paths of instruction. The other forty or so postulants attended classes in the novitiate. There were two professions toward which we were all heading as sisters of the Holy Cross—nursing or education. I had chosen education.

Among my classmates was Bridget, who had entered in September. We each fulfilled different requirements of our college curriculum, so I actually rarely saw her. Frequently I was the only nun in my classes. I was happy and busy and did not stop to think how I might look to others. I had never wanted to be a nun per se, but since being one was the means of giving my life as I wished to devote it, I found myself happy, excited about my classes, and pleased with the course my life was taking.

Our days were stratas of study, meals, work, and prayers closely packed one on the other. We maintained silence except when it was necessary to ask or to make reply. I found this beneficial to my progress. I had come to the convent to prepare myself for the Apostolate, so that I could go out and bring the good news of Christianity to others. I did not need distractions. I enjoyed being read to during meals. I found it more elevating than casual conversation. This was not to say that we lived in total silence. There were two recreation periods a day during which conversation was permitted, into which we squeezed all our pent-up

---

Of these, about twenty-five would continue the convent program.

chatter and laughter, sharing our experiences within, and before, our convent days.

It must have been my outstanding sweeping ability on that old porch which brought me the assignment of refinishing the library floors. Each of us was involved in duties of upkeep and continuance of life in the convent. Betty and I were to refinish the oak floors.

Until that time I had never considered my knees for anything but making locomotion easy and for praying. I discovered a most useful, but painful, purpose for them. Every afternoon of that autumn, I knelt on the planks of that floor, rubbing, scraping, varnishing, and polishing.

Wouldn't you have thought work clothes would have been provided for us? Indeed not! We wore every layer of our habits, plus the ubiquitous aprons up to our chins. Do you suppose we were provided with kneeling pads or gloves for our tender hands? I think it was expected that in one season I would acquire knee calluses thick enough to make praying forever a cinch for me!

There we were, two inexperienced girls, who had never done much housework, faced with a task which would have taken men and machines many hours to accomplish. We were given simple instructions and left on our own. Day after day, week after week, on those golden autumn afternoons, instead of crunching crisp colorful leaves under my heels, I bent on my knees, rubbing. Instead of inhaling cool autumn air, I breathed the fumes of paint remover and varnish.

At the end of my first day on that job, when I began unpinning my apron, I forced myself to stand straight. I felt my first inkling of discouragement. I ached from head to heel. Before me I surveyed my Herculean stable. No one had told me life in the convent would be all milk and honey. But I had never imagined a life's work involving physical labor. It was then that the memories of the lives of all those saints, which had been read to me, and the trials they had undergone to live their faith, flooded over me. The pain in my back and the ache in my knees seemed nothing at all.

We finally finished the floors of both rooms, so that they gleamed as light struck them. I was proud of the job we had done.

It was then that I discovered the blunder.

As our main source of varnish, we had been using a five-gallon drum. It was not full, but it was heavy. We had placed it in a convenient spot for replenishing smaller cans. Then, when we went to move it, to put it away, it would not budge. It was stuck to the floor. When I was finally able to free it, an ugly round mark, the size of my circled arms, was stained deep into the middle of the library entrance. Try as hard as we could, neither Betty nor I could eliminate it.

There was nothing to do but go to the mistress of novices and report the damage.

I had seen Mother Regina many times since our "holiday" on Bishop's Island. She had always been sweetly interested in me, but I doubted that this would be a similar occasion. As I approached her office, all I could think of was her beautiful, pure face. Obviously, such a person had never done any wrong in her life.

Timidly I tapped on her door, and heard her gentle voice say, "Yes, Sister?"

"May I come in?" I asked.

"Yes, Sister."

I entered and saw that regal lady seated, writing at her desk.

I crossed the room and fell on my thoroughly desensitized knees.

From my position of humility, she immediately knew something terrible had happened. She stopped writing and gave me her total attention.

In the quiet room her voice was like a rustle of silk.

"Yes, Sister?"

"Mother, in our refinishing project . . . the library floor was my responsibility. Sister Betty and I have completed our task. As we picked up the container of varnish to leave . . . we realized that the can had left a mark on the floor."

"A mark on the floor, Sister?" Mother Regina intoned with great preciseness.

"Yes, Mother."

"Will it come out, Sister?" she asked, scarcely louder than a breath.

"No, Mother."

"You are quite sure that it will not come out, Sister?"

"Yes, Mother," I replied, thinking futilely, "If it would, do you think I would be here?"

"How large is the ring?" the gentle voice pursued.

"Mother, we had the five-gallon drum."

"Sister, do you mean that the ring is the size of a dinner platter?"

"Larger, Mother."

"How thick is the ring, Sister?"

I was on my knees, my head bowed, hands clasped at my breast as she tortured me with these questions. Surely she *knew* the size of the drum. She had passed it many times. She was prolonging this questioning to agonize me. I was sick with fear and frustration. It was horrible enough that the floor was scarred. My record would be also.

"A little over an inch," I said miserably.

"Sister," the voice inquired, more loudly, but still with an effort to be reasonable, "is this ring in a place on the floor where we can possibly place a piece of furniture to cover your incompetency?"

"That would not be possible, Mother."

Now the voice was no longer gentle. I did not know how it was possible for such thunder to issue from this elegant lady, but it crashed in my ears.

"You know, Sister," she said fiercely, "this building has served the Sisters of the Holy Cross for over fifty years. Its floors were in beautiful condition. We simply asked you to refinish them."

"Yes, Mother."

"And now there is a ring on the floor! You say this damage cannot be removed or covered by a piece of furniture?"

"Yes, Mother."

With fury she demanded, "And why not, Sister?"

"It is just to the right of the door. It is located *between* the two library doors—in the passageway. . . ."

"Do you mean, Sister, that from now on, whenever anyone uses the novitiate library they will be reminded that Miss Dyckes couldn't manage the simple task of taking a rag and applying a coat of varnish to the floor?"

Mother's voice had risen until now it was extremely loud. Surely it could be heard in every room of the building. Through the utter silence it rang out like the bell from the tower.

As the admonition continued I felt my lower lip tremble. Never in my life had I been shouted at. No one had ever truly scolded me. I felt as though I would burst into tears.

"You," the voice went on, "who took a vow of poverty, have had total disregard for community property!"

I was appalled with myself. I had not realized the vast reaches of

63

my carelessness. I was totally humiliated. I knelt before her. I would not have been surprised to have received forty lashes, or a commitment to solitary confinement, or some other horrible imagined penance.

Above me I heard a sigh, as gentle as a passing June breeze, and then, in a voice so soft I could scarcely hear it, a *kind* voice, I thought I heard it say, "Now, Shirley, sit there."

I looked up. Mother was seated behind her desk, her smooth round face bearing a most benevolent expression.

"Sit there, Sister," she repeated, waving her elegant fingertips to a small chair placed to the right of her desk.

I pulled myself together, stood up, and walked to the little chair.

"Well, Sister," Mother Regina asked, "how are things going with you?"

We chatted serenely for four or five minutes, as though nothing had happened, and then she excused me, and I left the room trying to assess what really had occurred.

Such verbal castigation, I was to find as I became a nun, was not infrequent. Inside, I must grow in humility. It took some time before I was able to understand this type of punishment. Aside from expulsion, scolding was the only whip the nuns had with which to train us. As we served our Apostolate outside the convent, life might be harsh. It would not be even-tempered and pleasant. We must learn to buffet storms. By using her voice, the only weapon she had, this sister was preparing me.

On me, this punishment had double impact. We lived in a world of silence. Our bodies were trained to move without sound. There were never any noises in the dormitories or library or even crossing campus. We were decorous women moving silently about, speaking when spoken to, answering quietly in carefully modulated tones. Suddenly to be struck with harsh words was, to me, a form of being beaten.

Upon another occasion, while serving a meal, I accidentally broke a platter. The sound of crockery breaking could be heard throughout the silent dining hall. After luncheon, as it was her custom, Mother Regina stood by her chair where the nuns might file by her. If one had a petition to ask, a request for a visit from a relative, or to perform a special duty, that was the time one might make it. When it was my turn, on that day, I had to say, "Mother, I broke a platter."

As the other nuns stood silently in lines waiting to pass by, I was loudly berated, seemingly for an endless time. Before the sisters I was made to recognize my frailties. I was humiliated. Then forgiven—the incident to be forgotten—except, of course, that was not immediately possible. I continued to suffer. And so the punishment worked. I would rather have submitted to physical deprivation than to have incurred future verbal flailings from the otherwise gentle sisters.

One of my favorite jobs, granted in spite of my poor showing as a floor polisher, was to be portress for the office of the mother general. I would sit in the foyer and answer the bell to admit anyone who wished to see the mother general and other members of the council which ran the community. I enjoyed meeting both the visitors from the outside and the members of the council. Many of these latter were women who had been nuns for thirty-five or forty years. They gave me many little bits of information—everything from using lemon juice to remove stains from my white garments to detailing to me the history of the convent grounds and its many buildings.

Yet another job which I particularly loved was carrying dinner to the priests' house. At that time there were four priests living at the convent who performed the priestly duties of the community. Three times a day their meals were carried to them in a large metal container with two or three shelves. It took two of us to transport this receptacle. I enjoyed the service and my brief contacts with the priests.

The priests' house was run by an irascible nun who cowed most of the postulants. She was Irish, and spoke with a thick brogue, and had all kinds of rules and regulations about what was, and was not, proper conduct for young nuns. Fortunately, when I carried over my first meal to the fathers, I recognized her as an old acquaintance. It was Sister Samantha, who had helped me out as a freshman when I needed straps on a strapless evening gown. She remembered this encounter, joking about it, and after that, we got along famously.

The position I actually liked best of all was being laundry maid! Once a week for three years I spent most of an afternoon in the laundry. I learned to press sheets by feeding them through an enormous modern roller machine. This machine was so large it took four of us to man it at once. The equipment in this department was like a trip to a museum of laundry devices. There was everything in it from the time the convent had been founded, long before electricity. There were old-fashioned sadirons which had to be heated on a stove. All the equipment was still in use. Nothing at the convent ever seemed to be thrown away.

The laundry work also included mountains of items to be folded—all the clothing, bedding, and linens required not only for the 150 women in various stages of becoming nuns, but for the priests, and for the 100 or so aging nuns in the infirmary and the nuns who staffed the college.

The array of underwear which came across our tables never failed to amaze us. Most of our garments, as described, were convent issue. But through the years there had been variations in some of these. Some of the nuns in the infirmary were in their nineties, which meant they had entered the convent shortly after the end of the Civil War. Their undergarments had been designed and/or manufactured then, and carefully patched and mended ever since. The old nuns wanted nothing to do with newfangled underwear. Some of this intimate apparel was truly classic in design!

In spite of the many requirements of the convent, my grades at St. Mary's improved. The caliber of the work I was turning out was much better than in previous years. I chose political science for a second major. As theology, the study of God, is the queen of thought, political science, the ordering of men's lives, seemed a fitting complement. My interest in these studies grew with every class and every book I read.

At the end of the postulant year, we began to prepare to receive our habits. This may sound confusing—we were already wearing nun's clothing—but it was of an undistinguished sort. Our blouses and skirts were separate, not one dress. Our sleeves were plain, and we did not wear the distinctively beautiful headdress of the Congregation of the Holy Cross. At this time, several, who for one reason or another would not make good nuns, were weeded out. There were also departures for reasons of health.

The saddest of these, to me, was the exit of a splendid nun, Anne Gargan, who was a novice and had received her habit. We lived together in the same building and shared recreation together. Anne was an orphan, and a relative of the Joseph Kennedys who had made her their ward.

Anne dearly loved Joseph Kennedy. In spite of what we might hear of him in the political or business world, she said, he was a devoted father. When he was at Hyannis Port, he always found time for each of his children, and for the young Gargans, to take them walking, one at a time, along the beach, listening to them, counseling when they requested it, making each child feel special and loved.

An occasional visitor to the Kennedy compound in those days, though a renowned Republican, was Congressman Joe Martin, who represented his Massachusetts district for forty years in the House, holding minority leadership for many years, and two terms as Speaker. She recounted how that very colorful leader had almost lost his life in a sailboat in a bad storm off the Cape. The Speaker was not a good swimmer, and it had been a close call.

Anne, as a young girl, had attended a Catholic boarding school. One day, she told us, she had added ink to the holy water. When the nuns entered for worship and dipped their fingers into the font, eyes closed in prayer, to bless themselves, they stained their white coifs and collars.

While at Holy Cross, however, Anne was a model of deportment. She was assigned to take care of the chapel, a position most desired by all and rewarded only to outstanding nuns.

Toward the end of her novitiate year, she began having fainting spells. The day that she left the convent, under doctor's orders, was a regrettable day for all.

ॐ

My parents and Joyce were invited to the ceremony for my investiture of the Holy Habit and sat amid the congregation. By then, they had accepted my decision.

It was a most beautiful and significant pageant. Through it, the Holy Mother Church invested the spouse of Christ in the regal robes of those privileged, by His grace, to follow Him on the royal road to the Holy Cross. All the cloths and hangings in the church were white for the occasion, and the candidates wore long white satin wedding gowns, and their heads were covered with long white veils.

A few days before the ceremony we were taken to a wardrobe room which held racks of wedding gowns in various shades of white. It was amazing how age varied that color! Since I was a size six, it was necessary to alter mine to my particular proportions. When finished, I felt it was a sorry-looking affair. *Not* what I would have chosen for a bridal gown! It did nothing for me. However, I think it *did* do something for my parents. After seeing me in it, and how pale and plain I looked in all that white, with no makeup, they were relieved to see me later in the truly striking habit of the Holy Cross.

Robed in our made-over, much-used wedding gowns, we candidates paraded sedately into the church for the solemn and lovely service. Wearing the unbecoming gown was immediately forgotten as I allowed my spirit to become encompassed in the full meaning of the ritual.

The priest handed each of us a candle as he said:

Receive this light; let it shine in your hands as the symbol of good works of which you should give the example, and of the unceasing praises you should render to a God who has been so merciful to you. *

To me, this was a summation, the core, of my purpose in becoming a nun.

The service continued with prayers and a sermon, and then the bishop began his interrogation. "My daughters, what do you ask?"

We responded, "Your Excellency, we ask for the Habit of this Congregation, and the favor of being tried in the exercises of the Novitiate."

We then promised to observe the Holy Rule and the statutes of the congregation.

The bishop blessed our new habits and veils and sprinkled them lightly with holy water. Each postulant then laid aside her candle, and kneeling, received the holy habit from his hands while he said:

Receive, my daughter, this garb of humility and penitence, in order that, while wearing it, you may die daily to yourself, so as to live always as a true Religious.

He then gave us our veils, saying:

Receive this White Veil, bedewed with the heavenly benediction, and wear it as the symbol of innocence befitting those virgins who are to follow the Spotless Lamb, to the end that it may withdraw you from the indiscreet gaze of the world and conceal you in God with Jesus Christ.

With these two folded bundles in our arms, we rose, bowed to the

---

*This and following passages in this chapter are from Ceremonial of Investiture, Congregation of the Sisters of the Holy Cross.

bishop, and retired under the direction of the mistress of novices, to be clothed in our holy habits.

Dressed in them, with the high and sparkling white fluted head-dress of the order of the Holy Cross crowning our faces, we returned to the altar, where kneeling before the prelate, each was given a chaplet* and told:

Receive this Chaplet as the sign of your devotion to Our Lady of the Seven Sorrows, and recite it every day.

Then each received a copy of the book of Rules and Constitutions, a Directory of Exercises, and the Book of the Office, each to be used for our instruction and guidance.

The final portion of the service was the giving of names. The bishop sprinkled each novice with holy water and prayed for her, calling her by her new name.

Of course I had been curious as to the name I would receive. I expected to live by it for the rest of my life. If I could have chosen my own, I would have given myself the name Sister Joseph Sarto. This man, Pope St. Pius X, had been very important to the Apostolate, which meant so much to me.

In Roman Catholic life, all important occasions are marked by the giving of a new name. At birth my mother had named me Shirley, which was not a saint's name. At my baptism, as an infant, she chose a second name for me, Ann, for St. Ann. Yet another name was given to me at confirmation—Cecilia. This saint was the patron saint of music, and my mother thought that with the aid of this saint something might come of my piano lessons! So on my confirmation day, I became Shirley Ann Cecilia Dyckes. However, my new name had little influence on St. Cecilia. On the day of my piano recital, she did not give me any assistance. I had to play the final phrase three times before I could find the right note to end my piece!

As I knelt before the bishop in my new habit, I heard:

He who will be victorious, says our Saviour, shall receive of me a new name: Behold a new one which I give you on His part, to enable you to overcome the devil, the world, and yourself. Hereafter you will be called Sister Mary Bernardine.

---

*Rosary beads.

The bishop handed me a white card bearing my new name so that in the excitement of the moment I would not forget it.

I felt disappointed by his choice. Later, however, many sisters congratulated me. It seemed that Sister Mary Bernardine had been a well-loved sister of the Holy Cross, considered saintly by many. Several of the older nuns mentioned that among the novitiate nuns I was already known to be exceptionally prayerful. I found I had been honored by the choice of my new name, and my attitude toward it changed.

Later I was to read about St. Bernardino de Siena, with whom the name originated. As a wealthy, educated Italian, he had renounced many personal advantages to become a monk, and risked his life serving the plague-stricken. He was best known outside the Church as the man who introduced boxing to Italy as a more Christian approach to fistfighting. I found the saintliness of his life to be an inspiring example. In tribute to his holiness, it is said that his body, now deceased over five hundred years, is still intact in Italy.

Lettie became Sister John David, and Bridget—Sister Kathleen. Names were chosen by the mistress of novices with the assistance of other nuns. A name was supposed to inspire its recipient or indicate her talents or character strengths. Within our community a list of available names was kept and over the years they were used again and again. This list was added to as nuns died or left the convent, thus freeing the name for reuse. If a name on the list seemed to fit a new novice, it was used. Otherwise a name was chosen from that of a Catholic saint.

From the moment of my investiture, Shirley Ann Cecilia Dyckes became Sister Mary Bernardine C.S.C.*

Congregatio Sanctae Crucis—the Congregation of the Holy Cross.

7

Inside

A convent hedge does not a prison make.

During my novice year, I was confined to the novitiate building. I took no classes on St. Mary's campus and had no more outside jobs, such as portress or carrying meals to the priests, both tasks I had found outgoing and interesting. That year I rarely left the novitiate, but I found the confinement freeing!

I became the librarian—in the same room where the terrible ring on the floor leered up at me at each entering. I loved my job! It was exciting to be around all those books, and I wondered how I would ever find time to peer into each one and absorb its contents. New books kept coming in, and I could browse through them before anyone else. I found ways to expand the library in arrangement, so there was room for more books, and I learned the basic librarian function of cataloging. The library was a large cheery place, and it whetted my appetite for more and more knowledge.

I never went to bed a minute early. I would go to the study hall and read all the selections I had chosen in the library. Since I had first choice, I used my prerogative and knew the contents of all the books before anyone else.

I read two by Jews which impressed me deeply, *The Walls Are Crumbling* and *Pillar of Fire*. In Miami there had been a vast Jewish population, but I never really knew any of them. I was able to find great understanding for them. One of the authors was a brilliant doctor in Nazi Germany. His account of the psychological reactions of Jewish women forcibly sterilized weighed heavily upon me. As a doctor, he found himself in fearsome straits. He was able to escape to Canada, where he converted to Catholicism. The Jews I read about always converted to Catholicism. I understood the purpose of the material available to me, but I was grateful for the opportunity to study the intellectual depth and courage of these persecuted people. I came to admire Jews, and from then on enjoyed knowing them, and liked them instinctively.

The novitiate year was far more strenuous than the one before. It was particularly hard on my free-wheeling friend, Lettie.

Lettie and Mary Miller had a job in the sacristy of the big church on campus where they helped the sister in charge of the church with all its ceremonials. This church was two buildings away from the chapel where we held our daily prayers together.

The nun's clock in the big church was about two minutes slower than the novitiate clock. An arbitrary situation developed. The nun at the sacristy would not let Mary and Lettie leave the church two minutes early, which was on time by the novitiate clock. Every day the girls were two minutes late for prayers.

When Lettie and Mary arrived, breathless, but late, for service, the mistress of novices would scold them before all the other novices. At first this public denunciation seemed even worse to me than when she had privately upbraided me for the ring on the library floor.

During her reprimand the girls were required to kneel before her.

"Thoughtless girls," Mother would shout.

Their admission returned humbly, "Yes, Mother."

"Absolutely without consideration."

"Forgive us, Mother."

"What kind of sisters will you possibly make when you cannot even attend prayers on time?"

"We are sorry, Mother."

"Every day you are late. You will never be able to make it through the convent!"

"It will never happen again, Mother."

At the end of this verbal thrashing, Mother would be pink in the face, and the culprits pale.

After this had happened several days in a row, we other novices, standing to the side, were scarcely able to contain our laughter. We were all aware of why Lettie and Mary were late. The same scene happened again and again. It was a no-win situation. In a case like this, there was nothing for us to do but make a joke of it. But quietly. Later.

Finally Mother, after a last furious study of the girls at her feet, would say sternly, "Kiss the floor!"

Lettie and Mary obeyed, their lips brushing the floor while their backsides pushed up as though they were bobbing for apples. This all but exploded the rest of us, who were suppressing our laughter. An expression of derision could have meant being sent home, expelled from the convent. Most nuns had healthy senses of humor. Without one, many would have left the convent within the first week.

Later, it was realized by the sisters in charge that kissing the floor was neither humbling nor penitential. The practice ceased about 1954. We sisters referred to floor-kissing as "biting the dust."

It was following one of these sessions that I had a shocking encounter with Lettie. The repeated incident of the bells was humiliating and frustrating to her. *Nothing* was going to change the mind of either the sister at the church where the clock was slow or of Mother Regina, who was daily affronted by tardiness. There was no way we novices could approach either one. It would have to come from some other source—which, fortunately, it eventually did. But not until Lettie shaved off all her hair.

In our novitiate year our heads were always covered. We wore little skull caps over our hair with forehead bands topped by our beautiful headdresses.

Following lunch on one of the days when Lettie had just about had enough of those silly reprimands, I entered the bathroom to greet an almost unrecognizable sister. Lettie had cut off almost all of her hair. She looked like a female Yul Brynner.

"Lettie!" I gasped, still scarcely believing who stood before me.

"I had to!" she said. "I had to! If I didn't, I would have quit the convent—this minute! Not a minute more of it! But now . . ." She smiled happily, in a kind of giddy relief. "Now I can't—at least until my hair grows in."

I was still appalled.

"Sister," I said, trying to remember that now she was Sister John David, "if it is *that* bad . . ."

I felt awful. It was sad that convent life should be made so trying for as devoted a sister as Sister John David.

"It's all right," she said firmly. "I have blown my safety valve. Now it will be months before I would dare go into public. I will not be able to make a hasty decision."

She began brushing her collar and putting on her elaborate headdress. Without her thick hair, her little cap fit loosely on her head, but she fastened it tightly and covered her shorn head with her coif.

Sister John David survived other trials and became a splendid nun, spending many years of her religious life in Pakistan and Bangladesh fulfilling missionary assignments.

ৡ

At the end of the novitiate year there was another weeding out. Those of us who survived moved to the scholasticate, two buildings down from the novitiate, but attached to it through the huge kitchen which served us all.

This final convent year I returned to my classes at St. Mary's, carrying a heavy schedule while still having to maintain my household duties in the convent. Two of these were most interesting. My minor duty was in the dishwasher room of the big kitchen. Three times a day trays must be cleared and the dishes installed into the interior of an enormous commercial dishwasher whose appetite and feeding seemed endless! Besides the convent utensils and crockery, there were all the dishes from the infirmary—a multistory building. At that time there were sixteen hundred active Sisters of the Holy Cross. Whenever one of them contracted a chronic illness, she returned to the motherhouse for care. Other hospital beds were constantly filled with aged, bedridden nuns. The dishwasher room was always hot and steamy, particularly during the summer months. To some of the girls these duties seemed like previews of hell—but not to me! A job was to be done, and thinking badly enough of it to complain only intensified its odiousness.

I don't know how I was so lucky as to get my main job that year. I was one of the two sacristans for the Adoration Chapel, a hard job, but one which allowed much freedom. The Adoration Chapel was located in the infirmary. It was a most beautiful place for worship with exquisite stained-glass windows from floor to ceiling. In the mornings, instead of saying prayers in the main church, we said ours with the little old sisters in this jewellike setting.

The little old ladies, many in their eighties and nineties, were sweet and patient and, best of all, they thought I was perfect! A few were a bit senile, but I never found one who was crabby. Their bodies had almost completed their earthly cycles, and with some, their minds had already passed on, or were on long vacations. In others, their minds and spirits still raced with youthful joy. Every morning was an unexpected gift to them. They looked back on a lifetime of good works and loving service, with no regrets, and ahead with absolute assurance in the welcome of the Lord.

The priest, who was their chaplain, loved each of them. It was his duty to help prepare his darlings to die. Of course many of them had been preparing for that estate since they had taken their vows, long long ago, in another century.

The ladies told stories of the early days of the convent, which was founded in 1843 at Notre Dame. Some of them were the daughters of parents who had pioneered in Texas and Utah. From one of them I first heard a curious tale of Brigham Young, who believed, through his Mormon philosophy, that every woman must be married in order to be eligible for heaven. There were two nuns, the story went, who had gone to Salt Lake City to work during its earliest development. Brigham Young was impressed by their sincere quest for heaven in their missionary teachings. In order that they not be denied their hearts' desire, he married them, by proxy—though, of course, without their consent.

Throughout their history, nuns have turned up in unexpected places where there was a job to be done.

I heard of the nuns from Anderson, Indiana, who during a Civil War Battle, had manned a boat named *Red Rover* and maneuvered it around the Mississippi River, picking up the wounded from both armies. They carried them to safety and nursed them back to health.

At Gettysburg, the Sisters of Charity were like gleaners on the harvest field, after the battle was over, searching for, and recovering, the fallen wounded. There were no nurses' corps at that time, and any nuns who were available, with or without nurses' training, did what they could to alleviate the suffering of the injured.

From these dear ladies in the infirmary, I first heard the story of our Mother Angela Gillespie, who had founded the Holy Cross schools at South Bend. One day she called the sisters together and announced that she was going to southern Indiana to help out in the war. She invited any sister who wished to go to follow her. Before entering the convent, this lady had been a socialite in Washington, D.C. She was a relative of James G. Blaine, congressman, Speaker of the House, and twice a presidential aspirant.

Frequently the food in the military camps was of very poor caliber. It seemed unfair to expect the men to march and fight when they were undernourished. It made their recovery from illness or wounds much more difficult. The nuns invited the highest-ranking officers in the vicinity to tea. Along with their beverage they served food from the supply offered the sick. This was so inedible that the officers could not stomach it. They got the message.

At other times the nurses were able to protect the lives of soldiers wanted by the enemy. Frequently they would have men from both armies under their care. When soldiers from the opposing camp came and demanded a man, the nuns would guard his bed. They issued a rule, "No hanging from sickbeds!" They protected the men until they were able to convey them to safety.

This was the America of one hundred years ago, when, just by their presence, women had the power to civilize men. This was particularly true if the woman wore a nun's habit. It was unheard-of to rough up a nun.

Such tales gave me a deep sense of continuity. I began to feel that my small offering to the community was a link in an endless chain of selfless service. Far back before their accomplishments had been recorded, women in nun's habits, with love for *all* humanity in their hearts, had given the precious days of their lives to doing what they could to ease the suffering of the world. This human chain would extend into the future, giving of itself, its only reward the joyous knowledge that by ministering to mankind, its members truly served God.

The elderly ladies in their Victorian nightgowns bore in their thin bosoms a fierce loyalty for "our boys"—the members of the Notre Dame football team! Many of them rarely left their beds except to go to the bathroom or chapel. But on Saturday afternoons in the fall they would gather up their strength and hobble down the long uncarpeted stairways to sit by the television set and intently watch the game. In an effort to gain favor for the boys, they would make little personal sacrifices, such as denying themselves cream in their coffee, hoping through their good intentions to exert favor for their beloved team.

In those three or four hours of each day which I spent at the Adoration Chapel, I became acquainted with death. I was to see many dear spirits drift away. I would see Father walking with a particular quickness of step in a certain direction, and I would know that he was intending to administer last rites to a dying sister. I knew they could not possibly live much longer, but it was still a devastating experience to find their white beds empty, their pillows undented by their frail heads. The experience of having known them seasoned me in the pattern of the full circle of life.

Once every two or three weeks it became my turn to go to the Adoration Chapel to pray for two hours, and it always seemed my lot to pull a 1:00 A.M.–3:00 A.M. shift. Traversing the quiet infirmary halls, I could hear the heavy breathing of the sound sleepers, and sometimes the piteous moan of a sister in pain. The nurse on duty would nod to me, and we would pass, the soft sound of our garments sweeping behind us like wakes from small ships. The hospital atmosphere, mingled with that of the chapel, projected many new thoughts into my mind. I asked myself the unanswerable inquiries, "Why do people live and die? Why do bodies which start out so tender and soft grow brittle and feeble? What was the purpose between those two states?"

Watching old nuns crippled with arthritis hobbling and shuffling along behind their strollers in the corridors made a tremendous impression on me. How could a loving God do this to his people? The logic of getting rid of a body so pained must be the freeing factor. It seemed true to me that the spirit, which fights so valiantly against the ravages of time to the body, lives on. Within these ancient and pain-ridden bodies, only the spirit remained fresh, young, and ever hopeful. Surely *it* knew the secret of its final escape from the toils of this world to the releasing joy of the next.

As I would kneel alone in the chapel, though never truly alone, I recognized that far and beyond the scholastic education I was receiving at the convent, I was receiving an awareness and acceptance of life as it is within the sight and the will of God.

That winter my sister, Joyce, who was a senior at St. Mary's, came to see me during visitation hours. Our schedules rarely aligned, and I was delighted to see her.

She was more happy and excited than usual.

"I'm in love!" she announced, "and he's wonderful!"

"That's marvelous!" I said.

"He's very special. His name is John Slavsky. He lives in Detroit, and wants to marry me."

"That's absolutely great," I said, wondering why she was selling me so hard. If *she* loved him, she might have known that I would, too.

Then her attitude changed. "Shirley," she said, "when you wanted to enter the convent, I was on your side. I helped you with Mother and Daddy. You've got to help me! I know they will object. If God wasn't good enough for you, how will I ever get them to think John is good enough for me?"

Joyce was graduated that spring, and I was able to attend her commencement exercises and to meet John, whose ring she was wearing.

As to the possibility of attending her wedding . . . if we young nuns had been permitted to attend the marriages of our many friends and relatives, the convent would seldom have been able to collect a quorum for classes! All the leaves of absence were kept on an equal basis. When we traveled, to our retreats, home for vacation, or on convent business, the Church paid our way. That was necessary, or the girls from more wealthy families would have been able to travel to their distant homes, and the poorer ones would have had to remain in the convent. My father occasionally made donations to the convent, but this did not entitle me to any privileges. One year he gave a fine organ. His gifts were acknowledged, but I always felt that some of the nuns expected such offerings. There were those few nuns who seemed to feel that those who could afford to give had an obligation to fulfill. That did not necessarily require thanks.

My father could have afforded to pay my fare to Joyce's wedding, but that would have been unfair to others. As Joyce had predicted years before, I was unable to attend her wedding.

In that same month I completed my scholasticate year. There were still two courses I must take to receive my degree. I would take them the following summer, after which my diploma was mailed to me. But my basic period of preparation was over. I was twenty-two years old and ready to get out into the world and begin setting it straight. Shortly I would be given my assignment in teaching. What better place to make an instant impact than on young people, those fresh-faced creatures with minds like carbon paper which would instantly print any impression I made upon them!

What I failed to take into account was that all my courses in education had been between book covers. I had had no teacher training. I had never stood behind a desk and faced a student. After my many years of academic education, I was finally to receive a live one, myself.

8

The Teacher
Learns

As my classroom door opened that October morning for fifty fifth-graders to march through to the outside shrine, where the principal was to review a project of which we were especially proud, something which should never happen in a Catholic school did.

All hell broke loose.

Fifty excited children holding homemade banners extolling All Saints' Day, which they had proudly hammered to broomsticks and curtain rods, filed past me into the wide hallway, chests out, chins in. Then something happened. Who knows what ignites a riot? Somebody shoved, or one child banged another on the head with his pole. Suddenly fifty armed kids broke ranks, thrusting and poking at each other. Their banners became spears. Shouting and hooting, flaunting their flags, they raced to the stairway and down it. It was a stampede! And I was a lone cowboy in a nun's habit trying futilely to corral my dogies. The superior appeared at her office door, alerted by the racket, to head them off at the pass. It was awful!

The Teacher Learns

No one had taught me how to handle children. In my education classes I had not even been instructed in the teaching of phonics, arithmetic drills, or physical science. I had worked on a degree in secondary education. I knew little of the teaching of elementary subjects. At no time had it ever been hinted to me that I would spend my teaching days with fifty imaginative, active, preadolescent children!

I had expected to be assigned to a high school. In fact, I was given the fifth-grade class at Blessed Sacrament School on Chevy Chase Circle in Washington, D.C. By noon of my first September day of teaching, I was ready to weep. Just *seeing* that many children, all at once, fifty of them! row on row, in all stages of interest or inattention, had about undone me. Everything before me moved—in different directions. I felt like Gulliver at the mercy of the Lilliputian hordes.

After a long drink of water, I returned to the peace of my empty classroom. If I allowed myself to fold on the first day of my assignment, everything I had worked toward would cave in. As I fought to control my anxieties, there arose in my mind the lives of those saints who had surmounted apparently impossible problems, and by comparison, my challenge began to grow less. Within myself I held the undaunted conviction that I had something worthy to offer the world. I had elected to teach and been delegated these children to instruct in the rudiments of a fifth-grade education, and to further their knowledge and love of God. When the bell rang, I was ready.

Among my students were the sons and daughters of embassy parents and other wealthy and well-known Washingtonians. Although Catholic schools had been desegregrated in 1948, every shade of skin seemed represented except black, since none lived in the neighborhood. Our students were Catholics, or those who could afford to attend the school. There was no color exclusion. The variety of cultural backgrounds added richly to our development.

One of the early projects the class entered into was the All Saints' Day parade of banners. I had never imagined that fifty children, lacking implicit directions, would break loose and run yelling and jostling through the studious halls of Blessed Sacrament. The principal acquainted me with classroom dismissal procedures!

ॐ

Having learned by the end of that school year how to handle young children, I was then thrown into an entirely new world teaching seventh

81

grade at Blessed Sacrament School in Alexandria, Virginia. Only the names of the schools were alike! What happened to youngsters between fifth and seventh grades was unbelievable! At age nine, ten, or eleven, there was still a chance that an adult could be right until proven wrong. When one encountered seventh-graders, any idea that one might be the least superior was out! Fifth-graders looked up to their teachers. Seventh-graders looked sidewise.

I taught in that school for three years, and a series of events occurred which laid lengthening shadows across my heart, and brought to my pupils an early awareness of their fellow students and of life as a precious and mercurial prize.

Within a few days of the opening of school, a mother confided to me that her son, one of my students, was dying of leukemia. After great heart-searching, she and her husband had come to the conclusion that Edward would be happiest living as normal a life as possible for a boy so severely afflicted. She asked that he be allowed to continue in class and that he be treated exactly like the others.

This little boy was quite obviously ill. He was pale and thin, and had deep, dark circles under his eyes.

The demands of education in the seventh grade of a Catholic parochial school are probably the most difficult for a child. We had advanced grammatical analysis in English; our math program covered interest, percentages, net and gross product, simple algebra, and beginning geometry. In addition, there were courses in history, science, religion, penmanship, spelling, composition, music, and art.

Edward, with his many sedatives, found it difficult to concentrate. His grades fell far below average, and he could not participate in sports.

As time became short for him, Edward was sent to the hospital, and I went to see him in the children's ward. I had never before known a child who was about to die. It brought a question to my mind. Why should this young, untried spirit be so singled out by God?

Edward had already received the final rites of the Church, but still he continued to face each day with serenity. I found his lack of complaint most touching. He tried to comfort those around him who seemed troubled. On seeing his mother weep, I was told, he patted her arm and said, "Don't cry. It will be all right."

By then the children realized Edward was dying. We prayed for him daily in our classroom, and they never doubted that he would go to heaven. Still, when the word came that he had died, it was sad. When he was gone, we were less.

ॐ

The following year I again taught seventh grade in the same school, but with only thirty-five students.

In that class there was a sweet little girl named Marcia, who was an excellent student, quiet, and ladylike in behavior. In the spring she began missing classes frequently, and her mother explained to me that it had been discovered that a virus was attacking her heart. Marcia was being treated with intensive doses of penicillin. For some time she was in and out of school.

It was baseball season, and if there was one thing my class loved, it was baseball! Every recess the class divided into two teams, and we would cross the playground to a cleared space which we felt was our own particular ball park. We kept an ongoing competition from day to day. The teams played furiously, cheered on by a section of nonplayers who sat on a fence and yelled. Marcia was one of these.

One day, crossing the playground, she said to me, "Sister, I'm so tired, I don't know if I can make it back."

A few weeks later she was confined to the hospital for further treatment, and she died.

This was again a shock to the children. We talked together about our uncomplaining schoolmate, and the children came to the conclusion that "God had taken the best one of all."

Following an old custom in their family, Marcia's mother had the child's body laid out on her own bed in her room in her house, surrounded by her dolls and the things which were hers. The children were invited to Marcia's house to view her body and pray for her. That may seem macabre, but for the children, it was not. In the classroom we talked at great length about death, and our bodies and our souls. We were all comfortable in our discussions, and the children opened up to me, and to each other, speaking without fear or guilt about how they felt about dying.

ॐ

Yet another child in my class died during the following year of my teaching at Alexandria. During my three years at that school, no child in another class died.

Jack was exceptionally small for his age, but made up for it in brains and spirit. He was a ball-bouncer, and brought his basketball to school every day. In the hall, outside in line, any place where it was possible, he bounced that ball. Although he had no dedication to the intellectual life, I was determined that his bright mind was going to be developed. Jack had been equally impressed with me when he was a sixth-grader, and had witnessed my ongoing series of baseball games.

In my class I had some very strict rules of conduct. One of the most successful was that for talking which disrupted education, an equal amount of time would be subtracted, minute by minute, from our morning recess. I have mentioned our favorite baseball field. In order to acquire this, day after day, it was necessary to evacuate our room when the bell rang, and march quickly out of the building, where the children could then break into a run and cross the playground to secure this particular field for our games. This took organization. When we were late, we would find another team had our place.

Jack, who had been a talker and a time-waster, quickly caught on that minutes counted. He became less of a discipline problem, and his grades improved. He rallied the class to lining up and getting out of the building quickly so that no moment of our recess was wasted. Our baseball games waged hotly, becoming both a divisive and unifying force. We had class spirit!

But again, in the spring, a mother called to tell me that one of the children was ill. Jack had spinal meningitis and was dying. She told me that she had no idea that her son had such strength of character as to be able to endure his suffering. After a week of misery, he died.

Having three children die, three years in a row, in my classroom struck me as strange. In times of deeper superstition, this might have been considered a dark phenomenon. Some people alluded to the thought that possibly I had been especially chosen to prepare these children to face their afflictions. Who can say? However, I think that in a parochial school where religion is taught, there can be an extra measure in the relationship between student and teacher; more than is possible when the teacher is merely an instructor of academics. There can be value in a shared philosophy of life between student and teacher, into which, in time of crisis, a child can reach and find understanding and comfort.

Upon the completion of my scholasticate year, I had taken my temporary vows of poverty, chastity, and obedience. That had been marked by the giving of a royal-blue silk cord, called a cincture, which was worn doubled about the waist, and dropped with two tassels to the hemline. At that time also, each sister in my class made her will, granting, in the event of her death, everything she then owned, or anything she might thereafter inherit before the time of her death, to designated persons or the convent.*

Three years later, during the summer, I returned to the convent to make my final vows. Again there was a beautiful ceremony, though to me, it was not as impressive as the investiture of the habit. We each received the Silver Heart, which was always worn thereafter. It was attached to a small black cord and hung at the pointed base of the nun's large collar. The collar was made of plastic, which was practical as far as keeping it clean, but it was hot to wear.

The many Catholic convents around the world have varying vows which their particular nuns take. One becomes a nun, not of the Catholic Church, but of a specific congregation. The final vows I made were of poverty, chastity, and obedience *as a member of the Sisters of the Holy Cross*—forever.

One may wonder that I could promise poverty, chastity, and obedience forever and now be married in all good conscience in the Catholic Church. The reason is that when I made those vows, I made them in sincerity. Both being a member of a religious order and being married are states of life. There is a vow of marriage and a vow of religious life.

In the Catholic Church there are seven sacraments: baptism, penance, confirmation, Holy Eucharist, matrimony, holy orders, and extreme unction. When two people marry, their "I do" is the sacrament. Matrimony is a sacrament instituted of God. Religious life is not begun by receiving a sacrament. One takes a vow instituted by the Church, whose authority is the Pope. The Church law is that the authority who makes the law is the only one who can change the law. Therefore, upon application for release from a vow, with accompanying justifiable reasons, the Pope may grant dispensation, relieving the person of the commitment. Having received this release, a former nun would be able to marry and still remain a good Catholic.

It is appropriate also to explain why the Church, in like manner, can dispense a priest from the vow of celibacy and permit him to marry. The priesthood is instituted by holy orders, which is a sacrament.

In the event that she left the convent, the document was destroyed.

Beyond accepting this sacrament, the priest in the Catholic Church also vows celibacy. This is a vow instituted by the Church. When a priest receives a dispensation to marry, he is being dispensed from a Church-oriented promise. He may continue to be a priest. But at this time in the Catholic Church, he is not allowed to exercise his priestly powers—to say Mass and administer the sacraments—because the Church has not granted him the power of jurisdiction to do so while he exists in a married state. His case is similar to that of a man with a law degree who has not passed the bar, who is a lawyer, but without jurisdiction to practice until power is granted according to the rules of a particular state.

At last a fully endowed nun, I arose each day, eager to meet new challenges, to discover what might come next in the brilliant and ceaselessly changing kaleidoscope of my life. How could life be anything but an adventure when each morning I faced thirty-five to fifty children, avidly advancing in an exploration of life? It was my goal to keep them excited about learning.

My zest for excellence among my students had an unexpected benefit for me. I became an experimental teacher for the National Science Foundation and returned to Blessed Sacrament School at Chevy Chase, Maryland. Once again I was in a world of the children of the wealthy and renowned. That year a younger brother of Pat Buchanan, who was later an aide to President Richard Nixon, was one of my students, as was a child of Walter Jenkins, then aide to Vice-President Lyndon Johnson.

Among my school duties I managed the patrol boys who guarded the school crossings. One of my guards was a son of an embassy official from a Latin-American political dynasty. This boy was thrilled with the job of marching to the crosswalk each day to stand and direct his fellow students. Every afternoon I would see him step proudly to his position. Parked down the street, patiently waiting for him, was a seven-passenger Cadillac limousine with a uniformed chauffeur.

After seven years of teaching younger pupils, I was at last given an opportunity to use the talents I had developed for secondary education. I was sent to Norfolk Catholic High School in Virginia. This was just after the fomenting and hassle which had closed Virginia public schools because of the Supreme Court decision on integration. I had my first experience teaching blacks. It was a revelation and delight to me to discover that they had been prepared intellectually and socially and were able to hold their own with the white students.

At the start of my year at Norfolk Catholic High, a fine black student, whom we shall call Ken McDaniels, was not only cocaptain of the football team but was elected student body president. Ken was not elected because he was black, but because he was the outstanding person in the school—a true gentleman, serious student, and great sportsman. To me, integration was not something which would ever be worked out because a law was passed. Integration was when black and white students worked together, matched with equal skills, and among themselves, selected their leaders.

My life as a nun expanded in areas beyond teaching. I was elected to the Provincial Assembly of the Sisters of the Holy Cross, which examined the financial setup of the community for the Eastern Province,* and which discussed such needs as that for providing new schools or the closing of old ones where populations had shifted. If there were problems of morale within the community, they would be discussed there.

It has been asked of me if there was, or was I aware of, any abnormal behavior within the convent. That is a stream of speculation which seems to titillate the minds of those who are unable to understand the self-removal of priests and nuns from the daily life patterns of the world. First, I must say, I was continually busy. We were all kept busy with our work. To those not seeking an aberration of their own, such deviation might not be apparent. If there were any, since I was considered a leader among my age group, and had been elected to the Provincial Assembly, I would have been one of the last to find out. That is, such a thing would have been especially hidden from me. A sister with a morality problem (lesbianism, alcoholism, addiction to barbiturates) would have been most careful to have kept it from me.

There were two sisters in a convent where I lived at another time who, I later heard, were alcoholics—supplied by liquor brought in by "friends" from the outside. I heard a story, unsubstantiated, that one

---

*The Congregation of Holy Cross in the United States is divided into three geographical provinces.

sister—I suppose there would have had to have been two—was/were lesbians. I did not know it at the time. The thought never crossed my mind.

There were also stories of nuns and priests who withdrew from their orders because they had developed romantic attachments either inside or outside the community. I did not personally know any until my last year at the convent.

I was never a superior in charge of other nuns, or I might be better informed. Such a matter would have been addressed to the provincial chapter, but while I was a member of that body there were no such cases.

As for my personal observation, perhaps I am not the right person to ask. I am a happy, busy person. I do not use my time seeking faults in others. I do not mean to be insensitive to problems, but when a person is in a hurry all day merely to accomplish all the tasks lined up for herself and which have been lined up for her by others, there is little time to reflect on possible weaknesses in the people not actually close. There is little enough time for the people with whom one has daily contact. Although religious men and women are more likely to be stable, since they have been psychologically tested before entry, one must recognize that the same problems of sexual or addictive habits could exist inside the convent as without. Like everyone else, people with habits can have habits.

It is not frequent in teaching to find other teachers who work in the same department who have the same compatible attitudes toward teaching as one holds oneself. At Norfolk Catholic High, two other sisters and I composed the History Department. We were best friends, and marveled at our good fortune. We didn't think it could last.

Of course, it didn't.

9

"Boston Before Breakfast"

On the last day of October in 1963, I was notified that I was to report the following morning to St. Matthew's Convent in Washington, D.C.

I left Norfolk so fast I did not even have time to say good-bye to my students or my fellow teachers!

Upon arrival in Washington I was driven immediately to the Provincial House on Rockville Pike where the emergency was explained to me. I was to replace a nun at the Calvert School who, after months of deteriorating health, had had a breakdown while teaching her seventh-grade class. A nun of particular abilities was required to readjust the thirty-five impressionable children.

The mother provincial felt that I could continue the class with minimum disruption. She said to me, "Sister Bernardine, the sisters have been through a great deal. Go there, and do your job."

"I will, Mother," I replied.

She smiled at me. We had spent a week together the previous summer, when I had been chosen to attend the annual retreat with the Sisters of Mercy. Of the sixteen hundred Holy Cross sisters, six were selected for this occasion. I was younger than most and felt especially privileged to be among them.

The leader of the retreat had been a saintly Italian, Father Lombardi, who had started the Better World Movement in Italy after World War II. He lectured on "Love as a Healing Power." He also was an advocate of discussion. One did not simply swallow concepts in life and keep still. I certainly agreed with him! I was not averse to stating myself clearly on subjects which I felt deserved clarification.

The mother provincial was aware that I espoused the movement of Father Lombardi.

"Time is necessary for these sisters to recover from the experience they have been through," she said, looking me keenly in the eyes. "Save your big ideas for another time."

I almost laughed at her frankness, but I answered seriously.

"Yes, Mother."

She gave me one last warning look.

"Don't rock the boat," she said.

I sincerely meant to do exactly as I was told.

But something happened.

Before long Mother made an appointment for me to see her.

"Sister," she said, "what did I tell you to do? I asked you not to make any ripples, and all I hear is that you are making waves."

It came out that the other sisters were asking questions about me. They were alarmed because I received copies of the *Better World* newspaper of Father Lombardi, which they considered radical. I was appalled by this criticism of thinking, but tolerated it.

Less than a month after I arrived at the tiny convent next to St. Matthew's Cathedral, to teach at Calvert School, all the eyes of the world were focused on us. President Kennedy was assassinated in Texas, and his body was returned to Washington. He would be buried from St. Matthew's.

From far distant countries, people came to honor the fallen President, the youngest President the nation had ever elected, an appealing, though controversial figure. Political misunderstandings around the world were forgotten for a few days as the ceremonies of his burial, relayed around the globe by television, captured the minds of the populace.

In Washington, at the cathedral, it was soon realized that the throngs wishing to attend the services would be so vast that in order for the notables who were arriving from abroad, plus the family and close friends of the Kennedys, to be properly seated, tickets would have to be issued.

There was seething activity all around the church on the day of the funeral. Vast crowds gathered, both to mourn and to catch a glimpse of the many famous people who had come to the city. Two other nuns and I crawled out the library window and climbed to the portico roof to watch the proceedings.

As far as we could see, there were people, patiently waiting, standing elbow to elbow along Connecticut and Rhode Island avenues. It was a bright November day. Everything in the world seemed to have stopped except for those motions necessary to honor and bury the President.

Our habits blowing in the breeze, we stood on the rooftop amid the branches of the trees. When I happened to glance down, I saw a priest standing on a stairway below. He shook his head and smiled, and then disappeared from view. Shortly his head was again framed in a window. In his hand he was holding something white—three precious tickets to the funeral ceremony.

We were seated in the cathedral—not in a back row, not on the side, but in the sanctuary itself! I was only three seats away from officiating Cardinal Cushing. From my place I could look down and see Mrs. Kennedy and little John and Caroline; Mrs. Rose Kennedy; Attorney General Robert Kennedy and his wife, Ethel; Senator Edward Kennedy; the President's sisters; and all of their uncountable children. Prince Philip of England was present, as well as General de Gaulle and Emperor Haile Selassie. All the world seemed to be sharing our grief. It was an occasion of tremendous emotional churning, and I felt it deeply as the elaborate service progressed.

The most memorable part of the ceremony to me was the Mass. The tension of restraint amid the straight-spined Kennedy family who came forward was strengthening to behold. Their children, to the youngest in attendance, seemed to understand the impact of the occasion. Previously I had thought of Jacqueline Kennedy only as one who by her simple and modest style had made a needed contribution to women's fashions. Then I saw her as a bereaved woman of great dignity. Her face was a mask of crushed sorrow as she received Communion. I admired the Christian stamina of the Kennedy family in their hours of public suffering.

Apparently, I had a small problem of my own.

When I had made my confession during the retreat headed by Father Lombardi, the priest who heard me had told me that I seemed to be at a standstill in my spiritual life. He recommended that I seek a spiritual director to guide me in prayer. I had become adept at contemplative prayer, but to this man's thinking, I had reached a plateau and needed assistance to continue upward.

Reviewing this problem in my mind, I studied the religious qualities of the various priests in the local area, wondering who among them might best be able to help me. Finally I decided that Father Raymond was one whose thoughts both stimulated and advanced mine. We had several similarities which I felt would add to our accord. We were both about thirty and had attended college for two years before entering religious life.

He agreed to allow some time for me on his busy schedule. We would meet once or twice a month for half an hour, or an hour, at a time.

I told the principal I had an appointment with Father Raymond, my spiritual adviser.

She said, "Use my office, Sister. There is a window in the door."

I sensed suspicion in her tone. For a principal to vacate her office for a private prayer discussion was overemphasizing the occasion. I thought her a foolish woman. But, looking back, her viewpoint becomes more understandable. There we were, two attractive people, about of an age, with other similarities of interest than religion. As often happens with people like this sister, who do not seek to know the parties involved, physically attractive people are often construed as being intellectually shallow or spiritually weak. In opposition to this attitude, it has been my experience to discover that attractive people, being more acceptable in society, have more options in life, from which they often grow stronger in the field of personal discipline. Of course there are opposing examples of this, but I also think one finds in life what one's particular mind is seeking.

Several weeks later Father Raymond and I met again. We seated ourselves across from each other at a table near the office door. We kept the door closed, but its upper half was clear glass so that at all times we were in plain view of anyone seeking to look in.

In the middle of a teaching day, following this appointment, I was called from my class by the superior. She told me that a taxi was awaiting me at the curb. I was to report immediately to Catholic University to a Holy Cross priest who would "review my case."

What "my case" was I had no idea. It was most extraordinary to be removed from one's class. The issue must certainly be pressing. Traveling by taxi was an unaccustomed luxury. Sisters traveled by car or bus. As I neared Catholic University, I could think of no infraction I might have committed which had so aroused Sister's concern, and I found myself increasingly unhappy to have been summarily removed from my students. I was embarrassed that, in the small world of the convent, my career or my character might be under some illusive suspicion.

The priest was expecting me. I was relieved to discover that he was both friendly and understanding.

It had been reported to him by the superior that I was seeing the young priest more than seemed wise. It had been suggested to him that such an association, if permitted to continue, might lead to a sexual relationship. Father encouraged me to explain to him my reasons for choosing that particular priest as my spiritual director.

When I had finished, he leaned back in his chair and studied me thoughtfully.

"You are young, Sister, intelligent, capable, and . . ." He hesitated. Priests are not in the habit of remarking on the attributes of women, particularly nuns.

"Beautiful," he finally said. "Under some circumstances, when the critic is personally unhappy, so many good qualities arouse envy, even jealousy. I believe your sincerity in your choice of this director. I think that you should continue to see him—being always circumspect as to allow no occasion for criticism."

He continued to study me. Then he said softly, "The problem is not with you, Sister. It is in the mind of your critic."

I continued to work with Father Raymond. About once a month we met to discuss my prayer life. One might think that after so many years prayer would become effortless, flawless. There are many aspects to prayer. It requires both presence and absence of self. Through prayer one maintains one's stabilizing faith and the ability to offer serene guidance to others without personally entering the outside problem, as a doctor who faces heartrending physical conditions, yet to make proper decisions concerning them, keeps himself vitally present yet singularly apart. I began to feel myself growing again. I was spiritually uplifted. I was off my plateau!

⧦

That summer of 1964, when school was out, before continuing the work I had begun the previous summer toward a master's degree in Latin-American history, I made my annual one-week retreat at Dunbarton College.

On the final evening of my retreat, just after dinner, the sister in charge tapped me on the shoulder.

"I have a message for you," she said. "You are leaving on a plane for Boston before breakfast. You are to stay at Holy Cross Academy in Brookline. There you may enroll in any courses you wish to take at Boston College, but you are to remain there the entire summer!"

I felt as though I had been physically struck. I could scarcely breathe! All my associations in Washington were severed. My studies in my master's work were interrupted. I was shipped away like a recalcitrant sinner.

The superior had won her case.

⧦

At the beautifully situated Academy of Holy Cross in Brookline I met an old friend, a sister who had been at the novitiate with me. She was well acquainted with our superior in Boston and gave me some advice.

"Idle hands are the tools of the devil's workshop with this superior. It makes her nervous to see people relax. Never sit in her presence, Shirley, except to eat."

She offered me two keys to happiness for a summer at this convent. "Use the back stairs, and spend as much time as possible on the college campus."

I became an addict of the college library.

It seemed appropriate while in New England to study the American Revolution, and I also signed up for a course on "The City." This latter class offered two theories I found most interesting. The professor believed that the suburbs were contributing to the decline of the intellectual life in America. Driving a car to and from work each day, he reasoned, occupied one to two hours. Maintaining a suburban home involved cutting grass, mowing, gardening, repainting, and repair. None of these had anything to do with intellectual development. He did not condemn suburbia, but on these grounds he saw the rejuvenation of the inner city as a place for the educated to live.

Although he was Jewish, most of his class happened to be Catholic priests and nuns. He pointed out to us that we were a self-chosen few who had genuine freedom to stand against the wrongs of society. Without obligations to either family or spouse, we might protest, and preach against these evils without fear of risking the security of loved ones. Only the young and those in religious life had the freedom, he said, to make changes in life without hurting others. As I remembered the way I had felt when, as a college girl, I had fallen in love with Scott and had made a most difficult choice, I heartily agreed with him!

The summer was pleasant, but in the back of my mind there was the knowledge that I was in Boston as punishment. It is not easy to be happy and free in your mind when you feel defensive. I knew I was innocent of any wrongdoing. I had not even been guilty of wrong thinking! But there was no way I could exonerate myself.

One morning, late in August, I went down to the dining room for breakfast and found that the list of reassignments for the fall term had been posted. This was a register of the names of each convent in the province, under which was the name of each sister assigned there. I had not permitted myself to think ahead to that day and that moment. After the disaster of the previous school year and the suddenness of my expulsion from Washington, I had no idea where I might next be sent. By the upcoming choice, however, I knew I might be able to judge, to some degree, the regard with which I was then held within the Congregation of Holy Cross.

I had to study a map to discover my new location. It was Pericles,* New York—in the western, agricultural section of the state. It was not a large community, but it had a modern convent. Sacred Heart High School, in which I was to teach history, was highly rated. Most important to me was the further information I received about that particular school. It was one of only three in the entire Eastern Province of high schools which had an integrated faculty employing both priests and nuns.

I had been cleared.

Not its real name.

10

Love Is
Not for Cowards

Appointment to Pericles was a duty many sisters did not like, although most of those I knew on mission there were happy. The city of seventeen thousand was the center of an agricultural area which produced corn, lettuce, potatoes, onions, and other fresh produce for market. Quite a segment of the population was of recent foreign extraction, with communities of Poles, Italians, and a mixture of English, German, and Irish. Sacred Heart was a diocesan high school serving fifteen Roman Catholic parishes in three counties of New York State. I was to find my assignment there to be the happiest, most exciting of my religious life.

On my first day, as I walked down the hallway toward my classroom, I was introduced to Father Young,* a strikingly handsome priest of about my age. He was the head of the History Department.

All I could think was "Oh, God. I just *left* a situation like this!"

Father Young also served as a chaplain at a state prison and was

---

*Not his real name.

parish priest in a nearby town. In the medical profession his personality would have been called a "bedside manner." No matter how pressed he was for time, he was always able to *have* time and to give his total concentration to the problem at hand. As a result, he was loved and appreciated by the nuns, as well as the students.

You might think that a co-ed faculty might create tempting situations for the religious. You are right. Of the thirty Catholic high schools in the Eastern Province, only three had co-ed faculties. I served in two—Norfolk and Pericles. Sisters were assigned to those schools only after their emotional stability had been well proven. I was mindful of the fact that I had been removed from my position in the Washington, D.C., grade school because the superior, wrong though she proved to be, had feared my emotional entanglement with a parish priest.

It must be remembered that at all times a nun remained a nun. Wherever I was located, my home was the convent. I had a room to myself, but my duties outside its walls were constant. In all my years as a sister, there were few nights in which I had more than seven hours' sleep. My brief nights gave me long days. I needed them.

At Pericles I taught a full day of school, graded papers, prepared lesson plans, met with other teachers, met with parents, attended school and extracurricular meetings. I guided, counseled, rejoiced, and suffered with my students. That was between eight in the morning and late afternoon. At dawn I arose to a chapel bell and filled two hours with prayer and the Mass. Throughout the day there were further commitments to my spiritual life. Beyond that, I bore my share of the unceasing repetitive household duties required to maintain the human bodies and the habitat of the convent. It was also my plan, as part of my Apostolate, that I would move about the community, alleviating such suffering as I found.

The days were never long enough.

The History Department at Sacred Heart consisted of Father Young, a lay teacher, and myself. From year to year the lay person changed, but Father Young and I remained. He had a captivating manner. No matter who the other teacher in our group was, we had the most cheerful department in the school. Some called us "the Swinging Group."

Several times a year we drove together to Buffalo to hear history lectures, attend banquets, or meet with other history teachers. We continually strove to discover new presentations to share to improve the teaching of all. Our natures blended happily. In such an atmosphere, the students responded by working hard, and they performed well on New York State Regents and College Entrance exams.

A sister, on learning of my assignment to Pericles, had called it "the end of the world." Little did I know that, for me, it would be the setting for the discovery of an ever richer world. I met Father Xavier.*

Many of my feelings were changed by the entrance of this man into my life. He became a dear part of my Pericles experience. The daily adventures of teaching, year after year, overlapped, but the current that this man swept into my life seemed to carry me ever upon it, like a river always at flood tide. In knowing him, I began a relationship I had never envisioned.

We were introduced at a faculty meeting at the beginning of a school year. Our faculty was then composed of eleven priests, seven sisters, and eight lay persons of both sexes. Of the priests and nuns, several were physically attractive and well educated. They would have been superior people in any group. Not that one ever ran a Mr. or Miss Religious contest for physical beauty in an order, but comeliness, or lack of it, was outwardly visible and impossible to overlook. Possibly a handsome head or pretty face was *more* noticeable in a convent where so many things were so plain!

I was standing at the side of the faculty room when the principal touched me on the shoulder.

"Sister Bernardine," he said. "I'd like you to meet a new member of the faculty, Father Xavier. I want you to take care of him. You will both share the job of junior class moderators."

I found myself looking into two very blue eyes set in clear Nordic skin. Father Xavier was a large-boned, blond, square-jawed man, perhaps thirty-two years old. For a priest, he was exceptionally well dressed. The French cuffs of his shirt were a rare fashion in our community, and they were fastened with round gold cuff links. I thought the cut of his suit was excellent. Or was it the way he wore it?

Not his real name.

"Yes, indeed," I said to myself. "This is a job I won't mind at all."

"Father Xavier will be associate director of our sports program," the principal said. "But don't let this athletic ability fool you, Sister Bernardine. Father is a superb scholar. He has already edited and published a book."

I was impressed.

The following morning I heard the news that Father Xavier's father, who had lived in Buffalo, had died. A group of nuns arranged to drive to Buffalo to pray for the priest's father. I joined them.

Perhaps six of us made the trip. When we arrived at the funeral home where the body was laid out, we filed soundlessly inside. Together, by the casket, we said our prayers—so often repeated, one might think they had grown perfunctory, but to me, they never did. I was very aware of the individual, and prayed for his soul, and for the comforting of his family, from the depths of my heart.

At the completion of our prayers, we turned as a group.

To one side of the room we saw Father Xavier standing with a gathering of people similar enough to him in discernible ways so that we could tell they were members of his family. We moved silently to them, and Father Xavier introduced us.

I do not know how it happened that Father Xavier and I, after a time, found ourselves standing beside the casket containing his father's body. We stood there, and he talked to me, gently, lovingly, recalling characteristics of his father, his kindness, and generosity. It was a most natural thing to do.

I will never know how long we stood there—perhaps five minutes. Could it have been ten? I truly lost track of time. I was aware only of the handsome, well-spoken priest who deeply revered his father and the qualities which made a life well lived.

When I turned away from the casket to depart, I was surprised to find no one left in the room except Father Xavier's family. The sisters had all left. I had forgotten about them.

But something had begun. Something dear and important had passed between Father Xavier and me in those moments. It was the beginning of a friendship that was to mean much to both of us for years to come.

During our entire conversation, he had held my hand in his, lightly, understandingly, as we shared his loss. It was the only time during our long and interwoven association that he ever held my hand.

99

When I returned to the car, I was embarrassed to see the sisters sitting in their seats, patiently waiting, eyes straight ahead, not meeting mine. I apologized for having delayed them. Not a word was spoken. I had no idea of the time! I must have stood with Father Xavier much longer than it had seemed. What had he said? I could scarcely remember. The words had not mattered. Something else had. The seed of a very special relationship had germinated.

ॐ

A few days later Father Xavier, another priest, and I were relaxing between classes in the faculty room. It was furnished with upholstered chairs, tables with lamps, and another table which held an assortment of newspapers and magazines. One was a memorial issue to Marilyn Monroe, who had committed suicide a few years earlier. Her photograph was on the cover.

As the other priest rose to leave, he carelessly flipped through the magazine. "What could you expect for a girl like that?" he said in a deprecating tone of voice, and departed.

I glanced at Father Xavier.

"I felt sorry for her," he said.

"You did?" I was surprised. I had heard no other religious express any sympathy toward the life of that overly exploited woman. "I did too," I said.

We spoke a few sentences, sharing our understanding of the unfortunate life of the actress, and went on our way.

In the days, weeks, months, and years which followed, we were to discover that we felt similarly on many things. We also disagreed! We held involved philosophical and theoretical arguments, clashing our intellects together like lances in a jousting match. Conversations with Father Xavier were either harmonious symphonies or adventures in mental gymnastics. They were marvelous! Few priests I had ever met enjoyed a philosophical discussion as much as he. I was hard put to use my background in theology and philosophy to match his facile mind.

ॐ

Class moderators at Pericles always worked in pairs, one man and one woman. Father Xavier and I were advisers, sponsors, and chaperones for the junior class. We supervised the planning of their parties and outings and any activity to which they traveled on school buses. Their trips always required chaperones. My comoderator and I covered many jostling, cheer-yelling miles in those yellow chariots. I again became an avid rooter for a football team—the struggling, pounding boys at Sacred Heart. The enthusiasm of the young people was delightful. I enjoyed participating in it as I shared their sporting events, but I probably would not have attended their games so regularly if there had been a different sports director.

It is difficult to know when love begins. With us, because of our restrictions, it was a gentle, growing process. A moment we shared was brighter for me. The sight of him in the distance was a beacon, solid, guiding, strong, and safe. Between us there seemed a path of light. My eyes looked up to him in respect for the qualities I knew him to have. I came to love him.

How does one describe loving without sexual intimacy in today's world, in a time of acceptance of "instant all"?

There had begun between us an excitement of mind. There also followed a physical attraction. He was male. I was female. I had been raised in a society which had bred into me the distinction and purpose of the two separate roles. On entering religious life I had learned to sublimate my drives in favor of Christ. For me, this had been easy. The flint had not been struck. But then, as Father Xavier and I grew in our knowledge and understanding of each other, I recognized I cared for him. I was concerned for him. I found stimulation and satisfaction in our working and learning together. It was important to *be* together. I enjoyed looking at him. I found myself thrilled to be alive at the same time, in the same world, with him, to live in an area which daily brought us into each other's sight and hearing.

Attending sports events was a socially acceptable way of being together. We did not always sit side by side. We had the responsibility of a few hundred teen-agers who took a good deal of attention. At the games we would sit with groups of parents and students, two or three people separating us. Sometimes we would have seats on opposite sides of the field. But we were usually in sight of one another. There was an appreciation of his presence which gave pleasure and comfort to me. Mine was a loving state within the context of our condition in life. I recognized the added strength I had through my love.

I was sexually healthy, and at times the lack of physical demonstration was a torturous crucifixion to me. But I was not a teen-ager. I had chosen my religious state, and to compromise it would have been untenable. I regarded myself too highly and cared for him too much. If I had been interested in romance in the fulfilled sense of the word, I would have sought dispensation and encouraged him to do likewise.

Father Xavier and I were able to share, within the bounds of propriety, a most special part of our lives. I felt the joy of loving was worth the risk involved. The love I felt for this man gave me great personal happiness, developing within me a capacity for realizing another aspect of life. Human beings require love even when it is restricted in the measure of its sharing. Love is not for cowards.

ॐ

One Saturday in the spring I met Father Xavier coming out of his office. He took me aside, looking rather troubled.

"There is a woman in the hospital who slit her wrists last night."

I waited for him to go on.

"She lives in my parish," he said, his voice grave with concern. "She is the mother of five small children. When she was admitted to the hospital, she told the authorities that I would be happy to take care of her children."

What a picture! I shared his distress, but I was also amused. Five children in the priests' house!

"I've placed the children with Catholic charities. But I am concerned about the mother. . . ." He looked off into space.

"Don't tell me," I said, "she has a crush on you!"

"She doesn't quite understand our relationship."

That was not unusual. Patients fancied themselves in love with their doctors, clients with their attorneys, parishioners with their priests. But I had to comment. "So she slit her wrists."

Father Xavier was astounded. "Not over me!"

"Why, of course not," I agreed. "That wouldn't be reasonable. . . ."

"I would appreciate it if you would go to the hospital and check on her," he said. "I want her to know that I care for her as the parish priest, but I don't want her to misread our association."

"Of course not!" I said. "I'll call on her."

It was a lovely day and the hospital was only a short way from the school. I walked, enjoying the excuse to be out on the treelined streets.

The leaves were not yet fully uncurled. There was a readiness about the air, as though the world was making its final preparations before a party. It was pleasant to breathe the sun-filtered sweetness around me, to greet familiar faces, and to dwell for a few tender moments on the consternation of my love. Leave him five children! The nerve of that woman!

At the hospital, I entered the room where the woman lay. It would have been difficult to judge her age. Deep purple circles underscored her eyes. Her bony arms lay straight beside her on the white sheets, both wrists bandaged.

At the sight of me, she sat up.

Quietly I said, "Father Xavier sent me. He wanted to know how you are."

She stared at me, looking me up and down in my coif and long habit. Then she could not contain herself. She blurted out, "Isn't he a gorgeous hunk of man!"

I certainly agreed with her, but felt I should be more constrained. "He is a responsible priest," I said, emphasizing the final two words. "He is tied up with his sports program and won't be able to call on you. I will tell him that you are sitting up and feeling better."

In my mind I was saying, "You conniving woman! Don't you dare try to involve him!"

I was not about to let any woman besmirch his career. If he was going to reconsider his vocation and marry anyone, it would be me! But I had no intention of that. I was happy working by his side, doing my job to the best of my ability, and assisting him wherever possible.

11

Workers
of the Fields

Migrant workers in New York State?

At certain seasons of the year many might be found in an area with a most descriptive name—"the mucklands."

I had been representing the Sisters of the Holy Cross in Buffalo on a diocesan council to foster vocations. The council consisted of forty or fifty priests and nuns who met every two months to present to high school and college students various communities as attractive places for their life work. I had spoken to groups several times, and once been interviewed by a local radio station on why I had entered the convent.

One of the council sisters told me about the first Catholic migrant worker project in western New York.

"It is a shame," she said, "that the Catholic Church has been so slow in getting involved in this work."

Slow! I have never even heard of it! Migrants were something in John Steinbeck novels. They had lived in California during the time of the Oklahoma Dust Bowl.

She assured me they were here and now.

Another nun at Pericles, Sister Vincetta, who was also interested in the Apostolate, began to investigate with me. We learned that the parents of one of her students owned an onion farm in the mucklands. When I expressed concern for the migrants who might work the farms, she asked the student's father to give us a tour. He came for us and drove us to his extensive land, about forty-five minutes from the convent. It was late winter. Nothing was growing. The empty fields gave a sense of barrenness. Two sides were outlined by hedges for windbreaks to control the sweep of air from across Lake Ontario. There were, of course, no workers present. With justifiable pride, our host spoke of his farm and showed us his warehouse with its sorting and packing machines. I began "to know my onions."

As we drove away we observed several rows of cinder-block buildings, painted green, each divided into perhaps six apartments. The structures appeared solid, but there was a shabbiness about them. The screen doors hung on their hinges. Windows were broken and stuffed with rags.

"Migrant workers," the farmer said.

The quarters appeared uninhabitable. It saddened me to think of families living in such bleak compartments.

He read the concern on my face. With despair in his voice, he said, "We built this camp to service the workers. There were stoves and refrigerators and good plumbing. The beds had mattresses. They didn't know how to take care of anything. By the end of the first season, the mattresses were all torn or cut up. They threw things down the toilets and destroyed them. After one season, nothing worked. What could we do? We built a place that was sturdy and painted it so it looked nice, and in a few months, the destruction was incredible. They created their own pigsties."

His discouragement was genuine. He was a businessman. He had been willing to make initial investments in social welfare and even to reconstruct his buildings once or twice. But then he had quit. He could not see the wisdom of continuing to take a man-created loss each year.

On our way back to Pericles he showed us some other small dwellings where numerous ragged children played and a few untidy women moved about.

"Abandoned," he said. "They used to have husbands who came here to work. The men drifted off. Perhaps they intended to return. Few did. The women and children are here."

He said "are here" as though it was the end of the road for the

105

women. I suppose it was. There was little work for them. They existed on welfare and handouts.

As we traveled farther, the onion farmer pointed to a run-down two-story building.

"The real trouble lies there," he said, "with the overseer of the workers. When we want workers, we don't send to Texas or Florida, we contact the overseer and tell him how many pickers we want to hire for the season. He makes the arrangements. He sets the price. The amount of their wages that he keeps for himself is part of the problem.

"The people are trucked in. They can't get into town to shop in regular stores. The overseer sells them their supplies and their liquor."

The remainder of the drive home was mostly in silence, as we each thought our own thoughts.

Later, after I met Clarence Kelley, I would discover that the Miami I had always known and the Miami familiar to Clarence and the FBI were two different cities occupying the same territory. It was the same there in lovely western New York. There were two strata of human beings, neither knowing the other's world.

The migrants never came to Pericles. I had lived there two years and had never seen one. They did not come to stroll in the parks. They did not attend church. They were not customers in stores, nor patients in hospitals. They simply weren't there. That afternoon I discovered some facts of life about the area that my students, who had been born there, and lived every day of their lives there, never knew existed.

I wish I might say that I moved immediately to alleviate the circumstances of the dreadful discovery I had made, but my life was always lived at brisk pace, teaching, praying, working, and keeping up with extracurricular activities.

ও

It was on another of my Buffalo trips that a sister spoke again of the mucklands. A priest in Hercules,* the parish which included the mucklands, wanted some help in running a day nursery for the children of migrants.

"You know, Sister," she said, "those little children are not yet of school age. Each day they go to the fields with their parents. Father Zadar† is looking for some high school students to help in their care."

---

*Not its real name.
†Not his real name.

I had just returned from my annual retreat in Washington where I had taken further courses toward a master's degree in Latin-American history. It was summer. Vacation was still in effect for the students. I was able to locate four from my classes of the previous year, two boys and two girls, who were willing to help.

In midmorning of a hot August day we set out for the mucklands. Father Zadar met us at a one-story structure of aging, unpainted wood set amid weedy fields. He was a tall, slender, clean-cut man with a square face with strong, fine features. I was to find him a man of few words.

Waving toward a porch, recently enclosed with makeshift windows, he said, "Go in and see what you can do."

Followed by my students and Sister Vincetta, I climbed the steps and opened the door. The din of children's high-pitched voices was like an orchestra composed of cymbals and piccolos. We entered and became engulfed knee-deep in an eddy of hot, constantly moving young bodies. There were perhaps eighty children gathered on the glassed-in porch, all thin, black, and quite covered with dust from the playground which had caked to the perspiration on their skins and hair. They ranged in age from about three to eight. Only their hands were clean. Outside, I was told, was one faucet where they had all been lined up to wash.

Two other sisters, who arrived earlier, had assembled the ingredients for lunch. It was to be peanut-butter sandwiches, grape juice, and cookies. While the students seated the children on benches along low, homemade tables, we arranged the food on trays.

Twelve to fifteen children wiggled at each table. They had no table manners. They did not begin to understand the commands, "Sit down. Fold your hands."

When Father Zadar entered, his presence alone was able to still them.

"Before we eat," he said, "we will say grace."

The children had no idea of to whom they were praying. I felt that they did not even know that they *were* praying. What was prayer to them? It was a delaying process before food would be given to them to stay the hollow anger of their stomachs.

The students passed the food, which was devoured without being set down. We certainly hadn't needed plates!

I had observed bedlam before among children, but never with such a distressing quality to it. As elbows banged together, the tabletops became purple with spilled juice. Overeager, untrained hands made

107

more messes. Tears ran. Insults were exchanged. And above it all rose cries for "More juice!" "More sandwiches!" "More cookies!" "*More!*"

When, following lunch, we had restored some degree of order to the porch, I stepped to the next room. It was crowded with boxes of used clothing. Father Zadar was standing amid them.

"Please, Sister," he said, "do you think you could organize this room in such a way that we could know what size person would wear the clothes in these boxes?"

"I will be happy to, Father," I said.

I looked at what was sticking out over the tops of the boxes. Everything was old, worn, and brown. The sisters and I began sorting and organizing the clothing to the best of our ability. It was disgusting to see what sometimes people sent to "charity." Out of the boxes came musty-smelling, wrinkled, uncleaned, sometimes torn clothing. There were some nice things, but little to wear with pride. As I was to continue to observe the poor, I became more callous to this fact. What was better than nothing? Answer: something.

While I worked, I was able to observe Father Zadar and saw him to be a man of astonishing efficiency. He had a regular pace at which he moved about the four rooms and the grounds of the decrepit building. He continued from place to place, doing maintenance work. Never frenzied, he appeared relaxed, but he accomplished constantly. The path ahead of him seemed always to be filled with wreckage, but when he had passed, there was order.

That day was one of learning for me, as well as for my students.

I was on the playground, helping with the children, when one of my girls, Debbie, came running to me, a small child in her arms.

"This is a *real* emergency," she said. "This baby has *got* to have clean diapers"—a situation I had been able to guess from some distance.

"What am I going to do, Sister?" she asked, thrusting the child toward me. "Please take her."

"Debbie," I said, "if you were the mother of this child, if you were really poor, what would you do? Go into the house and see what you can find to make a diaper for her. Clean her up, and put it on her."

Debbie stared at me blankly, then marched off, mouth grim.

About fifteen minutes later she rejoined me. She held a clean baby and a new respect for resourcefulness.

After the school year began, our visits to the day nursery became less frequent. But I was gratified that with the many other more pleasant diversions open to my students, they continued to accompany me to the center. The students were not always the same, but those who experienced Father Zadar's day nursery mostly went more than once.

In the evenings after the children had gone home, and we had returned to Pericles, Father Zadar labored on. He drove his car to the migrant camps and transported the people back to his little store to choose items for themselves and their families.

My heart went out to him and his endeavors, but I found it difficult to maintain my initial enthusiasm. The weak sense of satisfaction I received could not equal the hopelessness I felt. There seemed no permanent sign of progress for our efforts. The children continued to be hungry, dirty, and mannerless. Each time I approached the center it looked more and more dingy to me. Every day there were more boxes of overworn clothes to sort. I tried to think of the happiness such contributions would make to their new owners. That seemed bleak.

The sacrifices of my students, who gave their time, went beyond giving. It involved taking into their minds sights and smells and sounds of ugliness which were forever unforgettable. To balance this to some measure, I made it a point, on our way home from our social welfare ventures, to stop and have some simple fun together, such as sharing a cooling drink at a wayside store and skipping stones across a small lake. Such little recesses were meant to be a healing time.

Between those who shared these experiences there developed a special comradeship. The students regarded each other with respect for their accomplishment in their shared purpose.

ತನ

Father Zadar stopped by school one day during a faculty meeting. When there was an opening, he asked, "Can you get fifteen or twenty students together on Saturday to pick cucumbers?"

Father Zadar frequently made surprising requests, but this seemed a bit to ask. Catholic schools are demanding of their students. For me to find twenty students to give up their Saturday seemed next to impossible.

"There's a farmer who says I can keep all the money I can get for the cucumbers," he whispered.

I presented the project to my classes, and early on Saturday morning, nineteen of them showed up, lunch bags in hand, smiles on their faces.

Father Zadar drove us in a truck to the field, its rows barely visible through the verdant entanglement of vines.

"I brought those out last night," he said, pointing to a heap of cardboard boxes and wooden crates. "All you have to do is fill them. As you do, I will cart them off to market and come back for more."

It was cool. Dew sparkled rainbows from the large leaves of the plants.

At Father Zadar's command, "Let's go!" the students chose boxes and rows and started picking, dragging their boxes behind them. They stooped ineptly from their waists, picked, turned, placed the cukes in the boxes, turned back, stooped. Soon their back muscles protested.

I knew! I was right with them.

Their shoes filled with dirt. They kicked them off and stuffed their socks in their pockets. They dropped down on their knees and picked, crawled, picked. When the boxes were full, we carried them to the ends of the rows and filled the crates and returned to pick again.

The hours passed, and with every one, the sun rose higher. Its rays became more intense.

The pickers sang musical rounds and echoing songs. They ran contests as to who would find the largest cucumber; who would pick the most; who could fill a box fastest.

I worked along with them in my nun's habit. Every bit of it. A nun could not take off her shoes and go barefoot, no matter how annoying the dirt that had collected. She might not remove her coif for a more suitable sun-visored cap. Under no circumstances could she ease off her hot plastic collar and open up the neck of her blouse.

I worked in the field in full regalia. Did nuns have summer whites? My! No! Year-round we wore our heavy black wool serge shirts and capes. They were supposed to insulate against the weather. Usually, they did. That day, I was miserably hot. Perhaps nun's habits were not designed for picking cucumbers. I picked. Leaning close to the sandy loam, the earth radiated its reflected heat upward. The sun beat down from above. In between, I felt like a burned hamburger in an overtoasted bun.

At the end of the day we replaced the cucumbers in the back of the truck with the weary, grimy bodies. Nineteen surprisingly happy students chorused their way back to Pericles, proud of their achievement.

Father Zadar was also delighted. For the day's work from his twenty field hands, including one sister with a sunburned face, he had received about $190.

A state school for the blind was located in Pericles, not far from our high school. Frequently we observed the sight of children tapping their way with their teacher as they practiced crossing the street to the park.

One Christmas the faculty was invited to attend the program presented by the blind children. From this, we decided to increase the awareness of both groups of students, the blind and the sighted, to the lives of the other. We exchanged students for a day, ten at a time.

At the state school, the Sacred Heart students were blindfolded and led to their classes by the unsighted students. The full day's program included lunch, and to the delight of the sightless children, peas were served. The ineptness of our students, who had difficulty finding their food, amused their more expert companions. When it became our turn to host the blind, the Sacred Heart students had another opportunity to become personally acquainted with their afflicted fellows. The two groups shared experiences and learned to relax together. Between the two worlds of darkness and light, barriers which had previously repelled them from each other through lack of communication were dismantled.

As my life became more and more filled with activities at school, my time with the migrant worker project decreased. There began to be trouble about the program. The people of Hercules had never recognized that there *was* a migrant problem. It was unpleasant for them to think about. Public criticism was made about their lack of concern for the social problem.

Those were the years when, for the first time, many Catholic religious began involving themselves with such injustices. This caused parishioners to complain to the bishop, and Father Zadar was one of their targets. He was not giving *them* enough time, his critics said. Others frankly admitted that Father Zadar's work with the migrants made them feel guilty, a feeling they did not enjoy, and which they did not like having thrust upon them.

In the course of time, Father Zadar was transferred back to Buffalo, where he was given a poor parish in the inner city in which to do his social work, where he could not offend the consciences of the Catholics of Hercules.

The migrant worker project continued, but not with as much impetus. Such undertakings, it seems to me, are always shouldered by someone already under a heavy schedule. It takes a worker with vast spiritual capability, and empathy for all people, to meet such needs. Such people are themselves aware of the best that life can be. What is often overlooked is that the people who are most deprived in our society do not have this wide view and understanding of the promises of life.

In social work the outsider who intends to alleviate distress is faced with a double enemy. Before him is the physical suffering of the deprived. There is also a lack of hope, a form of despair. The destitute are often resigned to their plight of life, and no longer fight to rid themselves of it.

For the social worker, there is outrage and spiritual suffering for the plight of the deprived. The poverty-stricken usually do not experience this. Eventually, the social worker realizes that no matter how hard he works, no matter how many plans he implements, there is rarely going to be any change for the better. I realized this acutely when, week after week, I would return to Father Zadar's child care center, always to be faced with that sorry collection of broken boxes filled with the sameness of old clothing. Everything grew gray to me. The original state of confusion I had met on my first day was there on my last.

A social worker, I found, must work to keep his spirits high, must continually revive himself against the repetitive dreariness of working with the poor. One of the terrible deprivations of poverty is the lack of beauty in the lives of the impoverished. People need beauty almost as much as they need air and water.

I began to understand why dissenters, such as the Berrigans and others who became revolutionaries in America, took to that road. When brilliant and talented minds give their all to a cause, and see no change, the next logical step is to think that there can *be* no change under the present system. Therefore, they work against the system, to shake it up.

My own life raced on, stopped short several times a day for quiet breathtaking during prayers. Then it sped on. I represented our order on numerous councils and committees. On each of my assignments I met new people who planted further ideas in my mind. An especially productive one developed in my association with the Oblate Sisters of

Providence, a black community in Buffalo. Through this group I was able to accomplish continuing charitable work which could include my students. Together we collected quantities of used clothing, happily of better quality than at Father Zadar's warehouse, to distribute to the poor. On one hand, thus, I was able to help those in need, and on the other, my students had an increased awareness of their better fortune.

Father Xavier coached the baseball team. Before entering the seminary, he had played professional baseball briefly with a minor league team of the Detroit Tigers. He particularly loved the game. With such a special coach, I tried to attend all the home games. They were played at Pericles stadium, near the convent. I always tried to be in the bleachers with the students and some of their parents before the games began. Father Xavier had enough problems with some of his sixteen-year-old ballplayers without having to worry about my support. I did not want him disappointed by not being able to find my face in the crowd.

But I had my convent duties.

The games began at four o'clock.

Our evening meal was served promptly at six.

Each night, in turns, it was prepared by two sisters. It seemed to me my turn came every afternoon that we had a home game. Absolutely I *had* to be in the convent in time to get dinner on the table on the stroke of the hour. But I hated to miss more of the game than was necessary. Fortunately, I was popular with my students. On those afternoons when I cooked, I had one of my junior class members with a car stand by to rush the other sister and me home at the latest possible moment. In the midst of the game, that loyal boy would dash Sister Mary Louise and me back to the convent kitchen.

There, in the last half hour, sister and I would run a marathon of food preparation to produce "gourmet dinners" for the fifteen waiting to be served. We sincerely tried to make those last-minute meals interesting and delicious so there would be no cause for complaint. That was my rule of thumb for any activity in which I might participate wherein Father Xavier was involved. It was difficult to argue with excellence.

My fondness for Father Xavier lay always deep in my heart. It never wavered. Through the years there was a gentle transition from the intense attraction which we had at first recognized, with its element of romance, to an easy, friendly, responsive relationship. We were model professionals, and successful and productive co-workers.

We never went anyplace alone. There were two sisters who enjoyed attending concerts and lectures such as those we found interesting. They could always be counted on to accompany us.

The only times I ever "went out with him alone" were when we were in the company of forty or fifty yelling kids. Riding the school bus was something most of the other sisters disliked intensely. Not I! If my friend was there, I rode those crowded, noisy, uncomfortable buses! Amid that confusion, Father Xavier and I could be out until eleven or twelve at night with our lively throngs, and nobody complained.

To describe our relationship through the years, I thought of it as a marriage of mind and spirit. We were together in the duties which were ours.

It was love at a distance.

Platonic love . . . feeling without touch.

12

Departure

In 1967–68 there were several changes within the Catholic Church. There was also a change in me.

In the Church there was a general softening of some of the more obsolete rules. Following a consensus of the nuns, and with the spirit of the Church, nuns who so wished might again use their parent-given names, rather than those taken in religious life. Thus I dropped "Mary Bernardine" and again became Sister Shirley Ann. Women's liberation had something to do with this. There were many nuns who no longer wished to answer to the names of males. Not even male saints!

The habit was modified, a step which had been under consideration for some time. The skirt was shortened to mid-calf. It was still made of black material and was very much a religious habit. The resplendent headdress of the Holy Cross was refashioned. No longer was the forehead band required, and our picturesque, fluted caps, which I had thought so pretty, were no more.

The following year the styles were changed again. From then on we were permitted to purchase off the racks in department stores(!) simple navy-blue suits of either polyester or wool. To wear with them I chose white blouses with short sleeves, tucked across the front, and with a tiny ruffle for decoration. The bodices were made of two thicknesses of fabric. No peek-a-boo exposure!

Beneath the remodeled costume we were able to wear our own lingerie. No more convent-issue petticoats! And our black cotton "can-can" stockings passed into oblivion, replaced by nylons—heavy, opaque, but nylons! Even our suitcases, those drab, dark badges that sisters toted while traveling, could now be colors of their own choosing.

Times leaped a century!

I, too, was about ready to leap.

I had not remained static in my observations and attitudes through the years. There were changes within me, though they had been so gradual that I was not actually aware of them until something happened which brought them into sharp focus.

When I returned to Pericles in September 1968, after another summer in Washington working on my master's degree, I received some disconcerting news. My good friend, Father Young, that charismatic priest, had moved to Buffalo. He had asked for dispensation from his vows. It was his wish to marry a young widow who had worked with him with his Catholic youth groups.

Father Young had joined the high school faculty several years before I had arrived. He was highly respected. In the four years I had worked with him I had developed great admiration and a genuine fondness for him. I felt a deep loss. As History Department head, he had been tops. His charm had brightened many a day for me, and his intellect and happy approach to life had eased my work load. It was the end of our "Swinging Group."

I had known him to be a conscientious man. In his appeal for laicization, I never doubted that he knew what he was doing. He was not asking to give up Catholicism. Laicization was the process whereby a priest asked permission of the Holy Father to be relieved of his vow of celibacy. It was Father Young's intention to remain a Catholic in good standing. Since at that time a priest could not practice the ministry and also marry, he had requested a return to the laity state in the Church. He was following the approved procedure of the Church and was resolute in his intention not to marry before the dispensation was received.

I felt that Father Young had come to a difficult decision and was handling it properly. There was no reason why his request to Rome for laicization should not be regarded with respect by his parishioners. He had given years of dedicated service to the parish where he lived, as chaplain to the inmates of the state prison, and, in my personal observation, to Sacred Heart High School. Beyond that, he was our friend. It seemed to me that we, who daily taught and received lessons in acceptance of the views of others, should uphold him in his right to his.

Therefore, I was astounded when I began to hear cruel remarks made by some of my students about Father Young and his fiancée. Unkind insinuations were made. One girl said of the young widow, "If she crossed the street in front of my car, I would run over her." Other students muttered similar affronts about the couple. I was shocked by this meanness of spirit. Murder was considered as quite the proper medicine for this couple because they loved one another! Father Young was the same priest many of the students had known for years. It was not sinful for him to wish to marry. I was outraged by the attitude of my students. It did not sound like them. I felt they must have been influenced by remarks they had heard carelessly expressed by self-righteous adults. Though an old Church law, in the sixties laicization was a new thought to many Catholics. To some it seemed to fight nine centuries of tradition. They were unable to accept it readily.

Among the faculty, while some were shocked and upset by Father Young's departure, no one questioned his right to do so, nor did they doubt the legality of his procedure.

I could not understand the attitude of my usually fair-minded students and decided it must be through ignorance of Church procedure. Through my classes I sought to help them by presenting a factual historical development of the religious communities of the world. I prepared a special program of study which explained that for the first thousand or so years of Christianity, marriage among the clergy had been quite common and considered the acceptable way of life. There had always been a distinction between the monks, who were celibate and lived in a monastery, belonging to a religious order, and the secular clergy, or parish priests, who staffed the parishes and local churches.

To my students I pointed out that the problem among the clergy in regard to marriage had not been one of being opposed to women. It had begun as a financial one! When a priest married, a thousand years or so ago, he normally had many children. In those times, in Europe, a daughter could not marry without a dowry. Those fathers, who were also priests, realized that since a priest had no property of his own, the only dowry available to their daughters was church property. That was all the family had. But it was for their *use*. They could not dispose of it.

Historically, the most important reason for the Church's decision for a celibate clergy had been the number of involved problems facing the Church in regard to raising priests' families and providing dowries for their daughters. The Pope decreed the celibate law to free the clergy from family problems and to simplify Church concerns for family support.

It was not the thinking of the Church that women, as a sex, were the problem or that a priest's relations with a woman made him less than holy. That aberration of thought, which was unwholesome, nevertheless crept into religious opinion. Obviously this idea was not valid. The vow of marriage was a holy sacrament. It was a higher order than the vow to become a religious, since the latter was only a Church vow.

I gave long hours of research to the subject of celibacy before presenting it to my classes, and we discussed it thoroughly, so that I felt all understood it. It was therefore distressing to discover that many of my students refused to acknowledge the truth of my teaching. My instruction was met with smirking faces or looks of boredom. Never before in my teaching had I come face to face with prejudice in my students which I had been unable to remove. For the first time in my life I questioned my teaching effectiveness. There I was, dedicating myself to developing Christians to make society a better place for all, and instead, I was fostering a group of bigots who not only refused to give their trusted friend, Father Young, a fair hearing, but would not accept the history of the Church.

I began to discover other chinks in the cathedral wall. There had always been rivalry between public school children and students in parochial schools. A "my school can whip your school" attitude. But the feeling ran deeper than that. Some parents of the students at our school looked down on the public school students. I began to recognize that some of my students felt socially superior because they attended Sacred Heart High School, and took it out on the Pericles High kids.

At the same time, I became aware that between our own Catholic parishes there were grave divisions. Within Pericles in the 1960s there were several Catholic parishes. Obviously, in a town of seventeen thousand, that many was not necessary to the population. But it *was* necessary for harmony within the Church. The Polish and Italian parishes were small and of strong ethnic character. There was a middle parish, and there was *"the"* parish, which included everybody else of Catholic faith within the area. The Polish and Italian parishes were considered to be of low economic stratum. More affluent was the middle parish, and *the* parish was the worshiping place of the elite.

In an effort to economize, it was at one time suggested that the Polish and Italian parishes should merge their grade schools. The hue and cry over this was unbelievable! Though all the people involved were Catholics, the families would not permit their children to mix with children of other ethnic backgrounds!

There was only one high school for all Catholics, so any inherited bigotry of the students must be quickly sublimated upon their entry into Sacred Heart. Quite a trick for those children who had been deeply indoctrinated to accomplish, though, I must admit, usually they handled it very well.

But apparently deep feelings of suspicion lay just beneath the surface of the minds of some of my students. What disturbed me was that we were all Catholics. All Christians. What kind of headway was the Church making when in small communities like Pericles there was such ill-will among men? Through the public sentiment leveled against Father Young, I was shocked to discover evidence of the lack of Christian principles in my students. Had ten or twelve years of Catholic education been in vain? I had not come to religious life to provide a free education for those who used our schools as nesting places for their prejudices.

Such aggravations planted seeds of dissatisfaction in my work. With all the effort I was putting forth, there seemed little true spiritual progress among my pupils. I could not see that our education was any more worthwhile than public school education. Nor did I see that our Sacred Heart students were any more Christian in their attitudes than the Catholic students who attended public school and to whom I taught religion on Tuesday afternoons.

I had not entered the convent to be somebody's maid, or because I needed a job or a sense of security. I had entered because I was convinced that the religious life was the most effective way to work in the Apostolate, to make the world a better place in which to live.

The catalyst that recast my life was the cruel denunciation of Father Young.

I am not ignoring the changes that had taken place within me, psychologically, which affected my views about Pericles. The world looked different to me. My need to work with others to perpetuate the message of Christ was no longer there. It had run its course.

When I had made my vow of chastity, instead of having one husband, I had many priest friends, five or six of whom shared their deepest thoughts with me. That type of relationship between men and women held many satisfactions. I was privileged to see into the hearts of many men. When one thought about that, most women married and were thereafter attuned only to one man's values, his needs, and his desires. My life had been more interesting. By sharing the thoughts of a variety of men, very different, one from the other, I had come to a point in my life where psychologically I was ready for the friendship, love, and affection of one man. That need for a loving companion, in itself, certainly was not strong enough to initiate a change of life-style. I had no marriage partner in mind. I simply had come to realize that the relationship I then had with the men in my life, too, had run its course.

The same can be said of poverty. For fifteen years I had had all my worldly possessions fitted into one small trunk and one suitcase. Even those were community property, for if I had died, they would have been passed on, and used by another sister. After all the years of non-materialism, I started to think about the fun of making money and spending it. I wanted an apartment of my own, with rooms I could decorate, a job I could work, and men I could date.

In regard to obedience, I began to think of being master of my own fate. It had been interesting and adventuresome to abandon decision-making for where I would work in the Apostolate—the city, school, and grade level—to a superior. The community had never taken advantage of that position. I had never been placed in an unhappy situation. Even the year at Calvert had had its rewarding aspects in the Apostolate. But now I began to want to chart my own course.

Deliberations about my future became a merry-go-round performing in my head to a dirge, with my thoughts thrusting up and down like its horses, which travel but go nowhere.

To replace Father Young, I had been named head of the History Department. This did not bring me any great sense of accomplishment. I was no longer satisfied with what I was doing. Even the presence of my dear Father Xavier was insufficient.

I am not a person who can stand much moping. I had given my problem much thought. It was time I came to a decision.

Departure

There was a little parlor in the convent where sometimes I could sit and be alone. It was the Sunday after Christmas when I entered that shadowy little room, and finding it empty, seated myself in its stillness. In the course of the next thirty or forty minutes I reviewed my life, my accomplishments, my failures, my dreams, my hopes, and the abilities and resources with which I had to work. Premise after premise passed through my mind. When I finally added them up, I had a conclusion.

I did not want to be a nun anymore.

I would leave the convent.

§~

The following afternoon I saw Father Xavier.

It was winter, and cold. He had just come in from outside. The fine-textured skin on his cheeks blazed red. His eyes were an intensified blue. His smile was wondrously warm.

We were alone in his classroom.

"I have come to a serious conclusion," I began. "I am going to apply for dispensation."

His mouth drew a tight line across his face.

"You are certain?"

"Absolutely."

"I admire you, Sister," he said. "You have always had the courage of your convictions." He stopped and looked over my head. "This course is different for me."

I understood what he meant. Were there any thoughts in his head I did not understand in those days? He referred to something he had mentioned often, something we had spoken of that day, which suddenly seemed centuries before, when we had stood at the side of his father's casket. His father had been German, and an officer who had known obedience and taught it to his son. He had been proud of his son, proud of his college education and his priesthood. Father Xavier felt a deep need to live the life his family had expected of him.

He sighed. "Even in your habit, Shirley Ann, you have always been a free spirit. I always knew the convent wasn't big or strong enough to hold you. You are no angel," he teased, "but you are a high flyer."

What do you say when you love someone and you are willfully saying good-bye? When you dare not pat him, or hold his hand, or throw yourself at him and hug him so he will never let go?

You say nothing. You smile, and turn, and go.

I never wanted him to leave the priesthood for *me*. If that decision ever came to him, from his own heart, for his own purpose, that might be his decision. But it would be wrong for him to leave *for* me. Any decision must be 100 percent his, or it might destroy him. He knew the callings of his conscience. I would not answer to any part of that.

৵

I was in no hurry to rush out the convent door. Certainly I would not leave in the middle of a term. The logical time to make my departure would be the end of the school year, six months away. Nor would I announce my plans to anyone else. The mood changes around one, once one has made such a declaration. I would keep my decision to myself.

When the secondary school supervisor made her annual visit to the province and began making personnel charts and plans for the following year, I felt it necessary to tell her that she should not plan on me to head the History Department.

I had not written to either the mother provincial or the mother general, one of whom always made an annual visit. I preferred to tell her my decision in person. That year the mother general visited Pericles. I was pleased, as the position at the time was held by Mother Olivette, the nun who had so impressed me as a college girl for her brave stand in the Japanese prison camp, Los Baños, on Bataan in the Philippines.

When I made my announcement to her, she told me that she was sorry that I was leaving. "You have been a good sister," she said, "and have made a fine contribution to the work of Holy Cross."

She told me the proper way to go about requesting a release from my vows. I must write to the Holy Father and receive his permission.

"If there was in my mind," she said with regret, "any way of coaxing you to stay, I would do it. But I can see that this is a thoughtful decision on your part."

I admired her good management sense. Merely to have a body in a nun's habit standing in a classroom was not enough. There was no advantage to the Apostolate when its adherents were dissatisfied. I was aware that some Catholics felt that the religious community was cheap labor for the Church—an attitude which I found appalling! I was grateful that in all my associations with the sisters of the Holy Cross, I was never treated as a cheap unit of labor. I had always felt myself to be regarded as a human being of considerable intelligence, personal integrity, and possessing the discipline to make responsible judgments about myself and my life.

I loved to swing on the garden gate of my early Miami home. I was nearly killed swinging on another door.

Daddy's three girls—Mother, Joyce, and me.

BETTY BARRETT JOHANNA BOURNE BETTY BRADFORD SIDNEY CROSS SHIRLEY DYCKES ALICE GABLE

PATTY BOWMAN
TREAS. '47
NANCY ROWLANDS
SOCIAL CH'M'N 48 · · PRES. '47
LIZ SAIGH
HISTORIAN 48
JANET FIELD
CHAPLAIN 48
ANN WEBB
REC. SECY. 48

BRUNIE JURGENS
PLEDGE CAPT 48
CORR. SECY. '47
JANE CLOUDE
CORR. SECY. 48
NANCY HUNT
PRES. 48
ANN ALDERMAN
VICE PRES. 48
JUNIE GARDNER
TREAS. 48
SHIRLEY FREBERG
SGT. AT ARMS 48
REC. SECY. '47

THETA SIGMA TAU ΘΣΤ 1948

PEGGY JEAN GROOVER JEAN HARLIN

MIMI LEFFLER MILDRED LITTLE JANET MacINTOSH MARION MacINTOSH CHARLYN MANNING CYNTHIA MANNING

JOAN MANNING DOLORES McALLISTER JOY PARKER IRENE PAWLEY BARBARA PRITCHARD

KAT ROBINSON MARY ANN SMITH ROSEMARY SPICER CAROL THOMSON JACKIE WRIGHT KAREN WYLIE

My high school sorority. Little did I dream I would go from this light-hearted sisterhood to the Sisters of the Holy Cross! Included are Irene Pawley, Karen Wylie, Janet MacIntosh, and Joy Parker.

Graduation in 1951 from Miss Harris' School, Miami, Florida. I am at the right.

Without a care in the world! Joyce and I the summer before I entered St. Mary's convent.

Sister Mary Bernardine (Shirley Ann Dyckes), C.S.C.

Out of the habit! Of course I had my picture snapped.

In order to save money to purchase furnishings for my new apartment, I walked all over Europe. Here I have climbed a mountain on the Isle of Capri!

A public school teacher—1971.

Clarence M. Kelley, Director of the FBI—the man with the gun who I found was such fun. (Rick Solberg, The Kansas City Star)

Clarence served 20 years in the FBI as a special agent. Here, as a firearms instructor, with a machine gun at Quantico, Virginia.

Press conference for Clarence. Everyone talks but the Director!

Grandad Kelley takes a bride. Part of my "instant family"—*Clarence's daughter, Mary Kelley Dobbins, and her children, Kent and Kelley. (Bill Sanders, Asheville* Citizen-Times*)*

"Happy the bride the sun shines on," October 2, 1976. Mr. and Mrs. Clarence Kelley.

No honeymoon! The first week of our marriage I attended a convention of ex-FBI agents with Clarence in Philadelphia.

Assured that Clarence was in good hands, Tom Moten, driver and bodyguard to Clarence, retired. His farewell party was held in the Director's dining room of the J. Edgar Hoover Building, Washington, D.C. Standing, members of Director's office (with Bill Reed missing). Seated, Mrs. Moten, Clarence and I, and Special Agent Tom Moten.

Fortunately for us, William Cardinal Baum, formerly of Kansas City and a long-time friend of Clarence's, was in charge of the D.C. diocese when we planned to be married. He was able to short-cut some red tape for us. Here he has officiated at the annual FBI Mass held at St. Matthew's Cathedral. (Reni Photos)

An evening "out" with some special agents from the Phoenix, Arizona, headquarters. At Pinnacle Peak Restaurant neckties are cut off overdressed diners.

A lady who gave me a new view of life—Virgie L. McNeal and her husband, Colonel Theodore D. McNeal of Missouri at dinner for St. Louis Police Department graduation, 1977.

Bureau changes were rarely more obvious—SAC Ronald L. Maley of the San Diego, California, office enjoys a domestic scene, seeing me shopping and the Director shelling out! Tijuana, Mexico.

aug. 7, 1976

My dear:

I am aboard the plane returning to Washington. The past two days have been about the most eventful ones I have experienced in many years. The discussion with the kids, the conference with the doctor, the phone call to you and the discussions held about the pending TV appearance and press conference all mounted to bring me to the peak of impact. I was tremendously pleased by the reaction of the children and your reaction to the news. It is as if a great load has been lifted from my heart. I was so anxious to have things turn out well and now that they have I could dance the Fairmount Stomp without a quiver of discomfort

In this letter dated August 7, 1976, Clarence told me of his children's reaction to our hopes to be married.

I particularly enjoyed the special regard between General Louis H. Wilson, Commandant of the Marine Corps, and Clarence. The FBI National Academy is on the grounds of the Marine Base, Quantico, Virginia. This dinner party was held in the historic Home of the Commandant, Washington, D.C. (Official U.S. Marine Corps Photo)

Here is my friend and former neighbor, Elizabeth Gullander, taking down my story as I tell it to her. (Werner Gullander)

&

As to the letter to the Pope—I had a little difficulty with its wording. No matter what I wrote, it didn't sound right. I kept on explaining, page after page—sort of a "Dear Holy Father, this is the way it is . . ." letter. After many attempts, I finally took what I had written to Father Xavier. My letter was six pages long, single-spaced.

Father Xavier read it, then handed it back.

"Shirley Ann," he said, "you don't want to get out of the Church, just out of the convent!"

He removed three of my six pages.

"Skip these. Do you think the Holy Father is ready for the full thrust of your personality?"

We laughed.

It wasn't that what I had written was so heretical, I had just felt the Pope should know my views on the Church and Christianity in general.

My friend recommended that I limit my communication to the subject at hand.

"Just send him a cable," he suggested. "Shirley Dyckes Quits Convent."

I revised my letter and sent it through the proper channels and on to the Holy Father.

&

Just before spring vacation, Margaret McCord,* a young woman I had met while doing some research at the Library of Congress in Washington, D.C., came to see me. She was a lively person. When I had been searching about for a way to uplift some of my problem children at Calvert School, she had helped me organize a cheerleader program which had been highly successful. Margaret was a sparkling-eyed woman of about twenty-three who brought freshness into any room she entered.

When she arrived at Pericles, I took her on a tour of the convent and the school, introducing her to sisters and priests we met on our way. I could see she was on a high step, bubbling with enthusiasm.

As we talked, she asked me if I would still be teaching at Pericles the next term. I told her no, that though I had not yet announced it, I was leaving the convent in June.

I pricked her balloon! I had rarely seen such a reaction.

Not her real name.

"You're kidding!" she said, her face undergoing a fast-moving series of expressions.

"What's the matter?" I asked.

"Shirley Ann!" she said. "You are my model nun! I came here to look into convent life. I had been intending to join."

I tried to reason with her quietly. There was no reason for my decision to influence hers. If, by herself, she had come to the conclusion that the religious life was right for her, then she should proceed.

Finally she pulled herself together. She looked half angry, half merry, as she put her hands on her hips and looked me in the eye.

"Shirley Ann," she said. "I have been planning a trip to Europe with a friend before entering the convent. Why don't you join us?"

I hadn't thought of such a thing, but it seemed like a great idea!

I had told my parents that I would be leaving the convent in June. Their reaction had been the same as when I came to any decision. If it made me happy, they would accept it.

When they called the next Sunday, I said to my father, "I want to remind you of an offer you made me fifteen years ago."

"Yes," he said. "What was that?"

"Fifteen years ago," I said, "when I told you I was going to enter the convent, you suggested maybe I would like a trip to Europe while I thought it over. How about a trip to Europe to get over it?"

He laughingly agreed.

෫෨

At Easter, when the school was closed, I went home for two weeks. On my visit home I always wore my habit. I put it on first thing in the morning and wore it until I took it off to go to bed. A nun was a nun, even at home. That visit home, I went shopping for clothes to wear when I left the convent in June.

I purchased a turquoise linen suit with an Italian silk blouse of many soft colors which matched the lining of the suit. The fabric against my skin was like nothing I had felt in years! It was as intriguing as a whisper. I bought slender, nonserviceable shoes with thin high heels, and a *pocketbook*. I had not carried a good-sized pocketbook in fifteen years! My most difficult job was to choose a hat. When the day came when I would take off my habit, I would have to have something to cover my uncoiffed hair, which through years of being tightly covered, and without sunlight, had turned mousy and dull. I bought a white hat with enough brim to look reasonably attractive on short, round-faced me.

Then I bought cosmetics! When I left the convent, I intended to look smashing! I would wear basetone and lipstick, the works! And to carry it all, I bought a sun-yellow suitcase.

Next I had to stop at a passport photo place and have a picture taken. Out of my coif came my head, with all my hair flattened and horrible. Those pictures are no longer extant!

In Pericles I began slowly to empty my trunk—so slowly that the average sister in the house did not realize that by the time June arrived, the trunk would be absolutely empty. My older clothes I threw away. One by one I added my books to the library shelves. I did this without show as I was not anxious for my decision to dismay any of the priests or nuns, or to cast any doubts into their minds about their vocations.

At last everything in my trunk was gone, and there were only the lovely new clothes in the yellow suitcase.

About a month before my departure I had an invitation to dinner with Father Young and his fiancée. I requested, and was granted, permission to visit with them. For a full year they had been waiting for permission to be married in the Church, and it had just been received. They planned to be married as soon as school was out. Nevertheless, they were still being openly criticized by some and snubbed by others. But I could see their happiness in each other was not dimmed. They had heard of my plans and were pleased that I was so enthusiastic about my life ahead.

When I think of those years at Pericles, I think of the special joy of working in the Apostolate with a man whom I loved. Then, I did not know if my friendship with Father Xavier would endure the test of time and separation, whether he would follow me or forever remain a religious. What mattered was that he had filled a need. When I fell in love, we were both in the Apostolate. The vow of celibacy remained the one obstacle that made it impossible for me to pursue the marvelous and beautiful adventure of loving one man.

When I left the convent, I was through with the Apostolate. I concluded it. It was over. I would not again volunteer my time for good works. I had fulfilled the obligation I had imposed upon myself.

Departure

After fifteen years and eleven months, I ended my life as a religious.

On that last day in June in 1969, Father Xavier called for me at the convent. I walked through the door in my beautiful linen suit with its whisper-soft blouse, my sheer stockings, tall-heeled white pumps, and my white hat. There was a blush dusted over my cheeks and lipstick on my mouth.

Father Xavier carried my yellow suitcase.

I had said good-bye to the sisters and priests, and all had wished me well.

Three of my favorite former students from high school, then all in college, were waiting in Father Xavier's car to drive with us to the Buffalo Airport to see me off.

At a restaurant, Father Xavier ordered an elegant pink champagne lunch for us.

How many nuns do you know who have left a convent in such style?

When I had first entered the convent, Mother Regina, after observing me, had said, "Miss Dyckes, you would like to have everything in life all gift-wrapped and tied up with a pink bow." I thought of that, toasting my champagne to the priest with the blue eyes sitting across from me, who had seen to it that I left the convent in such a beautiful, memorable way.

I loved him. He had taught me something exceedingly important. I needed the love of one man. Not him, but some *one*.

At the airport gate I shook hands with my three student friends, Rosemary, Debbie, and Diane. Then I said good-bye to Father Xavier. We shook hands, meeting each other's eyes.

I was no longer in my habit.

I was no longer a nun.

I reached up and kissed him, a fleeting brush of my lips across his cheek.

I would always feel for him in a most special way. Brother. Friend. Beloved human being.

13

Out of the Habit

"Don't make any left turns!" I shouted at Betty, who sat in her car, engine running, at the edge of the Hertz Car Rental in Washington, D.C.

She leaned out her window. "What did you say?"

"I said, 'Don't make any left turns!' "

Patiently Betty unbuckled her seat belt, opened the door, and walked back to the side of my rented car.

"Say that again, Shirley."

"I just said you will have to find a route to your apartment that doesn't take any left turns. I never learned to make them. It took me four tries to pass my driver's test. The fourth time, the examiner said, 'You were lucky you made that last turn all right, go get your license. Then go home and practice.' I haven't made one since."

"No left turns," she repeated hollowly.

I glanced out at the steady stream of Washington traffic pouring down the road, six abreast, past us. "Today is no day to start."

"But the Beltway is right over there," Betty protested. "All we have to do is make one little left turn, drive one block, and our troubles are over."

"I'll never make it."

"Shirley," she said. "It is fifteen miles from here to my apartment. It's the rush hour. Without left turns, it will be twice as far!"

"I'll follow you," I said, and watched her return to her car.

I studied the instrument panel before me. It might have belonged on a 747.

Ten weeks earlier I had left the convent and flown to Miami, where I had had ten days to learn to drive a car, buy a wardrobe, and pack for the trip to Europe. I had taken a crash course in driving. I had driven a car seven times. The day after I received my license, I left for Europe, where I had been ever since. Now it was the day before Labor Day. I *had* to drive a car. On Tuesday my new teaching job would begin. I would have no other way of getting to work.

I punched several buttons and gadgets. Nothing happened.

The attendant's head peered in the window.

"Try this," he said, turning the ignition key.

I stepped on the accelerator. Proudly I heard the motor catch and felt the car begin to roll.

৪৯

Still bubbly from the excitement and pink champagne celebrating my departure from Pericles, I had landed in Washington, eager for my job interview and to locate an apartment.

I had been determined to start out my new life by being self-supporting, but finding a teaching position, while still a nun and teaching in Pericles, had made it hard to job-seek. When I had written Dr. Cardoso at Catholic U. to notify him that I was leaving the convent, and going to Europe, and would not continue my work on my master's degree until fall, he had replied with a recommendation of a teaching position at Rev. Thomas Daniels Greek Orthodox Parochial School in Washington, D.C.

At my interview, the afternoon of the day I left Pericles, I discovered that the position was to teach fifth grade. I would have only ten to fifteen students, and the salary would be about six thousand a year.

The salary was nothing of which to be proud. I had had thirteen years' teaching experience, been a department head, and had almost completed my master's degree. Against this, I weighed my alternatives. My airplane for Europe left in ten days. I had to find an apartment, learn to drive a car, and buy clothing for the trip to Europe. All that I owned, I was then wearing.

As I hesitated, Father Kalaris asked casually, "Do you speak Greek?"

"Latin," I said. "Passable French. I am proficient in Spanish."

"I'm sure you'll manage," he said.

I should have taken time to ask him what he meant, but I had yet to choose an apartment and to catch the six o'clock flight to Miami.

ॐ

As a courtesy to my mother, who had heard stories of crime on the streets of Washington, and believed every one of them, I had lined up some apartments to inspect near Suitland, Maryland, close to where three friends, all ex-nuns, lived. It was late when I arrived there, patiently chauffeured by Sister Mary Louise, who had met me at the airport with the community car. The rental offices were closed for the day. There was no way either to know which apartments were available or to view them, except from the outside! We skirted around them while I made notes on favorable balconies and exposures, hoping this would help me to be able to make an acceptable choice by telephone from Florida.

Then we hurried to the airport, where Sister deposited me.

As I settled into the airliner, I felt it had been a long time since morning when I had arisen at the convent. And I had yet another appointment to keep.

My parents met me at the airport in Miami, but I didn't go straight home. They whisked me off to a beauty parlor. Mother had arranged for Pearl and Dan's Shop, the one I had frequented while growing up, to stay open to make me presentable. My hair was cut, shaped, and blond-frosted to brighten its drabness, permanented, shampooed, set, and dried. It was late before I was released, but the ordeal had been worth it. I was thirty-five years old, and my round face appeared much younger. My hair shone and curled. My fingernails were manicured and lightly colored. I studied myself in the long mirror by the shop door, and smiled, pleased by my reflection.

On seven of the next ten mornings, my instructor arrived to give me driving lessons. Every afternoon Mother and I shopped in the Miami stores. I needed everything for everyday living, plus the necessities for travel for nine weeks through ten countries of Europe. I must also pack. I would be traveling tourist class, and the overseas limit was only forty pounds. Every evening I removed price tags, turned up hems, took in, let out, folded, packed, closed up my suitcase, and set it on the bathroom scale to weigh.

On the tenth day I met Margaret and Joan in New York. They had made out our itinerary. We had a travel agent, and my father was my banker. That afternoon we happily winged out over the Atlantic to London.

In my pocket was *Europe on Five Dollars a Day*. If possible, I intended to do it on $2.50. My father had allowed $20 a day for food, side trips, and souvenirs. Since the duty-free allowance for purchases was only $150, he didn't think I would bring home much more than that. I had other ideas! I would have an apartment to furnish when I returned, and I had heard of bargains to be found in Europe. Light eating and a lot of walking, I thought, should enable me to spend all the money I saved by making fabulous purchases.

We walked, or bussed, wherever possible.

On our way to Stratford from London, as we boarded a bus, I saw sitting on the front seat a friend, a sister, from New York. She was as surprised to see me out of my habit as I was to see her in civilian clothes. This sister had left the convent temporarily to take care of her mother, who was extremely ill. She was under exclaustration, a Church law that is rather like a leave of absence, during which she was taking a week's vacation to visit London to see the plays she dearly loved. Under exclaustration she was still a nun, though she might wear conventional clothing.

Exclaustration is not a new custom. The Church is anxious to assist its religious in times of personal trial. For example, I remember when I attended the funeral of the wife of an FBI agent. The couple had ten children. As the mother was in terminal illness, her sister, a nun, was granted a leave of absence to assist with the little children during the mother's long illness.

During my first weeks in Europe, I was surprised to discover how little I felt any effect from the radical change I had made in my life-style. For almost sixteen years I had lived according to convent rules, rising early, answering bells, spending long periods in meditation and prayer, thinking almost nothing of myself, but being always concerned with the needs of others. Now I was on a glorious holiday. My horizons were limitless, and so was my outlook on life. Perhaps the change I felt most often was a certain light-headedness—from not wearing at least a veil on my hair! My head had always been covered. Now my hair was out in the sunshine, curly and fluffy. For some time it was a surprise to me to reach up and touch my hair.

Only on one occasion did I find myself reverting to a thought pattern instilled while in the convent. Once, on a train in Spain, while Margaret and Joan shared a neighboring compartment, I found myself paired off with a sweet little Spanish lady. She retired to bed, but I found myself delaying as long as possible. I had had a single room for so many years that I simply couldn't take off my clothes before a stranger! I finally threw myself, fully dressed, into my berth and slept a fitful night in my clothes!

ह✤

We walked through Europe. I think we placed our shoes where American leather had rarely trod.

I found walking had three side benefits. One, I enjoyed all the interesting foods of Europe, including their vast and marvelous varieties of bread and desserts, and came home as trim as when I left Miami. Two, when one walks, one sees. And three, there were all those open doorways to pass through, alleys to explore, and little shops in which to make purchases. I chose Royal Doulton china in England, painted trays in Italy, crystal and stainless-steel flatware in Vienna, table linens in Switzerland, sterling silver candelabra in Denmark, and a cobra-skin pocketbook and matching shoes in Spain.

Whenever possible, I shipped my purchases, but still, the night before departure, I was faced with an enormous European Care Package, all designed for needy me. There seemed nothing I could throw out. Surely not the dear letters from Father Xavier which had been awaiting me at every stop, or the fine pipe I had purchased for him in Innsbruck. No, there was nothing I could leave behind.

ह✤

Throughout my visit in Europe I felt a vague uneasiness about what I would be returning to at home. I had been casual about renting an apartment, finally leaving my preferences with my father in Miami,

131

hoping he would accomplish a miracle in Washington, D.C. He did. On our last stop, in Paris, a cable arrived for me.

"Apartment available. Go right in. Welcome home. Dad."

By continuously phoning Washington, he had found a one-bedroom rental, the apartment of my first choice, at Holly Hill. He had also ordered a new car for me, which would be available within three days after my arrival.

Can you imagine being thirty-five years old and having a first place of your own? I fell in love with my apartment on first sight! It was down a half flight of stairs, with a balcony overlooking a garden. Those rooms were the first of my very own in which I was allowed to express my feelings about decorating. When I thought of the years of general barrenness with which I had lived at the convent, and the simplicity which had surrounded me in all my quarters, I could scarcely wait to fill the walls with paintings and chairs with cushions; to be surrounded by color and forms and pleasing designs, all chosen by me!

The day after I arrived at Holly Hill a shipment of furniture was delivered from my parents. I had asked them to limit their contributions to my living, as I was anxious to have everything about my new life reflect me, my ideas, my wishes, my way of living. They sent a fine antique hand-carved bedroom suite of white oak that had been put together with pegs, and a nine-by-twelve white rug with stripes of green and rust, yards of fabric, and even my grandmother's fifty-year-old electrified sewing machine. Oh, it was fun playing house!

But in between bouts of decorating, I was going to have to make a living, miles away, in Washington, starting the following day.

❦

Without Betty to lead me, I arrived at the Greek Orthodox School on Sixteenth Street. It had been an involved run, but it had included only one left turn—and that was into the driveway of the school parking lot!

Barely recovered from jet lag, I entered the fifth-grade classroom of the Greek School.

Within minutes, I discovered why, during my interview, I had been asked that casual question, "Do you speak any Greek?"

A few of my most recently arrived immigrant children spoke no English! They thought in Greek. They spoke in Greek. I had been hired with the knowledge that I would be unable to understand a word some of my pupils would say to me!

My students were the sons and daughters of the Greek working community in Washington. Their parents were willing to make sacrifices to pay tuition for their children to attend the school. The Orthodox Church was a bit of homeland transported to their strange new country, and they felt a deep affinity to it. Some of the parents spoke only Greek and had small incomes, but they had large hopes for their futures in America, and especially for those of their children. In their children they instilled an early respect for education.

Our studies included American and Greek subjects. Report cards had Greek subjects listed and graded in Greek, and American subjects in English, graded in English. Aside from that, the school program was identical to that of any other American fifth grade. No subject in the curriculum was watered down to meet language difficulties. Some of the school books were the discarded volumes from the public school system. Our purchased books received many years' wear. There was no elaborate equipment to use in the school. We had no gym program, though we had two recess periods.

The children, I found, were every bit as competent as those I had taught in the Catholic parochial grade schools. Soon they could all speak, read, and write in both English and Greek. Everyone was multilingual. None seemed overwhelmed by the homework expected of him. In that, their parents cooperated fully. They were anxious for their children to take full advantage of their learning years. Impossible though it may seem, the reading level of those children, in the 1970s, was among the highest in the District of Columbia.

క్లు

If America is the "land of opportunity," its capital, Washington, D.C., surely must be the "Oh!" in that opportunity. Vast cultural richness was at hand for the edification of my class. Its small enrollment made it easy to arrange outings. We attended the children's concerts given by the National Symphony, toured the Capitol, the Museums of Art and Natural Science, the Archives Building, and of course, the Smithsonian. A world of information, attractively arranged for easy learning, stood at almost every street corner in that beautiful city.

There were also programs for children frequently overlooked by other school programmers. A fellow teacher, Peggy Hogan, and I found some prime ones offered by the DAR. Since 1939, when the DAR ladies had erred in the eyes of many Americans by refusing to allow Marian

Anderson to sing in their Constitution Hall because she was black, many events for children went begging for participants.

There was an art contest and a scrapbook project and most important, it seemed to me, for my little Greek-Americans, a good-citizenship essay contest. Since my students were almost the only participants in the art contest, they handily won first, second, and third prizes! And, believe it or not, they did as well in the essay contest. My students won all three top prizes. We were all invited to hear the children read their essays in the DAR Chapter House. There we were, a bilingual school, many of the children with parents not yet American citizens, reading their compositions in the auditorium of the national organization.

Before starting on such an outing, we discussed proper and polite behavior. Refreshments would be served, and I wanted no unmannerly children. Definite guidelines were established. I allowed no second chances for miscreants. If there was bad behavior by a child on a trip outside the school, the next time that child stayed home. I had found that only one such concrete example of punishment was required about every five years in teaching. The classroom was a grapevine with endlessly extended tendrils. Word that Miss Dyckes meant what she said got around. As a happy result, I rarely had an occasion not to be proud of my students.

At the end of the summer after teaching my first year at the Greek School, I received my master's degree in Latin-American history from Catholic University. This event gave me cause to appraise my situation. I was thirty-six years old, had fourteen years' teaching experience, and held a master's degree. My salary was then the highest paid to any member of the teaching staff except the principal, but it was still only about seven thousand a year. My darling apartment was shaping up slowly under the financial stress of living in an expensive city during an inflationary period. I could only make one expensive furniture purchase at a time, and then start saving for the next one. With all my teaching experience and education, it seemed as though I should be receiving higher pay and living better. I began to consider other school systems which would provide some retirement and medical benefits, as well as more salary. I enjoyed my Greek students and their families, but it was time I started thinking of myself.

At that time there was still no man in my life. I scarcely had time to think about men. Twice a day I had the long drive to and from school, though I had learned to make left turns and took a much shorter route! Much of my free time was spent shopping and choosing furnishings for my apartment. Frequently I saw my dearest friends, three former nuns, all of whom lived in neighboring apartment houses. We had many male friends: brothers, husbands of sisters, and friends of friends. I saw these men frequently. They kept a balance in my life. Surely, few people enjoy a life surrounded only by people of their own sex! I know I certainly wouldn't.

In my work, and in my classes at Catholic U., there was a complementary ratio of men to women. But I was over thirty-five, and the college men I met were generally in their early twenties. My man/woman life was still rather a continuation of the pattern which had been established in the convent. I was friends with many men. Many men were my brothers, but I was not singularly interested in any one.

Three of my ex-nun friends taught in Prince Georges County, Maryland, public schools, and their salaries were approximately fourteen thousand each, plus benefits. At the end of my second year at the Greek school, I started my applications for a position in Maryland and Virginia public schools. There I ran solidly into the money crunch. Would you believe, my teaching experience was against me? Teachers with their college sheepskins still unrolled under their arms, with no experience, were to be hired because they could be paid lower salaries. One and a half teachers could be hired for one with my experience and degrees. More teachers supposedly could teach more students. What they taught and how they taught were not the criteria. There was no opening for me.

I renewed my contract at the Greek School.

In January of that school year, as several of us were eating our lunches in the teachers' lounge, the principal entered. "I have this paper," she stated, "which I am to hand to you personally. You will each sign it, signifying that you have received and read it."

The Greek School had elected a new president of the community whose position would be superior to that of the director of education and the school board president. The new president's letter notified us that no more paychecks would be received until each of us had been personally approved by him as to our standards for teaching.

My reaction was to feel professionally and personally insulted. I felt we should meet with him immediately.

Impossible, I was told. He was on a two-week holiday in Hawaii.

I was infuriated. I had no desire to be kept in a state of limbo until this man got around to grading my teaching abilities. I inquiried into *his* qualifications to decide educational standards and discovered he was an officer in a cement-mixing company!

For months Betty's principal had been pressuring her to help him locate a teacher with my qualifications. I had turned a deaf ear to her suggestion that I accept the position. In this new situation at the Greek School, I wondered if my contract had not been violated and sought the advice of an attorney. He assured me that it had and drew up the necessary papers for my release.

With these in hand, I returned to the Greek School and told the principal of my decision. She called in the president of the board.

He was surprised at my dissatisfaction.

"You are most valuable to the school," he said.

"The school can't get along without you," the principal echoed.

I told them, "You have changed the laws under which I signed my contract. Therefore, I no longer feel bound by it."

"Now, Miss Dyckes," the president said in a voice which pleaded for reasonableness, "this is not an ordinary school. There are many ways in which we may show our love, affection, and respect. Just think, Miss Dyckes, of Archie Bunker and the way he fusses at his wife. Without that type of abuse, she might not be regarded in the particular affectionate way that she is."

I was horrified by this rationalization.

"I don't watch Archie Bunker," I said. "And I don't come from a society which shows its regard by dwelling on abuse. I will not work under such conditions."

"But you cannot leave your position unfilled," the president said.

"As to my replacement," I said, "I will find one."

I had heard of an ex-nun who was looking for a position, and I was able to fill my place with a teacher who had qualifications similar to mine. I began public school teaching the following week.

ৰ❧

One day, while returning home from the Greek School during the spring of 1971, I heard an ad on my car radio saying, "Come visit our model apartments—700 New Hampshire Avenue." The name that caught my attention had a descriptive ring to it. It was "Watergate."

The last section of that vast complex on ten acres of land between the Potomac River and Virginia and New Hampshire avenues was still under construction. Its final building, with its distinctive open-circle architecture, was Watergate South.

I parked my car and got out amid the mud-and-plank walkways and toured the sample apartments.

The apartments were compact but thoughtfully designed, the bathrooms were sumptuous, the kitchens tiny but complete, the living and bedrooms open and yet private. With the same sudden but firm conviction which had marked the major decisions of my life, I decided to live at Watergate.

The Watergate complex consisted of three apartment buildings, each with an outdoor swimming pool and lounge area, plus a large hotel, with a health club and indoor pool, gardens and fountains, and two office buildings. It was in one of these latter that a minor break-in was to be turned into a world-upsetting burglary, which would enter the word "Watergate" in modern dictionaries, to be defined as: "any political activity that is grossly illegal or unethical, usually involving unfair tactics, concealed contributions, special-interest deals, and abuse of governmental trust for partisan advantage (from the name of the building in which the break-in occurred)."*

This event did not occur for more than a year after I became a Watergate resident. For neighbors I had some seven hundred families, including some interesting Washington names. Martha and Attorney General John Mitchell's balcony was across the gardens from mine. Madame Chennault had a two-story penthouse apartment. Secretary of Commerce and Mrs. Maurice Stans lived in an extensive apartment. Other notables came and went. Congressmen and senators, judges, writers, people of the media, and representatives from many foreign embassies all lived together. My neighbors were interesting and intelligent people. Becky Nagel, a daughter of General Carl "Tooey" Spaatz lived across the hall from me. She had a box in the Concert Hall at Kennedy Center, where I was a frequent guest.

Watergate was not a child-centered world. It was a place for professional, busy people, both men and women, generally in an older age bracket, their children raised or away at school. The marked differences between us was that I was an ex-nun and had not been in the job market long enough to command an impressive salary. I had had to

---

*Random House Collegiate Dictionary, *rev. ed., 1975.*

balance the additional monthly payment I would have to pay against the convenience and excitement of living in such a lovely spot. Watergate won. All I had to do was to get a second job and I would be able to eke out an existence. I found one, in a women's dress shop.

The Watergate offered more than just a home. It was an entire way of life, a most sophisticated village with even its own branch post office within its walls. One could be snowbound for weeks and never lack supplies! One might even have meals delivered, hot or icy cold, from the hotel restaurant.

A little known fact about the Watergate was that for a period during the development of the complex, a majority ownership was held by the Vatican.

But most important in choosing my new residence was the neighboring presence of the Kennedy Center for the Performing Arts, which held its grand opening in September 1971. It was right next door! From Maryland, when I had sought entertainment, it was a long drive, frequently alone, at night. From Watergate, which was well lit and policed, I could walk back and forth to the endless variety of programs offered in the three theaters of glorious Kennedy Center.

I moved into Watergate and was to find the fringe benefits even greater than expected.

14

The
Watergate Years

On the top of his desk, an eleven-year-old giant towered over me.

I looked him firmly in the eye as I told my fifth-grade class to line up for lunch.

"Not me!" Jim shouted from high over my head.

"Not me! Not me!" Other children took up the cue and raced around the room, shouting.

"Line up for lunch," I repeated. "Jim, I will meet you in Dr. Keeney's office." The rows quickly assembled, and we proceeded to the cafeteria.

The principal's name was magic. He was not a big man, but he had a large reputation. Aware of the individuality of students, he met each accordingly. He was interested in and understanding of them. He also had an invisible weapon. It was known that he had once *spanked* a child. In his office hung a paddle painted with the words "Board of Education." To my knowledge it was never used, but its potential carried a lot of wallop.

A changed Jim met me in Dr. Keeney's office. He was taller than the principal, but he seemed much smaller.

"What do you mean, Jim," Dr. Keeney asked, "not minding your teacher? Do you want that nice lady to leave us?"

To my surprise, instead of a smart retort, tears appeared in the boy's eyes, and he hung his head.

The power of the right approach was never presented to me more strongly. The principal really knew which chord to touch.

Unfortunately I was with Dr. Keeney only one year. Other principals did not have his disciplinary control, and I really earned my first ten thousand dollars and later fourteen thousand a year.

I taught in Prince Georges County public school for four and one half years and found it a vastly different experience from teaching in the parochial schools, where discipline was almost routine. In the public schools maintaining order consumed so much of my teaching time that I was never able to use as much material as I had. The situation worsened every year. There was a marked deterioration among the children in respect to authority which could only result in less quality teaching. Punishment for even serious offenses was light, and even when it was to their academic detriment, students had no serious concern about passing to the next grade.

I felt that teaching and attending school were work. School was not all playground, though it could be fun. When a child went to school with the idea that he was to be entertained, he was limited. Learning could cause intellectual pain. As in mastering a sport, until muscles are trained, it hurts. A child must be put into an atmosphere where he wants to dig in and learn. Such a climate was not always possible in the public school system. Some fine teaching was accomplished, but it seemed to me the product was inferior to what should have been expected, considering the money, effort, and time dedicated to it.

I found the federal government, through its many branches, to be like an octopus reaching its tentacles into the public schools.

One day a principal came to me and asked if I had all the slips signed by parents for all the students that I had detained in detention for the year. The father of one of my black students felt that I was prejudiced and punished more of my black students than the others. He had advised the principal that an Equal Opportunity officer was to be notified.

Fortunately, I had a complete file. When I checked it, I found I had punished one more white child than black.

The assumption of wrongdoing infuriated me. The child of the complaining parents was not even at grade level and needed every moment in school he could receive.

I showed my records to the principal and said, "It just happens that I have punished one more white child than black this year. Would you like me to find a black child to pick on for a day to show that I am not prejudiced?"

The Equal Opportunity officer did not show up.

At another time HEW sent out a notice that they had a new process which we were to use to determine if there was a fair racial mix in our classrooms. We received involved IBM forms which allotted ten spaces for sex and racial backgrounds—black, white, Oriental, Indian, Spanish extraction, etc. Numbers were used to identify the specific combinations.

In the first place, there were such mixtures it was sometimes difficult for a teacher to determine the exact background of a child. I analyzed my class to the best of my ability and turned in the forms. Much later they were returned to me with IBM scorings to place with my permanent records. There were so many machine errors that the HEW files could not possibly have the correct totals. On one of my cards, a Vietnamese boy had come back as an Indian girl!

Some of the unexpected fringe benefits from having moved to the Watergate began to become visible to me. I found it a most fascinating place to live. I made friends with several people, and they, in turn, introduced me to many others. My neighbors were busy people with only short hours for socializing. This suited me fine! Informal, short-notice cocktail parties and dinners could be quickly arranged. Many times these extended into an evening at Kennedy Center. Friends had season tickets for the symphony or the theater or opera. I was often included.

This type of living afforded me introductions to a wide spectrum of men who were available in the nation's capital in the 1970s. I was able to preview my dates at cocktail parties. Everyone knew that Washington had a high crime rate. Casually made dates in cars could be dangerous. The Watergate gave me freedom. A single lady could be gracious and enjoy an evening with a new acquaintance without leaving the Watergate complex. I never had to enter a car with a stranger.

I had always found it easy to be friends with men. In the convent, this had been most advantageous. As a single woman, out of my nun's habit, I might look toward men for something more. However, I did not wish to marry merely to *be* married. I *did* want the full experience of living with a man, but I had no inclination to cohabit without marriage, as had become widely accepted in the world outside during the years I was sheltered by the convent. It was not that I wished to legalize a relationship with a man, or become his dependent—after all, I was perfectly capable of maintaining myself—but I wished to have a natural and growing relationship of a woman living with a man with rightness about it, a rightness considered by both parties before entering into the relationship. A commitment. Such a relationship could not be entered into on one evening's notice, or a week's. It required communication, conversation, and consideration—a courtship!

I certainly met some interesting people.

I was scarcely settled at the Watergate when I met Richard.* He was without doubt one of the handsomest men in the country, and the descendant of a "name" family. He was tall, and dark, and three or four years younger than I. He taught history, and it seemed we had much in common.

He invited me to dinner at the Watergate Terrace. Afterward we went to my apartment and sat out on the balcony sipping an after-dinner drink, enjoying the beautiful spring evening.

As a recent nun, there were many areas of conversation which were still new to me. My young friend began to speak of the beauty and enrichment which bisexuality offered. He went on to say that he was staying in Alexandria with a friend who was having a party that evening, and that other bisexuals and homosexuals would be there. He invited me to join them.

There I was, supposedly a sophisticated lady, who had lived for years in a convent, acquainted with homosexuality only through rumor or what I had read, and I was listening to an invitation to a bisexual party! I was almost sick! I couldn't even speak! I got up from my chair and went into the bathroom where I poured a glass of cold water. I drank it and lay down on my bed for a few minutes to recover.

---

*Not his real name.

My friend courteously sat through this on the balcony.

Finally I rejoined him, and he thought it was time to go. We parted pleasantly, and of course, I never saw him again.

However, as a truly naïve woman, I appreciated his honesty. Although I had not been prepared for the experience, I felt he was wise to clear the air in regard to his preferences before our intellectual simpatico might lead us into a more involved relationship. So that Greek god turned out to be a Janus.

ॐ

I met many single men who were residents of Watergate. Of course there is an advantage to having one's date under one's roof, but with separate doorbells. Busy men found it particularly convenient to have compatible women handy, and impromptu parties could be formed.

In the convent I had read about Jews and had come to admire them. Now I finally met some. One was a dedicated doctor, a divorced man, gentle and kind. He enjoyed being a man and loved the differences between men and women. He also liked being a Jew. He told me that when people let him know that it bothered them that he was a Jew, it saved him a lot of time. With such prejudice, he felt, they wouldn't be worth knowing anyway.

Nathan* struck a romantic chord in me. I felt myself more and more attracted to him. He responded similarly to me. But he had been burned by his first marriage and was not considering another. He really wanted an affair.

I told him frankly, "It has to be friendship or marriage."

This infuriated him.

We were relaxing at my apartment after dinner.

"You don't need a priest," he shouted, "you need a *man!*" and slammed out of my apartment.

We remained friends, and for one thirty-six-hour period, sincerely considered marriage, but then decided not to spoil our friendship!

Another man whom I dated was partially crippled by his racial inheritance. He told me his lack of success was due to his race. I was in a party with him at the Second Inaugural Ball for President Nixon. There was such a crush of people at Kennedy Center that we did not stay to greet the reelected President, but found a small dance floor at one of the Watergate's restaurants, to spend the evening.

Not his real name.

I dated younger men, and men in their sixties, up-and-coming White House aides, and philanthropists, men who were doing great things with their lives, and some who still felt the burden of some psychologically inflicted wounds of their youth. This included a man who had escaped from Nazi Germany, under horrible circumstances, in the trunk of a car. Thirty years later he still found it difficult to enter an automobile.

ॐ

Friends invited me to a cocktail party especially to meet a famed doctor from India.

As the rather short, undernourished-appearing gentleman met me, he said with effusive appreciation, "I deserve you."

"Oh?" I asked.

"Yes," he said. "Don't you notice anything unusual about me?"

I didn't.

"My earlobe is punctured," he said proudly. "I am of the Brahman caste."

Under the gaze of his dark eyes I felt like a harem girl about to be purchased for his pleasure. He "deserved" me! Because I was an ex-nun and he was a high-caste Indian! There *had* to be more to communication than that!

ॐ

Of course I saw congressmen. One invited me to my first office party on the Hill. We were both single and Catholic, and our first dates had been interesting. He worked late, so it was arranged that, with another girl, I would meet him at the Longworth House Office Building. When we arrived, on a snowy night, the party was late starting. A group of congressmen, lobbyists, and businessmen stood on one side of the room. Three office girls sat on the other side. There was an open bar between. My glamorous congressman barely nodded to me as I entered and continued speaking with his group. Other people began arriving.

The first congressman who spoke to me shook my hand and said, "Hello, honey, don't you want to take your clothes off?"

Innocent me! I had expected to meet people dealing in the most noble of human sciences, and I met this character! I had never seen him before! Moreover, none of the assembled people came to my defense. No one seemed to think he had said anything amiss!

Another congressman, tall and gray-haired, with a family back home, regarded me with obvious personal interest. I knew his state. My father was a friend of one of its wealthiest residents. It gave me great pleasure to ask if he knew this man, who had been "like a second father to me." The change in his behavior toward me was radical!

On other occasions I met many fine congressmen who did much to enhance my basic faith in the men who run our government. Of course, in any large group, such as Congress, there are always a few whose poor behavior compromises the reputation of the many.

For a time I dated an ex-FBI man, who proudly took me to Harvey's Restaurant for dinner—a restaurant so often frequented by his former boss, J. Edgar Hoover, that a plaque had been placed on a booth. He told me that an FBI agent never sits with his back toward a door, but always tries to sit against a wall. When I began dating Clarence Kelley, I was to remember that.

As I dated men in Washington, I continually received advice from well-meaning women on how to capture one and make him my very own. It was amazing how important it was to those who had ever been married to make sure that everyone else tried it at least once! I was not concerned about my single state. Why should I rush to the altar with the first man who proposed marriage? The criterion of one's status should be happiness, which I already had.

I was in no hurry to make a decision. I was the one who would be living for the rest of my life with whomever I married. He would be *my* choice, and chosen not out of some ridiculous sense of embarrassment over my singleness. I think I was not alone among women in the early 1970s in wishing to find genuine romance in a relationship with a man. I felt it should include tenderness, and a deep and abiding interest in one's proposed mate's well-being and joy in life. Love should never be hurried, unless it was certain.

One of the women at Watergate gave me much free advice, though I never asked for it. When I was dating a man who was at least fifteen years older than I, and with whom I certainly was not in love, she advised me, "Marry him. You aren't getting any younger, Shirley."

She seemed to feel it was necessary for me to get a man even if I didn't love him. Then I would be successful!

Talking with this woman, she said, "Have an affair! Get rid of your virginity! Virginity frightens men!"

I whooped with laughter. "I have no intention of doing such a thing!" To my thinking, virginity was not a bad thing. At the convent, where I had done much counseling, I had listened to hundreds of people pour out their hearts, and I knew she was giving me poor advice. The most important thing for a person to remember was to be faithful to oneself.

It was not virginity or the lack of it that I thought was important. It was the reasoning behind this advice of giving it up that lacked integrity. Many, many girls, who had sound basic value systems, were squeezed under social pressures to compromise their principles so that they would not be considered "squares."

Whatever I did, I enjoyed myself. I had a marvelous time. I joined friends skiing in Canada and at Vail, Colorado, and spent a summer traveling through Europe with my mother. Life's adventures never let up. They multiplied!

The men I met were a cross-section of what was currently available for dating. They were not youngsters. They had either been married or had pretty definitely decided on permanent bachelorhood. The formerly married frequently had problems connected with their earlier marriages—children, alimony, a cool regard for women. For me the times were not conducive to marriage.

I was happy with the life I had had, and was having. No one had entered my life who I felt, by sharing it with me, could make it any happier. I was proposed to, but never by anyone with whom I could imagine a future as happy as my present.

15

Saigon

My home away from home during my five years at Watergate was the apartment of Bill and Mary Peterson. Both were economists. Mary had authored *The Regulated Consumer*. One of Mary and Bill's avocations was a continuing search for a knight on a white charger who might sweep me off my feet. Through them I met many interesting people. The Petersons were literally willing to extend their efforts on my behalf to the ends of the earth!

During a business trip which Bill made to Vietnam, he met a man who was in banking there with an American firm, and decided that this young man, Andrew,* was a promising candidate for me.

When Bill returned, Mary decided that her next party would be to celebrate the upcoming Vietnamese New Year. I was invited and met some more of my neighbors, including Chairman of the Federal Reserve Arthur Burns and his sparkling-eyed wife, Helen. Madame Chennault and Ambassador Phong from Vietnam were present, as was Andrew, who was in the United States on business.

Not his real name.

Andrew was indeed as charming as he had been touted. He was a fine conversationalist, tall, slim, and blond.

As the cocktail party broke up, Andrew asked me if I would have dinner with him next door at the Watergate Terrace. I couldn't imagine anything more fun than knowing more about this man who lived in Vietnam. Even though I had eaten enough hors d'oeuvres not to need dinner, I said yes.

As we were departing, matchmaker Mary called after him. "Andy, if you miss your flight to New York, feel free to sleep on our couch!"

Over dinner Andrew and I became deeply involved in a discussion of Roman Catholic philosophy. He was a convert to Catholicism. Having made this decision as an adult, he had researched church law, and our conversation sharpened some insights for both of us. He was comfortable in his religion, although he had a personal problem because of it. He was divorced and the father of a small child. He felt heavily the burden of this as a constraint against remarriage. We talked about this and about many other things. Time passed so enjoyably, and we conversed so long, that he missed his New York flight and slept on Mary's couch.

He flew to Europe the next day.

About a month later, who was announced from the reception desk in our lobby but Andrew! I was delighted, and we spent a busy weekend "doing" Washington together.

On the final evening, before his return to Saigon, we went to the Tombs, an informal little restaurant in Georgetown. It was in the basement of an old building and had low ceilings. Small tables for two, each with a flickering candle, crowded the room, as did an active, noisy, laughing group of college students from Georgetown University. It was a happy place, but hardly one in which one might expect to hear a proposal of marriage.

"Shirley," this man whom I had seen four times said, "I want to marry you."

I was surprised at his directness.

With a lift of his hand he gently stopped anything I might have said.

"There are a couple of bridges we have to cross," he said thoughtfully. "I hope we will reach the other side together.

"As you know, I am divorced and have a child whom I dearly love. If we plan to marry in the Church, this could cause a problem. I expect that with your background, this would be a condition of marrying. I respect that. Therefore, a dispensation from the Church will be required for me. I know that this all seems to have happened fast, but this is all the time we have. I love you, and I want to marry you. I feel a dispensation is worth pursuing. In our hearts, we must both feel happy about our religion.

"The other consideration is," he said in a tone so solemn that my heart sank, "if you marry me, you will probably never again live in the United States. My work will probably always keep me based in a foreign office. This concerns me for you. The Oriental culture is very different from ours. The customs, language, value system, even the appearance of the people, require a tremendous adjustment. I want you to feel sure you could be happy there. I wish there was some way you could come to Vietnam and see the country as it truly is before you make your decision."

Now, I am a woman who makes up her mind quickly. I could think of nothing more exciting than a trip to Vietnam! There was a war going on, but other people seemed to live through it. The idea sounded vastly intriguing to me. What better way to see that country about which so much of the world's thinking was directed, but which so few people ever saw, than with an escort who knew it well, and with whom I was rapidly falling in love!

"I think that can be arranged," I said.

My mind was already halfway to the bank to request a loan.

I had six weeks until spring vacation to hack my way through the red tape that entangled travel to the war zone. Women were simply not being admitted at that time! I pulled every string I knew, including reminding the ambassador that he was in a way a participant to my plight, since he had been in attendance at Mary's party when I met the delightful man whom I wished to see.

Wonder of wonders, my appeal won! I was granted a visa for the week of my spring vacation from school.

At the bank, I expected no trouble. The loan officer knew me. I had used his services before. Banks, I had found, were always curious as to how one intended to spend their money, even when one was paying interest to borrow it. On my previous visit I had obtained money to buy a fine Oriental rug for my apartment—not a frequently expressed need for a loan.

The loan officer remembered me.

"No problem," he said when I stated the amount. "Just answer a few questions."

When he arrived at the reason for my need, he looked up expectantly.

"A trip to the Orient for my spring vacation," I said.

"Any collateral?" he asked.

"The Oriental rug," I replied.

My flight landed in another world, a split world, part war-torn, part business as usual.

As I was going through customs, an American, who had been on the plane with me all the way from New York, approached me.

"I see that you have someone here meeting you," he said. "Do you think that you could give me a lift to the Jehovah's Witnesses Hospital? My mother-in-law is sick there."

I told him I would ask my friend, which I did, and Andrew immediately offered the man a ride into town in his waiting Mercedes.

On the way into Saigon the man explained that he had been in Vietnam on a tour of duty and had married a Vietnamese girl. When he had arrived back in the United States, he learned that his wife's mother was critically ill. He had returned to be with her and to assist her to the United States for further care. Andrew and I were deeply touched by this story. The man was obviously not wealthy, but was prepared to spend thousands of dollars for his new family.

As we drove into Saigon, on every side I saw military men with machine guns. Displaced persons seemed everywhere. The President's palace bristled like a fortress. Through the streets thronged masses of people. Others jostled by in rickshaws. Past them rolled hundreds of splendid Mercedes-Benzes, each chauffeured by a native driver, transporting in the luxurious back seat one foreign entrepreneur. The sidewalks were cluttered with a population of quiet, squatting people sitting behind little stoves on which they seemed endlessly to be stirring some meager brew in pots.

Yes, the Orient was different.

In the buildings beyond the sidewalks life functioned with astonishing matter-of-factness. People went to work, provided services, enjoyed life. Restaurants served fine food. There were beautiful things to buy in the stores. Orchestras played. Life was enjoyable.

On the other hand, in the midst of this city was a building which we passed several times. It was a large, solid structure—a prison. When we drove by, army trucks, loaded with prisoners, were driving through its gates. Hundreds of men entered. Yet amid the teaming life of the city, this grave building sat surrounded, it seemed to me, by the most eerie stillness. Not a sound issued from its depths. No sign of life moved about its grounds. What was happening to all those inmates I had seen enter? I dared not wonder.

Of course I was overwhelmed by what I was seeing. But what I had really come to see was Andrew. He was all I had hoped for, and more. He made every effort to make my visit comfortable and worthwhile. Particularly, I enjoyed being introduced to several of his Vietnamese friends. Through them, I began to feel as though I were truly seeing Saigon. Four times I was invited into their homes.

Each house, I found, was a compound of two life-styles. In the large front house, the owners lived. There were always at least two servants. The families of the servants lived in small sheds in the backyard, complete with generations of children, siblings, parents, and grandchildren. These people, with their chickens and ducks and little gardens, lived off the employed member of the family. Side by side these two classes existed, the owners and the relatives of the servants. They never mingled, but each respected the territorial boundaries of the other.

The furnishings of these upper-middle-class houses surprised me. With the rich markets of finely carved woods of China and Taiwan relatively near, I was perplexed to see in these homes the least expensive of furniture, rattan, and other poor pieces. There was no porcelain china, silver, or crystal. When I inquired about this, Andrew told me that many felt that defeat might come. They were quietly shipping everything of value out of the country. If it happened, they did not want to have all their eggs in one basket.

I found that the Vietnamese handle their unemployment problem in a most unusual way. When I went to a beauty shop for a shampoo, seven ladies attended me. One shampooed my hair, another set it, a third removed the curlers, a fourth combed it out. A fifth waved a fan over my head during the warm process. For my manicure, one lady removed my old polish, another applied fresh enamel. In the United States these women would have been represented by two, or at the most three, attendants. In Vietnam more people did less work, so that all might benefit. Each received less, but there was a bit for all.

Can you imagine figuring out tips for such a bevy? I left mine with the cashier and asked her to distribute it.

One night Andy took me to an especially fine nightclub for drinks and dancing. The dance band there was reported to be exceptionally good. When we arrived, we were told that this particular group was no longer there. For the past week, no one had been able to locate even one of its members. It was rumored that they had all been drafted into the Army. I felt the long reach of the uniformed sleeve into that business-as-usual world.

My most frightening encounter in my visit to that war-torn land did not come from a man or a bombing, but from two ladies. As I approached the women's lounge one evening during dinner in a restaurant atop a tall building, below which a splendid view of Saigon was spread, two long-taloned ladies accosted me. They began picking at my dress.

One exclaimed in English, "Oh! what a beautiful dress!"

The other, as their hands with their brightly painted long nails began touching me all over, said, "Where do you suppose she got it?"

I freed myself from them and rushed back to the table.

"Andy," I said, "I can't get into the lounge. Two ladies seem to think I am encroaching on their territory."

He stood up. "C'mon," he said, "I'll take you to the men's room. You'll be safe there." He carefully scouted that chamber, and then stood guard at the door for me.

That was the only time I was ever afraid while in Vietnam. It was also the only time in my life I was ever invited into a men's room. And to think, I was safer there than with the ladies!

The days passed far too rapidly as I studied the country and the possibility of living there. I knew it would be vastly difficult. But isn't that what produces adventure? It is not the samenesses, but the changes, which make life interesting. With a loving husband, who himself had mastered the difficulties of such a foreign country, learning a new life-style, and sharing it with him, would be one more exciting voyage in living.

When I left Andrew in Saigon, I had made my decision. I told him I would marry him. We planned that he would come to the United States in the summer.

ॐ

One does not live forty years without undergoing heartache. I ran into a big one.

I loved Andrew.

He had said he loved me.

I felt we might happily blend our lives and create a better one for each other together.

We were both Catholic. I was also a former nun. Surely I understood what my Church meant to me.

Catholic views on divorce and remarriage were widely quoted but frequently misunderstood. Each case was individual. To remarry while a former mate was alive one must present one's case to the Holy Father and receive dispensation. That was a step Andrew finally did not take.

Since we did not feel we could marry outside the Church, we could not be married.

I accepted his decision.

Naturally, I was heartsick. For many years I had expected to experience complete love with one man. As it was just about to be mine, it slipped away.

I had been jilted.

I wept.

The days following the arrival of his written message were exceedingly difficult. It was summer. I was not teaching. I had more time to think than I needed. All my plans had been directed toward my marriage.

On the sixth floor of the Watergate, there was a door where another couple lived. I had seen a great deal of them, and they knew Andrew. I turned to them in my unhappiness, seeking their understanding.

They heard me out, allowing me to pour out my feelings.

At the close of the conversation, the lady smiled brightly at me and spoke some prophetic words. At the time I did not believe them.

"Shirley," she said, "forget him. Such joy lies ahead for you as you could never imagine."

How right she was!

16

The Man
With the Gun

"A very special party," Janet said, handing me an invitation to read.

It was May 1976, the bicentennial year, and there were parties everywhere as the nation approached its two-hundredth birthday. This one was to be held in a beautiful old Virginia mansion, Selma, in Leesburg. Guests were to wear authentic Colonial costumes, or dress which would blend with the centuries' old theme.

I was sitting in the charming country home of my friends, Janet and Bill Reed in Middleburg.

"Wouldn't you like to go?" she asked.

"It sounds like fun," I said, reading the small engraved print where it said "$25.00 a couple." "But I'm not dating anyone just now that I'd care to bring along."

"Come by yourself," she urged. "We're making up a group."

"Do you really want me without a date?" I asked, thinking of being without a dancing partner.

"Of course! It's a party!"

I wrote out a twenty-five-dollar check for "a couple," knowing it would only be "for one."

Later, as I drove out of her driveway for the fifty-mile return to Washington, Janet called after me.

"See you June twelfth for the ball!" Then she added gaily, "You never know, Bill may find an available bachelor down at the Bureau!"

William L. Reed was executive assistant to the Director of the Federal Bureau of Investigation. His wife, Janet, was the sorority sister who, years before in Miami, had had her mother's Cadillac overly soaped and undershaded in our car wash.

A week or so before the ball, she called, breathless with excitement.

"Shirley," she announced, "Clarence Kelley is going to be your date for the ball!"

"Clarence Kelley." Aside from Bill's stories of him, I knew almost nothing about the Director of the FBI. Vaguely I remembered having seen him on television, and I had heard Bill mention him. I also knew that his wife had died the previous year and that Janet had liked her very much.

Janet continued to talk.

"Now you know, Shirley, the Director always has to have a bodyguard. He will be driven out to our house in his bombproof, bulletproof limousine. You come on out and meet him here."

She certainly made it sound like an interesting evening! I thought it would be fun.

The following day, Janet called again. This time she sounded upset.

"Shirley," she said, "the Bureau is very concerned. The Director insists on picking you up himself, in his own Chevrolet. Not only does that mean that he will be without protection whatsoever, but he has hardly driven in this city in the three years he has been here! His driver picks him up every day. Now, Shirley," she insisted, "you make it very clear to the Director that *you* will do the driving!"

By the time she hung up I felt as though I was going to be not only his driver but his bodyguard too! She had thrust tremendous responsibility upon me. I was entrusted with the care, comfort, and conveyance of the Director of the FBI for a fifty-mile trip which would take over an hour to drive.

Such thoughts were not calming as I dressed for the ball.

I had had no problem in selection of what to wear. Working part-time in a department store had given me a closet full of beautiful evening gowns. I worked several evenings, and Saturdays, at Lord and Taylor's, whose expensive dresses during sales were sometimes marked down to a third of their original cost. Being on the premises, I never missed a sale. I adored bargains, whether I needed them or not!

When I walked down the wide carpeted hallway to the ballroom-sized foyer of Watergate South, with its Italian mosaic floor and sparkling crystal chandeliers, I was wearing my most diaphanous, floaty gown—layers and layers of white chiffon. I had spent the afternoon in the beauty shop and was pedicured, manicured, and coiffeured. I felt wonderful! And I was a half hour early for my date. As I approached the door my head was full of possible devious plots which might be brewing against the Director. When he arrived, I didn't want him to have to stand around waiting, with the chance of being recognized and endangered.

But, what do you know! As I entered the lobby with its floor-to-ceiling window walls, I saw, parked across the driveway, Clarence Marion Kelley, the Director of the FBI. He was sitting in his white Chevrolet, coat off, sleeves rolled up, one arm hanging out over the door, for all the world to see and take a shot at!

I had never seen the man before, but I recognized him immediately. He saw me and stepped out of his car, looking like a live cutout of his newspaper pictures. He was a large man, with the broadest shoulders I had ever seen. His head seemed squared-off, solid, with a strong jaw. Black-rimmed glasses contrasted sharply with his silver hair and hazel eyes. He had a most encompassing smile. His entire personality burst forth through it, warm, genuine, interested, and fun-loving.

I walked toward him.

"Hello, Clarence," I said. "Give me the keys. I'll drive."

I had only one thought in my head, to get him to Middleburg in one piece.

"Hello," he said, and meekly handed over his car keys.

A couple months later, as we discussed our first meeting, he told me he had been made absolutely speechless by my approach.

"Here," he said, "this little twerp walks out of the Watergate and bosses me around before she hardly even says hello. And there I was, the chief of thousands of FBI men, obediently handing over the keys of my car to a girl I had never previously seen."

157

He topped that by inquiring, "C'mon now, weren't you even a little bit afraid of me?"

Of course I wasn't!

ဦ

Accompanied by Bill and Janet, we approached Selma, a white-pillared mansion with broad chimneys at either side, magnificently placed on a hill above a sloping lawn so that one could thrill to its beauty long before stepping inside.

The members of the receiving line were each dressed in suit or gown of a century or more past. I was transported into history, and so lost in the gracious charm of the house that I was quite unprepared for our hostess' exclamation, "How beautiful you are!"

Many turned to look at me. I was embarrassed, but pleased.

"Good," I thought, "maybe I look fine enough to be the date of the Director of the FBI."

When we reached the top step, Clarence turned to me and took my chin in his hand. He looked in my eyes, but didn't say anything. Then I heard a purring sound deep in his throat. He was proud of me.

We walked through the house and out to a bar beyond the swimming pool, where chairs had been placed. The sun was sinking, and the evening, amid the trees and hills, had begun to turn cool. I shivered. Clarence, who wears "extra large," took off his suit jacket and draped it over my size six shoulders. I must have been a vision in that enormous coat, though at the time it scarcely crossed my mind. What *did* fill my eyes and mind was a gun! As my escort sat beside me in his shirt sleeves, a gun stuck up from his belt!

Never before had I knowingly been in a room with a man who toted a gun. Now I sat beside such a man. Danced with him. Laughed and chatted easily with him.

ဦ

Following the party we returned to the Reeds' home, Foxchase Farm. Clarence had a room on ground level. My romantically imaginative suite was above, on the first floor. It included a den, bath, and a loft, reached by a ladder, where my bed was located. There were two other rooms above where Bill and Janet and their daughter, Noel, slept. I lay in my storybook room listening to the night sounds, my imagination beginning to run away with me. I was not accustomed to being around a man whom "somebody might be out to get." Few cars passed on the country roads, but when they did, I raised my head, expecting to sound an alarm as intruders approached us. For hours, I envisioned impossible plots against the soundly sleeping Director below.

Following breakfast the next morning, the four of us drove to Antietam. Clarence's reaction to the battlefield moved me. After all, it seemed to me, he worked in a kind of one. As a part of his work, he saw evidence, almost daily, of heinous crimes, and was well acquainted with unnecessary death. Still, he was visibly distressed by the number of young men who had been killed at Antietam. "Why could not men satisfy their differences at the conference table?" he asked.

We lunched in a lovely country inn. As I think back on that first meal Clarence ever bought me, I realize I was certainly not out to impress him! Mama had always told me that to be polite one should order from the middle price range of the menu. That day, lobster was the most expensive choice, and I ordered it. It was delicious!

I have had a life of many "firsts" with Clarence. That afternoon I had my first experience of being in the company of a nationally recognized public figure. Four people stopped him and asked him if he was not the Director of the FBI. I was amazed by the pleasure, and even awe, with which people regarded his office. Later, as I discovered his popularity, I was to realize that that had been a rather slow day for well-wishers.

It was late on Sunday afternoon when we returned in Clarence's Chevrolet to the Watergate and said good-bye. No bolt of lightning had hit. My directional compass had made no violent swing. Goodness knows, Clarence Kelley was an interesting man, and we had both had a good time, but I never really expected to see him again. He had been fun to be with. We had been comfortable in each other's company. But that was all. His presence had been pleasant, but it had not been "a date."

Two days later he called and asked me if I would like to go out with him Thursday, Friday, and Saturday nights of that week.

"Yes," I said, thinking, "How refreshing! No phony dating games. Here was a direct Director."

On our first date, Clarence arrived for me in a seven-passenger limousine driven by Special Agent Tom Moten. A sumptuous beginning! In elegant style we rode to his condominium, where we were discharged beside his Chevrolet, in which we continued on to Billy

Martin's Carriage House Restaurant in Georgetown. Alone with Clarence, without his driver, who doubled as a bodyguard, I felt the full burden of his security. After all, if he needed protection during working hours, who was looking out for him now? I was the only one left! Not only was I concerned for his life, but I soon discovered he was in considerable pain from a pinched nerve in his back. He was really suffering. Anyone else would have been home in bed. To top my other concerns for his health and well-being, he next seated himself with his back to the door! Even *I* knew better than that and told him so. But would he move? Of course not! Clarence Kelley, I early discovered, could be as determined as I!

Our napkins were scarcely unfolded in our laps when our conversation got around to "us." Clarence had to make certain he was not wasting my time. He had signed me up for three dates, thereby obviously depriving any number of fascinating people of my time. No, I assured him, I was not currently dating anyone, or ones. I was happy to be with him. Then, he reminded me, he was a recently widowed man, who had enjoyed a long and happy marriage. His interest in me was only as a friend. He needed someone to take out to dinner occasionally.

"That's fine," I assured him. What I was really curious about was what he did. I had a million questions to ask about the FBI. Practically all I knew about it, I had gleaned from the TV series on the FBI starring Efrem Zimbalist, Jr.

"Surely," I said, "you must have won uncountable awards in your years as a special agent."

"No," he replied casually, he had won none at all. "As a matter of fact," he said, "the most spectacular event in my twenty years as a special agent was a stakeout in a men's room. You wouldn't believe how difficult it was to appear nonchalant for three or four hours in that place."

He was obviously not in the mood to discuss his job. The more I tried to get out of him on the great cases he had solved or been a party to, the more it began to seem to me that in one hour a week, Efrem Zimbalist, Jr. accomplished a lot more!

After dinner Clarence said, "I really haven't seen enough of this city. I'd like to go see the Jefferson Memorial."

I laughed. "Do you really want to go there? Congressman Wilbur Mills got into a lot of trouble at the Tidal Basin."

We drove through the park beneath the overhanging, shadowy elms.

While we were standing beneath the vast dome above Jefferson's statue, reading some of his hopes for the nation which are engraved on its walls, the guards began turning out the lights. It was closing time. Regretfully, we returned to the Chevrolet as the lights behind us snapped off.

Clarence began patting his pockets, first one, then another, in that manner that says louder than words, "I can't find the keys."

All I needed was for Clarence Kelley to have to identify himself at the Tidal Basin an hour before midnight in the company of a blonde, and it would be all over the morning paper!

The chink of metal, as he finally found his keys, was music to my ears.

Our Friday date was to attend a meeting in Baltimore given by B'nai B'rith, during which Clarence would give the principal address.

Tom Moten arrived for me in the seven-passenger limousine before picking up Clarence.

At that time the Bureau had three seven-passenger limousines, all purchased under J. Edgar Hoover and built to his specifications. The newest was purchased in 1972 and was four years old. The others, of vintages 1968 and 1970, were kept in other cities which the Director frequently visited.

The cars were most interesting. They were extremely heavy, having been armor-plated at a cost of $29,000 apiece. Each was equipped with extra safety devices, with two-way mobile radio units, and telephones, heavy-duty batteries, and all the glass was bulletproof.

Hoover had the cars built with a glide-up window between the driver and passengers. Clarence, I would find, never used it. Of course I had to try it out. The phone was out of sight, nestled in the hollowed-out armrest in the middle of the back seat, covered with matching upholstery. The cars, while huge and powerful, were strictly utilitarian. No frills. Their extreme weight held them solidly to the roads, which was good for Clarence's frequently painful back—almost therapeutic.

The eventual disposal of the cars interested me. It would be easy to imagine the delight of a crime syndicate member who discovered one of them on a used-car lot! But that could never be. Any of the cars that was ever offered for sale to the public first had to be dearmored, an expensive job. When President Carter took office, in conformance with his suggestions, the bulletproof, bombproof limousines were removed from the FBI for economy measures. They were turned over to the Secret Service, their security being replaced by a Mercury Marquis. A second car, a two-year-old Chevrolet Impala, was used as a backup car. It was equipped with a two-way mobile radio and a telephone, and was always kept at a state of readiness for the Director. That car could be used in case the first car was in need of repair. It was also used to transport FBI members or staff to meetings or on official visits. Use by the Director, however, was always given first priority.

Economy on the use of official cars of the Bureau began during the Nixon administration, at the time of the energy crisis. At that time a Mercury was the backup car to the limousine, and it was used to transport the Director to and from work. The larger car was kept for official evening events, or to use on short trips where it would be cheaper to drive than to buy airplane tickets.

On the evening of my second date alone with Clarence, I felt very small, but elegant, riding by myself in the wide back seat of the limousine with Tom driving. As he had settled me into my seat he had apologized because it would be necessary to stop at a gas station for fuel. Of course I didn't mind. In fact, I enjoyed it!

For the first time, I found myself looked upon as a celebrity! Tom, a handsome, courteous man, an FBI agent himself, sat smartly behind the wheel as we drove into the station. He rolled down the window and gave the station attendants his order.

Two young men scurried about, one attaching the gasoline hose, the other making motions at the windows, which already were spotless, with a chamois.

I quickly realized why.

He was studying *me*. Trying to figure out who *I* was. In such a car, obviously I was somebody important.

"Nice car, lady," he said.

"Thank you," I replied, feeling as if I was cheating, but enjoying the opportunity to play to the hilt the role of Cinderella.

We drove to Clarence's apartment, which then was at the Grosvenor Park. As we were slowing to a halt by the front entrance, I noticed Tom wave to some men parked down the street in a brown car. Then he picked up the phone and called Clarence in his apartment upstairs. Within moments Clarence appeared. He, too, waved at the men in the brown car before getting into the seat beside me. I was tickled by the whole neat package—the huge car, the phone, the fun, of this enchanting world!

Tom started the car and we drove off. The brown car also began to move and followed us out to the highway.

"Friends of Clarence," I thought. "Probably going to the same party." How right I was!

We were on the Beltway, headed northeast, when Clarence said, "I received another threat today. We have an escort." He waved his hand toward the brown car.

At first I didn't want to believe what I thought I had heard. A threat? A threat! I was not used to threats of any kind. My life was usually more direct than that. Things happened, or they didn't. I guess I looked my puzzlement.

"A death threat," he said simply. "It happens. This time it sounded pretty convincing, so we are taking extra precautions. We take these things seriously," he went on, "but we don't allow them to keep us from going on about our business. Actually, I am not the man they are after. The gunman really wants to kill the mayor of Baltimore, but the mayor isn't going to show. There is always the possibility that when the fellow gets to the meeting place and is disappointed at not finding his most favored target, he will look for a good second choice—in this case me."

I was horrified. I began to wonder what I was doing, speeding along in a huge limousine with a man I had only seen twice before, and now I was sharing with him the possibility of getting killed by some little punk who wasn't going to be permitted to change his plans.

Clarence saw me tense up.

"Don't worry," he said. "This car is very special. It is armor-plated, and all the glass is bulletproof. It is even built so that if an average bomb went off under it, the car would simply rise a bit off the ground and then settle back down again, not much damage done."

I heard him, but my imagination went to work. It would be one thing if a bomb exploded beneath the car while it sat at the curb. But suppose it was traveling at fifty-five miles an hour?

I peered through the bulletproof glass windows at the summer evening and then back again at the strong, calm face of Clarence Kelley. It couldn't help but be an interesting evening. I relaxed.

We arrived at a Baltimore hotel where we met a party of perhaps forty people, all FBI special agents and their ladies, with whom we had cocktails and dinner. Then Clarence and I were escorted back to the car and were driven to another hotel where the B'nai B'rith function was being held. Three cars filled with FBI men accompanied us.

As we entered the garage, two Bureau cars preceded us. The first made a quick U-turn across the exit lane, thus blocking any cars from that direction. The second car stopped directly ahead of us, blocking the entrance road. Behind us, the third car stalled traffic from entering the garage. It was just like a movie—all those G-men! Five men sprang from the second car. One raced to the door leading into the hotel, quickly checked out the corridor behind it, and returned to hold the door open for us. Another man came to my side of the car. Two men approached Clarence's side and opened his door for him. There seemed to be G-men everywhere! There was not one moment of hesitation. Clarence proceeded to the hotel door, escorted on either side by two bodyguards. I was ushered in just ahead of him. We were whisked into the building, where we were taken to a suite of rooms with chairs and couches, a television set, and a bar. Already assembled was a group of FBI agents and their ladies.

I received my next shock.

It was a warm evening. Summers in Baltimore are humid. The men were at ease. They had removed their jackets and were sitting or standing about in their shirt sleeves, and *every one was wearing a gun.* I simply couldn't believe it! I looked from one to the other. Every man carried a gun, either in a shoulder harness or attached to his belt by a small hook, with only the butt sticking up, dark, metallic, and handy in either location.

To me, to be in a group of people on a social occasion with all the men nonchalantly wearing loaded weapons was a stunning shock. I don't think I said a word until I absorbed the stark reality of the situation in which I had placed myself by accepting a date with Clarence Kelley.

I had ridden in a car built to withstand the explosion of a bomb and viewed the world through bulletproof glass while seated beside a man who was frequently the recipient of death threats, and who was at all times vulnerable to attack from someone who had not first bothered to notify him of his drastic intent!

And how did I feel? I could not help but respond to this outgoing, warmhearted, and amusing man. He was such fun! I had never in my life had so much fun as on those dates with Clarence Kelley. Fun? On a date when his life had been threatened? That sounds perverse—but I remembered how it had been in the car when Clarence had first mentioned the threat. He had made fear seem bearable. Almost comfortable. He had no fear of his own. Being with a truly brave person is rather like entering a church.

Our Saturday date was to have been aboard the presidential yacht *Sequoia,* as the guests of Attorney General Levi, but instead, it was in the hospital.

Clarence was in a state of almost unrelievable pain from his pinched nerve, for which his doctors had prescribed total rest. He phoned from Bethesda Naval Hospital to say he was sure a visit from me would inestimably speed his recovery.

He remained there for a week, attached to his office by direct telephone, performing all his duties except the presenting of awards and picture-taking ceremonies.

During my several visits to the hospital, we had time for backgammon and conversation. Every day I learned more about him. I admired his humor, which throughout his pain, kept effervescent. Even lying flat on his back, he was determined, and forceful, his mind seizing ideas and making summations. He was very much in command.

We spoke of our earlier lives, and from the stories he told, I was able to piece together the happenings of his life which had created the man and had brought him to that time and to my side.

In Washington, D.C., Clarence Kelley was considered a VIP, but during that week, he began to become personally important to me. A very special relationship began to develop.

17

Clarence Who?

What does it take for a boy to grow up to become the Director of the FBI? Well, first of all, it requires the absence of a current Director—which possibility was precluded for generations of American youth while the first Director, J. Edgar Hoover, held the position for forty-eight years. During that period Hoover's name became synonymous with the Bureau, and the Bureau became so entangled with his image that in the public mind the two were one.

Hoover became Director of the Federal Bureau of Investigation at the age of twenty-nine. During the 1930s and 1940s he did much to make it nationally and internationally effective. Through his innovations, and with the assistance of his skilled and trained staff, he created an almost unbeatable machine for crime solving and orderkeeping. But in later years, some of the Bureau's compelling character was diminished as the agency more and more bore the personal stamp of its aging leader.

J. Edgar Hoover had served under eight Presidents and held his powerful position through four Republican and four Democratic administrations. The limits of the Director's job had never been defined.

No precedent had been set for his office. Time passed, but Hoover would consider no possibility of retirement. Nor was pressure brought to bear. Within the FBI files, which he held under his control, there was the possibility of enough clout to quell any inquiry as to his status by lawmakers and even Presidents. On the American political scene, the Director held a most unique position. Only death could dislodge him from it. It did, on May 2, 1972.

By what process could a possible successor to such a man in such a position have arrived at the right moment in American history to assume his spot?

Possible answer: through personal character, will, and luck.

The position required a man who felt for humanity as a whole, and for every person as an individual. He must have had the will to work with determination toward the fulfillment of the duties and ideals of law and order. He must have had the luck and opportunity to have made the right decisions at the right time, decisions that brought him to the right place to be recognized as a candidate capable of serving his country in the particular requirements of that most specialized position.

Clarence Marion Kelley, the only son of Bond and Minnie Kelley, was born in Fairmount, Missouri, a small suburb of Kansas City, halfway between that city and Independence, in 1911. In those days this area was sometimes referred to as "Truman territory." As Clarence Kelley was growing up, Harry Truman was first a haberdasher and then a judge in Jackson County, from which he was later elected to the U. S. Congress, still later to become the thirty-third President of the United States. When Clarence was a small boy, Harry Truman sometimes stopped over in Fairmount on his way home to Independence, to visit friends with whom he enjoyed playing poker. On those occasions Clarence was warned by his mother, "don't you go to so-and-so's house. Harry Truman is there playing cards, and that is nooooooooo place for a boy!"

Although Harry was much admired, he already had a full array of expletives, for which he would later become nationally renowned, and Minnie Kelley had no intention of allowing her son to be exposed to such talk.

ह∾

Minnie and Bond Kelley were descended from German and Scotch-Irish ancestors who had migrated to the Midwest. Bond's grandfather,

Clarence had often heard as a child, had married an Indian named Missouri. His imagination was fired by this relationship to the past. Clarence's parents were proud of their strong pioneer background. Family ties meant a great deal to the Kelleys. They were devoted to their only child.

Soon after the birth of his son, Bond, who had had only three years of grade school, returned to school. He hoped to provide more choices in life for his son than he himself had had. For seventeen years he worked his full-time job, and then attended classes, not only completing high school but earning a degree in electrical engineering.

In his "spare" time he built a family home across the street from the Christian Church of Fairmount, where the Kelleys were faithful members.

Bond Kelley believed in duty and discipline. Young children should contribute to their world by performing tasks, and they should practice accepting the will of their parents.

On this latter discipline, Clarence, at the age of three, received a swift and severe accounting when with his parents he boarded a streetcar for a trip to Kansas City.

Walking on ahead, while his father deposited their fares in the box, the little boy seated himself beside his mother. When his father came up beside them, he asked Clarence please to move to the single seat across the aisle.

Clarence refused.

A second time, Bond said, "Sit over there, son."

"No," Clarence replied. "I am going to sit here."

Bond picked him up and spanked him. Immediately. There. On the streetcar.

If Clarence had previously been in doubt as to who was boss in the Kelley household, he no longer had reason to speculate. He had learned an immediate lesson. Yet he felt nothing but love for his father, and his respect for him deepened through the years.

The Kelleys never had money to spend foolishly, and the acquisition of any new piece of household equipment was always an event. A fine, heavy lawn mower, meant to last many years, was bought to make ten-year-old Clarence's weekly task of lawn mowing easier for him.

When he had finished using the new machine, he attempted to put the tool away, as he had been taught. It was to be stored in the basement. As he carried it down the stone steps, it became too heavy and unwieldly for him and fell from his grasp. It crashed down the stairs, its iron castings breaking as it dropped.

When Bond returned home, he found a tearful boy in the basement helplessly attempting to rebuild the machine. Realizing what had happened, he voiced an important message.

"Son," he said, "this was not your fault. I am a big man, and I gave a little boy a man's job. I should have known better than to have told you to put the lawn mower back into the basement by yourself. I asked too much of you."

No wonder Clarence loved his father!

His mother's chief despair was that both her husband and her son were extremely active. There was always so much to do, and they were constantly about its accomplishment. To keep up with them, Minnie required afternoon naps.

Clarence, on the other hand, needed little sleep, and even when forced to go to bed, always took toys, or later, a book and a flashlight, with him.

Seeing his light on late one night, Minnie gently scolded her son, reminding him that his body required rest to grow.

Upon returning to bed, she groaned to Bond, "What will ever become of that boy? He will never amount to anything. I can't even get him to sleep at night."

Minnie Kelley did not live to share in the honors which were bestowed upon her son.

ॐ

After the example set for him by his father in his long search for an education, there was no doubt that Clarence would go to college, though there was a big question as to where the money would come from. The answer, he found, was to work one year and attend college the next, alternating work and study until he attained his goal—a law degree. This desire, to be in law, not as a judge, but as a law man of the people, was so firm in him that in his memory it had no beginning.

He entered college and affiliated with Sigma Nu fraternity, which gave him two honors in life. When he was an undergraduate, his fraternity brothers noted a resemblance between Clarence and the drawing of an Indian chief featured on their school tablets. He was dubbed "Chief," a name well suited to his future role. In 1977, as Director of the FBI, Clarence M. Kelley was proclaimed the Sigma Nu alumnus of the year.

During the third year which he worked between college years, Clarence began to feel a growing discouragement over the slowness with which he was approaching his goal. He was employed by an electrical company. For a single man, the pay was good. Perhaps, he thought, if he kept working and saved his money, he would have enough security to ask his longtime sweetheart, Ruby Pickett, to marry him.

At the time his thoughts were traveling along that line of thinking, he was in an open field, where his assignment was to repair an electric transformer. He had been told that the equipment was disarmed and safe to work upon. He reached toward it and was within a hair's breadth of the mechanism when across the field he heard his co-worker's voice call, "Stop! The juice is still on!"

His reflexes were so quick that he stayed the forward thrust of his hand, saving himself from instant electrocution.

In that second, Clarence Kelley set himself straight on his life's path. There might be shocks in life as a lawyer, he thought, but none of them would hold the deadly possibility of those faced by an electrician.

In the fall he returned to college, and he received his A.B. from the University of Kansas in 1936. Four years later he was awarded his degree as Juris Doctor from the University of Missouri in Kansas City.

While still in law school, Clarence was approached by a representative of the FBI who asked him if he had ever thought about becoming a special agent for the Federal Bureau of Investigation. The Bureau, he was told, was on the lookout for apt young men who had degrees in law or accounting and who could qualify for their physical and intelligence tests.

Clarence thought, "Why not?"

The FBI was certainly an important branch of the law, and under the direction of J. Edgar Hoover, the Bureau sounded as though it offered a worthwhile and stimulating career. Starting salaries for young agents were attractive and quite adequate in compensation and benefits compared to those of a young lawyer. Probably, he realized, as a lawyer, he would make more money at a later stage,* but the FBI held a special attraction. The agency was gaining fame throughout the world as a nucleus of special, dedicated men who offered selfless service for the safety of their countrymen. There would be excitement and purpose in such a body. Clarence passed the bar exams for the state of Missouri, married Ruby Pickett, and at the age of twenty-eight began a career as a special agent of the FBI.

He quickly distinguished himself as an excellent marksman and for a year was assigned to the National Academy for FBI agents in Quantico, Virginia. Of the thousands of men who have been FBI special agents over the past fifty years, only about two hundred have ever received the Possible Medal. Clarence was the twenty-sixth to receive it. This test uses a paper target silhouetted with the figure of a man. The marksman must hit the vital areas of the dummy fifty times in a row, using a pistol held standing, sitting, lying prone, left barricade, right barricade, rapid fire, and from the hip. Clarence accomplished this feat. He was also one of the few men in the country who could hit a target behind him by holding his gun over his shoulder and sighting into a diamond held close to his eye. I found that to be an interesting experiment. Properly held, even a very small diamond will reflect an entire locale. A truly steady eye and hand, such as Clarence's, was able to shoot accurately, even from that awkward position, with reverse sighting.

FBI special agents each carried at least one gun. They were trained in its handling and were required to practice their marksmanship. They were instructed never to draw a gun unless they intended to use it; never to use it except when certain of the need. An agent did not shoot to wound, which might permit the criminal to continue his attack. Agents aimed for vital areas, which meant to kill. They shot only to protect others and themselves. Knowledge of their marksmanship and that the agents could, and would, shoot to kill was a great crime deterrent. During his many years of service in the FBI, Clarence had never had to shoot a man. His only experience in shooting had been on the range practice field. He believed competence gave a man a cool head.

The appearance of Clarence Kelley, with the oversize breadth of

---

*Prior to 1976 the Director's salary was $47,000 a year—upped in that year to $57,000. The chief of police in Los Angeles makes about $60,000. In other cities, the C.O.P. and heads of sheriffs' departments are paid considerably more.

his shoulders (he wore a 17-by-36 shirt), created a strong physical presence. He was a definite man, with an all-seeing, penetrating gaze from his hazel eyes and a boxlike jaw. It was understandable why almost any criminal, merely in meeting him, would feel the lesser person. As I came to know him, it was easy for me to see why, when he pointed his gun at a lawbreaker, and stated, "FBI—put up your hands," without fail the wrongdoer would do so. This, he said, made it unnecessary, as an old-timer once told him to say, "If you move one muscle without my permission, one minute from now, you will have been dead sixty seconds."

In spite of the fact that FBI agents never knew from one minute to the next what extreme service might be asked of them, those I knew were the most gentle, peace-loving individuals I had ever met. Among the people of the FBI I found the same dedication I had found among some priests and nuns. Possibly that was one reason why I felt so comfortable with them. They did not waste time complaining that they were underpaid and overworked. It seemed to me that their whole effort was to get the job before them done.

As had happened during my life in the convent where I had had nothing to say about my annual assignment, so it was within the FBI. The men were constantly shipped from city to city, wherever there might be a need for a particular talent, specialty, or for further training. I had thought that the seven places where I lived during my almost sixteen years as a nun involved change, but for many FBI men, the change was almost annual. Wives and children of the agents were thus frequently required to restart their lives in new communities, with new housing, new schools, and new friends. That was a lot to expect of adults and could be particularly distressing to children. The Kelleys moved seventeen times in twenty years.

Aware of the effect of this disruption, Clarence had promised his family that if any particular move ever made either Ruby or the children, Mary and Kent, truly unhappy, he would go to Mr. Hoover himself to ask for a change.

One year Clarence's job was that of inspector, which required him to be away from home over long periods, as he checked field offices. Returning from an extended trip, he was greeted by nine-year-old Kent, who reminded his father of his promise and then said, "Daddy, I'm unhappy."

Clarence studied his son's face for a moment, knowing he must make good his word. "All right, son," he said, "I'll make an appointment to see Mr. Hoover tomorrow."

Appointments with the Director, in those days, were not easy to come by. There were thousands of people in the Bureau who had never even caught a glimpse of J. Edgar Hoover. Most only saw him once, at a service award ceremony. Mr. Hoover did not believe in being highly visible to his men.

From the reception room as he waited to be admitted, Clarence studied the outside of the Director's door intently. *That,* he knew, was *his* side. When he would see the other side of that door, Mr. Hoover's side, he would be on the way out of that venerable office. In between, his whole life could well be changed. Since he was obviously not content with his job, he might no longer be a special agent, or else he could be demoted to some less responsible position from which he would have to work his way back up again.

What actually happened was a possibility that had never crossed his mind.

When he had explained his problem to Mr. Hoover, the Director said, with far more patience than Clarence had dared expect, "Well, if that is the way you feel, Mr. Kelley, would you be interested in the position of SAC* in the Birmingham, Alabama, office?"

Clarence could scarcely believe his ears. He was being kicked upstairs!

As he went on to tell me this story, he laughed. "Then I found out why! No doubt, as I had walked in, Mr. Hoover thought, 'Lo and behold! Here is just the fall guy I have been waiting for!' "

Birmingham, Alabama, was not the best place to be at that time.

Police Commissioner "Bull" Connor had just purchased some new equipment for his department which had aroused nationwide comment. He had acquired some vicious attack dogs which he intended to use in the event of black rioting or to disperse black gangs who might gather.

Clarence was assigned to supervise the Birmingham FBI office and ordered to "keep things civilized." His office was to side with neither Connor nor the blacks, but was to keep the city, which was on the edge of interracial turmoil, on even keel. The method he chose was in sharp contrast to that of the Director. He chose to be almost constantly visible

---

Special agent in charge—head of a city FBI office.

to the citizens of Birmingham and to its police commissioner. He might have been his own shadow those days. He was everywhere. He wished always to be within eyesight of those who might commit crime and those who might attempt to quell it. The fact that day and night he was known to be aware and watching proved to be an excellent crime deterrent.

Clarence made every effort to maintain an amiable relationship with Commissioner Connor, realizing this would be best for all. They occasionally associated outside their jobs.

One day Bull invited Clarence to attend a football game with him and used it for his political advantage. As they were taking their seats in the stadium, the commissioner startled Clarence by calling out in a loud voice for all to hear, "I'm in pretty good shape. I have the top FBI man in town with me!"

Connor was a skillful politician and, Clarence felt, often played the tough-cop role because it brought him votes.

Clarence never saw the attack dogs unleashed, though he had no doubt of their cruel capability. One day Bull asked him to come see the dogs. They were standing in a corridor where a trainer brought them in on a leash. As commanded, the dogs sat quietly.

Bull said, "Now watch this, Mr. Kelley. You'll see how these dogs hate niggers."

From the end of the hall, a black man was approaching.

Bull nodded, and the trainer uttered a command.

Immediately the dogs alerted toward the man, teeth bared, tugging at their leashes. "An appalling sight!" Clarence said.

A result of this overt hatred was a backlash in public thinking which favored the blacks. Rev. Fred Shuttlesworth, a black minister in the area, felt that Bull Connor did more for the blacks than anyone else in their locality at that time. His red-neck attitude was so unappealing that whites became more aware of the true nature of the racial conflict and more understanding of the human relations involved.

Conditions in Birmingham improved.

At the end of Clarence's tour of duty there, things had indeed remained civilized, and Connor marked his departure by presenting him with a fine silver tray engraved "to CM Kelley from Commissioner Bull Connor and members of the Birmingham Police Department 1960."

ह्~

From his hospital bed, Clarence regaled me with many anecdotes from his past. When he was ASAC* in Houston, Texas, it was verified that a man considered dangerous, whom the FBI had been seeking, was working as a farmhand on a ranch outside the city. Clarence and his men drove out to the farm.

Since the man would probably be armed, the best way to reduce the possibility of bloodshed would be to take him by surprise. At the farm, the man was spotted driving a noisy tractor down a field away from the FBI men. Moving rapidly, but without sound, Clarence ran down the field and came up behind the fugitive. With a strong arm, he grabbed the man and jerked him off the tractor, holding him firmly while he frisked him for his gun. The man was in too great a state of shock to resist. Holding the slippery character firmly in his grip, Clarence straightened up. Moving rapidly away from him, its speed unchecked, the tractor was heading directly for a barn. Stabled inside, Clarence knew, were some valuable Appaloosa horses. He was faced with a difficult choice. Should he let go of his catch, run after the tractor and stop it, in order to save the horses, and lose the fugitive, or should he hold on to the man, watch the barn be destroyed, the horses maimed or killed, and find himself facing a bill from the farmer for thousands of dollars of damage? As he stood there wondering, reluctant to let go of his charge, he saw, to his great relief, the tractor make a slight turn which brought it crashing into a supporting post on a lean-to. It brushed against only one horse and caused no serious damage to the building.

He told me the apprehension of the tractor by the post brought him greater relief than the capture of his prime target.

In Kansas City, Clarence served as supervisor in charge of the criminal division. At that time he was again in a problem office. It was there that last-chance-Charleys were sent by Director Hoover. One more mistake, and they would be booted out of the Bureau. To dress up the office and give it a better quality of responsibility, a number of young first-assignment agents were also sent there. To organize this not-the-best-of-mixes, Clarence sat down with the group and announced, "Gentlemen, we are going to work together. We will share our strengths. The experienced men are going to teach the new men all they know; the

---

Assistant special agent in charge.

young men will help the more experienced members write up their reports in the latest and most complete fashion that has come out of Washington. Together, we will do a bang-up job!"

৵

When Clarence retired from the FBI, he had planned to practice law in Kansas City. A friend suggested that he apply for the job of chief of police. The Kansas City Police Department was in difficulty, and a search was on to find an honest, competent man to take over. Clarence interviewed for the job and answered all the questions asked of him. He was then told that one board member was absent, and he would have to return. In the second interview, that man, Roy Swanson, asked Clarence a question none of the others had thought to ask.

"Now, sir," Mr. Swanson asked, "is this job simply a fill-in or a stepping-stone you wish to use until you get yourself established as a lawyer?"

That was exactly what Clarence had had in mind!

The question lay squarely between the two men. A solid decision must be made.

"No, sir," Clarence said, therewith committing the next ten years of his life. "I am interested in the job of chief of police of Kansas City and in serving this community." A long friendship between the men began that day.

Just as he had worked while with the FBI in Birmingham, Clarence used "high visibility" on his job as chief of police in Kansas City. He became known as the chief who never seemed to need rest. At two or three in the morning he would wake up, and get dressed, and go out to cruise around the city in his car, observing the activities of his men. Many a policeman in the act of an arrest, or leisurely sipping a cup of coffee during a break, was surprised to see Clarence's police car, Cruiser #1, come into view at an odd hour of the night.

Alerted by his radio, Clarence would arrive at the scene of a major accident or murder. Weekends were no exception to his surveillance. Sometimes the chief would show up with his high-school-aged son, Kent, or with daughter, Mary, and his future son-in-law, Edward ("Scrappy") Ragland Dobbins, Jr. He was not content merely to sit behind his desk. He wished to see what was occurring on the streets of Kansas City. This ubiquitous approach was intended not merely to keep his men on their toes, but to let them know he shared some of the tragic scenes and ordeals of the city streets with them.

Through innovations he brought to police work, Clarence began to gain national recognition. It was he who first introduced helicopters into police work for patrolling in large cities. He also instigated use of the computer system through which patrolmen in their cruisers were enabled to check with headquarters for a possible criminal record connected with cars or drivers they had stopped. This system is now used nationally. Through it, within a matter of seconds the current status of any licensed driver or vehicle may be referred back to the inquiring officer as he stands at the roadside by the radio-telephone in his car.

The Kansas City Police Department, under Clarence, became so well known as a model law-enforcement system that it averaged four hundred visitors a year from all over the world who came to study it. To keep himself current on the latest improvements and techniques of the field, Clarence frequently attended seminars and took courses, including those offered by the Harvard Business School.

It was after Clarence had reorganized the Kansas City law-enforcement agency, so that it was able to control the riots which started in the city in the 1960s, that Governor Reubin Askew of Florida asked Clarence to go to Miami, during the summer of 1972. He was put in charge of a team of law officers who were to make the city safe for the upcoming Republican and Democratic presidential conventions.

Clarence's work in Miami gained him recognition by the national press, but more meaningful to him was the renewal of an old friendship there. He remet Bill Reed, who was then the crime commissioner for the state of Florida, through which office Bill had installed an IBM system for the Florida police. When Clarence assumed directorship of the FBI, Bill would become his executive assistant.

ह्≽

Amid Clarence's collection of photographs, which fill volumes, boxes, and cover walls, is a prophetic one. It was taken in 1971 at the White House meeting of chiefs of police and law-enforcement personnel from all over the United States who had assembled to discuss riot control in the cities. In the picture, Clarence is shown seated directly across the table from President Nixon and FBI Director J. Edgar Hoover.

After Director Hoover's death in 1972, two interim selections, L. Patrick Gray and William Ruckelshaus, briefly filled his chair, though neither was given the title of Director. Nineteen hundred and seventy-two was a fateful year for United States domestic politics. It was a presidential election year during which some overzealous employees of the Committee to Re-elect the President were caught illegally entering the headquarters of the Democratic party. That was the start of the Watergate affair which was to change American history. As the country rocked under barrage after barrage of accusations and denials, the newly reelected President, Richard Nixon, sought a man known for his integrity, who lacked the stigma of strong political party suasion. He chose Clarence Kelley, politically an independent, and experienced FBI career man and chief of police, a man internationally known as a reformer of police systems, and the recipient of countless awards (nine boxes, at current count!). Among these, his most prized is the Veterans of Foreign Wars' J. Edgar Hoover Medal of Honor. This commendation was given him in 1971 "for his outstanding achievement in law enforcement, and for his comprehension of the sociological implications necessary to bring new and creative techniques into his police department to effect a thoroughly modern institution."

Having been proposed for the position of Director of the FBI, the wheels of the United States system of selection and investigation began to whirl. For four days Clarence was interviewed by several different people in the White House on his ability to comprehend fiscal management and the problems of intelligence, organized crime, white-collar crime, and the everyday criminal problems abroad on the streets of America, plus other aspects of the job. On the fifth day he was reintroduced to President Nixon, who offered him the position of Director of the FBI in June. For the following two weeks he was subject to intensive questioning by the Senate Judiciary Committee, from whom he finally received unanimous approval. No time limit was set for his service except that he must leave at seventy years of age. On July 9, 1973, Clarence Marion Kelley raised his right hand and was sworn in as the second Director of the FBI.

It was a happy day for law-enforcement people everywhere. Clarence was the choice of the International Association of Chiefs of Police (IACP). He was a policeman and had been an FBI special agent. He was keenly aware of what the law-enforcement men on the streets of America faced. He had seen and felt and heard and knew their problems. He knew what it was like to have the man by his side injured in the line of duty. Like all the other chiefs in America, he had had to go to the homes and face the mothers or wives of sons or husbands killed. He knew at first hand the heartaches that were the frequent companion of the man on the job of keeping America safe.

Actually, Clarence accepted the directorship with reluctance. In fact, he almost turned it down. In the first place, he enjoyed being the chief of police of Kansas City. It was a job that used his talents well. But more importantly, a situation in his personal life weighed heavily upon anything he might consider. Shortly before his consideration for the appointment, he had had to give his wife, Ruby, her medical report. She had an advanced cancer. Clarence has told me that of the many ordeals he had faced in life, nothing compared with the anguish of that assignment.

In the family there was much discussion as the pros and cons of the change were reviewed, with its tragic implication of a life in which Ruby would be little able to share. The President himself, anxious to assist his new appointee, intervened with the solution that Mrs. Kelley would be able to receive treatments for her cancer at the National Institutes of Health in Washington. The decision to accept was made. Clarence went to Washington and chose a condominium apartment within a mile of Bethesda Naval Hospital.

Actually, Mrs. Kelley's particular cancer kept her in such a state of weakness that she was not able to travel frequently to Washington or to participate in social life when she was in the capital. For the next three years, Clarence commuted on weekends to Kansas City to be with Ruby. He would fly out to Missouri on Thursday evening and work out of the Kansas City FBI office, and by telephone from home, returning to his apartment in Washington on Sunday evening. He never had time adequately to furnish the apartment. Acquiring a simple decoration for it would become, at a later date, a national issue. In Kansas City his son and daughter assumed the many duties in regard to their mother during the week. It was a time of sacrifice for all the Kelleys.

One might wonder how Clarence could put himself through such a torn-up life during a time of such personal sorrow and strain. I came to understand this as I lived with him. He is a man who fervently and dearly loves his country. He had worked in the Federal Bureau of Investigation for twenty years before going into police work. He knew, and highly respected, the Bureau, but he was also aware that there had to be changes in it. He felt that he could make a permanent contribution to it, and hence the country, by remaking the FBI into a stronger, more effective, and more efficient law-enforcement agency. He had received the nod from the President and won the approval of the elected Senate. For years he had seen people cope with problems of personal suffering within their families while they staunchly continued their service in the Bureau. He could not ask less of himself.

Ruby Pickett Kelley died in November 1975.

Alone, Clarence immersed himself even more into the involved responsibility of administering the FBI during a period of national political upheaval. For many intricate and sometimes inexplicable reasons, forces, both within the Bureau and from the outside, were working against him. The Watergate affair, which had toppled a President, had given heady clout to the press. The media flexed its power. Some members of it roamed, dug, ruthlessly insinuated, and trampled political figures under rapid, frequently unsubstantiated, often vicious attacks. Paper bludgeons unmercifully battered at the mettle of many in government, and if those public servants were not beaten, they were often bruised; sometimes their entire careers were made suspect. All authority—the presidency, Congress, the CIA, and the FBI—was a prime target. Clarence began to feel his lumps.

As I pieced together the life of this man, flat on his back on a hospital bed, he stood tall and resolute in my mind. I found myself laughing at his humor, touched by the sentimental experiences of his life, and enraged by the injustices he described. I fervently wished to fight his battles with him. As I listened and studied him more and more, I realized I was falling in love with him.

18

The F. B. and I

I first met Clarence Kelley because he considered me "safe." I was an ex-nun, a schoolteacher, surely a woman of upright character, introduced to him by a man whose judgment he trusted. I have never asked him if he "ran a check" on me before agreeing to escort me to the Bicentennial Ball, but I could scarcely have blamed him if he had. In the 1970s in Washington, D.C., there was a twelve-month open hunting season. Items which could be "gotten" on public figures were headlined first and researched later. Sniping was sport; character assassination acceptable. If a person was willing to accept a high rank in government service, let him be aware. He was watched! When he raised his right hand at his swearing-in, he relinquished many of his rights to privacy. Reporters, cameramen, television interviewers, had an unquestioned right to waylay, surround, trail him. His doorstep became a camping ground; his lawn, public domain.

Clarence realized he must live more than his usual circumspect life. He must permit no incident which might be misunderstood or improperly interpreted. He was pleased when Bill Reed had described me to him.

From my point of view, I certainly didn't expect meeting Clarence Kelley to change my life. To have such a distinguished escort for an evening added extra sparkle to a festive occasion, but I never dreamed the relationship would develop into a personal one. I was charmed by him at once. In him, I found all that I had ever felt was admirable in a man. He was moral, religious, patriotic, and endeavoring. He worked hard. He played hard. And was more fun to be with than any man I had ever dated, even twenty years younger!

From the very first, our age difference concerned Clarence. Not me! For one thing, I think my years in the convent made my age, to a degree, indeterminate. I had been protected from, and yet faced with, many problems of life, but always within the other-world detachment of my habit.

I have been described as both naïve and wise, as young for my age, and old beyond my years. When one enjoys good health and views life enthusiastically, it is difficult to know how to categorize one's age. It certainly didn't bother me that Clarence had lived a score more years than I! His charm to me could not be computed chronologically. He just was! And I was happy that we were both alive at the same time and that our paths had met.

At the end of the 1975–76 school year, I decided I needed a vacation. I didn't want to work. In fact, I had been invited to visit in Australia, and that sounded like a great idea! But when I suggested to my father that he underwrite the trip for me, he answered, "If you don't want to work, come home, and you can paint the fences."

During my years at the convent my parents had moved from Miami to the mountains of North Carolina, where they had purchased a farm of rolling fields and woodlands. It was, in every season of the year, a beautiful, restful place to be. The pastures were dotted with black Angus cattle, and a little tobacco was grown. White fences outlined the green fields.

I had made the decision to visit the farm before I met Clarence. Then, just when I was getting to know this most interesting of men, it came time to leave him. Without working, my schoolteacher resources were rapidly diminishing. Reluctantly, I packed up and drove to North Carolina.

Of course, I told my parents about my friendship with the Director, though I had the feeling neither of them realized what the relationship was beginning to mean to me. When it became bedtime, I said, "Don't be startled if the phone rings, Clarence will be calling."

My father was amused by my confidence.

"He won't call you here, Shirley," he said.

He had just fallen asleep when the phone rang.

It was Clarence.

After a couple of nights of this, Daddy finally said, "Shirley, tonight I'm going to get some sleep. I'm turning off the phone in my room. If you are expecting any late calls, you will have to sit by the phone in the living room."

At this time Clarence was in Cedar Rapids, Iowa, where he took the stand as a defense-summoned witness in the Cedar Rapids federal court murder trial of two men charged with killing two FBI agents the previous summer on the Pine Ridge Indian reservation in South Dakota. Though Clarence had failed to honor a subpoena directed to him to be present in court, he did respond to the order of U. S. District Court Judge Edward J. McManus by appearing—a precedent-setting event. It was believed that this was the first time the Bureau chief had ever responded and testified in a trial.

The defendants in the case were both members of the American Indian Movement (AIM), which Clarence stated had "some fine goals and many fine people." In general it had "something worthy to offer. It was not," he said, "tabbed by the FBI as an un-American subversive organization."

Defense lawyers in the case had argued that for years the FBI had waged a covert attack on the movement.

The Director stated that the "cointel program," started in the late 1950s under J. Edgar Hoover and continued until the early 1970s, in an FBI effort to prevent violent extremist activities, was not now continuing under any name.

Attorney William Kunstler made the statement that Clarence should make a public apology for past abuses of the FBI, to which Clarence replied that there was "a need to admit mistakes, but there was also a need to retard oppressive legislation which might hamper the operation of the FBI."

The first of his letters began arriving for me.

On July 7, from Cedar Rapids, he wrote:

The F. B. and I

Dear Painter Buddy,

. . . the appearance in Federal court was not too travailing, and I would say the counselors are greatly over-rated. . . . I was on the stand for five hours with a continuous stream of questions hurled at me. Unquestionably I was to be their patsy, but I believe I emerged unscathed. . . .

I may go back to the hospital Friday night and get some enforced bedrest. I haven't improved as I think I should have, and feel that four or five days flat on my back in the hospital will be helpful. I am so tired of this incapacity.

My desk is probably 5 feet high with mail. I have a speech in Washington Friday; after a dinner—black tie, I will report to the hospital. Probably one of the few to come in so formal.

Your busted back buddy,
Clarence

Regular evening phone chats, sometimes lasting up to an hour, continued, and his letters arrived frequently. From Bethesda Naval Hospital, July 11, 1976:

Dear Shirley,

Another day in the hospital and another day closer to recovery. . . . I know I have already made some progress for I have been able to move my legs higher and easier than I have for some time. The worst is the fact that I have to stay in bed all the time, not even sitting up.

Another news report that is critical. This time in New York, where accusations "from sources" that new offenses have been reported as attributed to the bureau office personnel there. I'm going to take some drastic action quickly. Otherwise I'm fearful there might be inferences, justifiably, that I condone some of these things. Too much is at stake to stand by and let events take their course, rather than for me to guide them. I had hoped the opposite could be true, for really, there is no proof of the accusations.

You know, I am now down to a svelte 199½, and still, hopefully, going down. At the expense of not satisfying my truly fine appetite. What I wouldn't give for the opportunity to tie into a batch of brownies, steak rimmed with fat, baked potatoes—I can't go on. It's punishing.

184

. . . I do hope you take full advantage of the opportunity to see your parents. I treasure my memories of visits made to mine. Both of mine are now gone.

I must tell you something I have been thinking about. I told you recently I missed church attendance, and had no good reason for my neglect. I have decided we are going to start to attend, yours or mine, but I am going to root you out, and insist. I don't think either of us has an adequate excuse, and I will not listen to any. So get ready, because we are going to church.

Fondly,
Clarence

The "drastic action" referred to early in this letter resulted in the removal of Nick Callahan and the withdrawal of Andrew Decker from policy-making sessions.

July 14:

My girl,

The doctor told me today I will probably need to be here until Friday, July 23. I plan to arrive in Asheville about 11:30 A.M. . . . to be your lounging guest for a couple of days. It is felt I need to give the easy life more of a chance to see if nature can do the job. . . .

It has been good to talk with you during our 9:30 P.M. dates. I make all the widows swish out at that time, but some are a little stubborn. Poor kids, they don't realize how futile are their efforts.

The only real break in the monotony has been the visits of some of my associates, and from the Dept. of Justice. All in the aura of doom and gloom. That's what I get and deserve after having carelessly raised my right hand July 9, 1973. I will make one more move 7-15-76, and more later. These are calculated to give us [the FBI] a greater degree of stability. I think they will. The Attorney General [Edward Levi] was in for about half an hour. A fine person.

I am now at 197 ½ and believe that is about the leveling point. I am beginning to look spare and gaunt, and if I don't watch it, I may have to buy new clothes. If I have to do so, I'm going to be forced to get a second job painting fences. Sometimes it makes me so depressed. I want to get out of here and drown my sorrow in cottage cheese, of which I have plenty, having had a quart sent to me. Really, I don't believe I'll ever reform.

So I sit here and pine away waiting for better days which won't begin to happen until I get to Waynesville. . . . I wish that you were here so that I could see and be with you. It is strange how much has happened in such a short time. "The Florida Flash swept through Washington with devastation and chaos"—as told by a victim. Can't you just see the headline?

Stay happy and eat lots of good food so you won't be puny. . . .

Goodnight my girl and God Bless you—

Your boy,
Clarence

July 17:

My dear Shirley,

. . . I am concerned about your mother suffering distress because of concern about you. I don't quite understand it and hope I can get more details when I talk with you later. I am concerned that possibly it stems from fears about the risks you might take being around me. If I thought for a minute that there was any reason to be fearful I would not subject you to danger, real or fancied. I suppose I sometimes overlook how other people view my presence. I do not feel there is any real danger, and as a matter of fact, if I had to be ducking and dodging, I would give the job back to them. Yes, it is true there are some nuts who may get ideas. I don't attract them for many reasons. First, I am not important enough for them. Then, they know I am armed and have had considerable experience in defending those around me. Also, I don't take any chances, and try to be alert to anything unusual. I do hope, however, that the "risks" you mention are because of me. I can't fight fear. That is something subjective, and I wouldn't want to cause you or your fine parents any concerns. Tell me straight. I don't want it any other way.

Another day in this palace of fun. I get so tired of these dancing girls and fancy food. All I would like to see is a little girl named Shirley. I had become accustomed to you, and enjoyed so much our discussions. The fact I had an opportunity to talk over some of my problems, and just to be near you, lifted my spirits. Harm you? I wouldn't harm a hair.

The doctor told me about the operation I may have to undergo. Substantially, it is to chip away some of the vertebrae to relieve the pressure on nerves going down my legs. However, I am going to continue therapy for at least three weeks and then make up my mind on the basis of

186

my own analysis of my progress. So far I don't detect any appreciable improvement.

I had a tough job yesterday. I asked for the resignation of Nick Callahan, 42 year veteran, and #2 man in the bureau. He looked like he was whipped and I know I felt like I had been. He was injudicious in his actions, and although [he] left the possible appearance of illegal activity, I really feel he meant no harm. So you see, it's not always a soft spot.

I'm anxious to see the garden spot of North Carolina. From the way you describe it, it must be Youthful Valley. At this point that air would do old Kelley some good. Don't do a lot of planning to keep me busy. I'll sit around with your Dad and tell him what a great daughter he has. All Pops like to hear that. I have some anxiety inasmuch as I feel the need to convince your parents I'm not such a bad guy.

I have received several plants. . . . Tom Moten drops by once in a while to water the plants I already have [at the apartment]. I'd like you to do that job if you lived nearby. I don't believe I would want to live at Watergate, however. I understand there have been numerous burglaries at the posh spot. No problems in the ghetto where I live.

Stay as sweet as you are,
Clarence

I was indeed pleased that Clarence was coming to visit in North Carolina. Not only was I anxious to see him, but I knew both he and my parents would enjoy one another, once they had met.

He flew in from Washington accompanied by Bill Reed. This was part of a ploy to detract from any curiosity that might be aroused, either inside or outside the Bureau, on why the Director would be spending a weekend in a far-out place like a farm in North Carolina. Bill's wife, Janet, and their daughter, Noel, were to drive down from Middleburg to join us for the "family weekend."

My father and I drove over to the Asheville Airport to meet him. Clarence had told me that it would probably be best if we waited in our car out in front of the airport, as some FBI men would be there to meet him. Remembering my happy moments watching Efrem Zimbalist in the TV series, I deducted that the five well-dressed men assembling from different directions in front of the airport might possibly be from the FBI. My conclusion was assisted by several observations; there were no women with the five men, they did not look as though they were about to travel, they each appeared of more than average intelligence, and they were far and away the five best-groomed and dressed men in the airport.

I got out of the car and walked over to one of them.

"Hello," I said, "I am Shirley Dyckes."

Before I had finished my sentence, I had captured the total attention of all five.

They asked about the Director's back, and when I confirmed that walking was painful for him, they told me they would drive a Bureau car onto the runway and transport the Director from the airplane steps directly to our automobile.

I thought that would be exciting.

Beaming from ear to ear, Clarence had frequently told me that I did not have the proper respect for his office. Meaning, of course, that I saw him as Clarence Kelley, the person, not the Honorable Clarence M. Kelley, Director of the Federal Bureau of Investigation. Which was true. Therefore, whenever special services, which would assist his office and station, were evidenced, it was always a surprise and thrill to me.

I looked across to the airplane which had landed and was disembarking passengers, and there was my boy, coming down the steps accompanied by Bill Reed. At the foot of the steps, five agents were ceremoniously placed in an arched line from the plane's steps to their waiting automobile.

I ran back to our car as the auto with Clarence and his entourage, which included a second, backup car, came flush with the back seat of our car. Rarely had I ever felt it necessary to feel grateful for the family Cadillac, but after all the ceremony of respect I had just seen, I was certainly happy we had not decided to bring our Bronco, but could offer a more luxurious ride.

ॐ

During that afternoon at the farm, Clarence and I took a brief walk about the farm, coming to rest on a stone wall about two hundred feet from the house. This was the first opportunity we had had to see each other and be alone in almost three weeks.

Knowing that he was the first suitor whom I had brought to the farm, he asked what my parents thought about that.

Immediately the subject of matrimony came up.

Now, as you know, I do not dilly-dally over decisions. I leaped from his very simple question to a very outspoken statement.

"Clarence," I said, "I have decided that I am not going to spend one agonizing moment over our relationship. If you have decided to marry me, I'm going to accept. But it is *your* problem."

And he had problems!

He was twenty-two years older than I.

He had been happily married for thirty-eight years to a wife whom he had adored.

His former wife had been dead only nine months.

He had children and grandchildren.

He had a serious physical condition in his back.

And my parents were the type who would question the advisability of a marriage in which there was such an age difference. Clarence, it so happened, was one year older than my mother.

In spite of this array, of which we both were aware, Clarence looked at me with a mixture of bewildered joy. "You mean," he said, "you would really marry me?"

There I was! I had fallen in love with a man who couldn't walk more than two hundred feet, who was in constant pain. Yet, in spite of that, I found him more fun to be with than anyone I had ever met. From some directions, I was later to hear, it was projected that my "do-good" attitude had finally found a nesting place. But that was not the case. Aside from the fact that he was in constant pain, Clarence did not seem handicapped to me. He was perfect! His smile and his wit, the solid, kind, intelligent man that I knew him to be was like twenty-four-hour-a-day sunlight.

About marrying me, Clarence felt that he had three problems which concerned him in his responsibility to me as a husband. The first was his back. He did not want me to be burdened with an invalid. Second was money. He wanted to be sure that he could provide for me in his later years, or if he died suddenly. That was the first time I heard about the widow's pension in the Bureau. To receive this sum of money, a widow must have been married to an FBI man for at least one full year. So, since Clarence had expected to resign his position as Director of the FBI if he could find no relief for his physical condition, he could not promise that he would be in the Bureau a year after our marriage.

I said to him, "Clarence, if that is the way you feel, you should have married me yesterday!"

189

He agreed that from that point of view, every day our marriage was postponed was a day wasted. And that brought us to Clarence's third worry.

He had not been widowed a full year.

The problem of Clarence waiting a full year after Ruby's death before he remarried meant no loss of respect to her memory to me. In North Carolina I knew numerous examples of close, loving couples, separated by death, from which the surviving partner had again entered into marriage before the first year of mourning was up. The reason put forth by my father, who approved of these remarriages, had been that when two people were truly happy, there was a terrible void left upon separation which could not be filled with passing relationships. It was therefore understandable why the bereaved reached out again for another loving mate.

Clarence's interest in me, only seven months after Ruby's death, was thus by this line of reasoning a reaffirmation that he had truly been a good husband. As we discussed his feelings on this matter, I said, "Clarence, I have no difficulty with your memories of Ruby. In heaven, I am sure, your heart will hold us both. You have two arms, one for each of us. I am sure you have enough love for both of us."

The weekend was spent pleasantly. Clarence and my parents sincerely enjoyed one another. If they had had questions about him, they evaporated. We had a happy time together. Neither to them nor to the Reeds, however, did we mention that we were considering marriage, though our fondness for each other must have been obvious. I am sure that the possibility of our friendship leading into marriage must have crossed their minds. But at that time, nothing was said.

On a later visit, after my parents knew of our plans, my mother discussed with me the differences in our ages, about which she had some reservations. Suppose, she worried, he became irrevocably ill? Or died? She reminded me of the many sobering occurrences which inevitably happen as one grows older.

Finally I said, "Well, Mother, I have no other option except to marry Clarence. I love him. If I give him up for some reason which may never happen, I will sit around long-faced. He will too—for a while. Then he will marry someone else. I am not going to leave him to make some other woman happy when he makes *me* happy. If he is going to marry, which he *will*, it will be me!"

At the end of that first weekend on the farm with Clarence, I got up

190

Monday morning, dressed in my blue jeans, and drove the quarter mile or so to the guest house, sipping my coffee from a mug as I drove along.

Clarence and Bill were up and ready to drive to the Asheville Airport for a flight to Washington, where Clarence had an important meeting to attend before noon. He looked like a fashion plate in his summer suit as he gave me a quick kiss. The other agents with the backup car had arrived and viewed our embrace. I knew that rumors would soon be flying.

At the door, Clarence turned back to me for one more hug, bumping into my arm which held my coffee mug. Warm brown liquid poured down his jacket front and sleeve.

I was embarrassed.

Bill hurried to the bathroom for a towel and cold water, and I stood watching, repeating, "I'm so sorry," as he dabbed away at Clarence's suit. Such aid as was possible was given, but Clarence no longer looked the total fashion plate as he departed. But his spirit was undaunted by his dunking. He gave me a big smile.

Later that day Janet, Noel, and I drove to Middleburg and from there I returned to Washington. Clarence and I had many details to work out in our lives before the back surgery which he had scheduled for August 16. We also wished to spend every possible moment together.

Evenings, Clarence would close the door to his office at 6:00 P.M. at the FBI building, and Tom Moten would drive him to the Watergate, where I would be preparing his dinner. It was necessary in my apartment building for all guests to announce themselves to the clerk in the lobby, who would then check by inside telephone to make certain the visitor was expected. I was aware that several members of the media were fellow-residents, and so as not to alert them to my romance with my newsworthy friend, I made it a practice of meeting Clarence in the lobby, where Tom deposited him every evening promptly at 6:15.

To further continue his anonymity, I transported the Director of the FBI to my eighth-floor apartment by freight elevator. This convenience is located close to the lobby and is mainly used for moving furniture in and out of the apartments. Its availability is also encouraged for transporting a rather large household of dogs—eighty-four or so, an assortment of setters, poodles, pugs, basset hounds, collies, and various other breeds, who, several times a day, lead their masters for walks about the grounds. Riding the freight elevator eliminated a long walk down the hallway to the resident elevators, and many chances of recognition and speculation concerning the regularity of the Director's visits.

Toward the end of July I had my first look inside the FBI building. Clarence had a trip to make during which he would stop over in Kansas City and see Mary and Kent.

"I need a picture of you to show my children," he said. "This will also be a good time for you to see my office."

He arranged for Tom to pick me up and drive me to the Bureau. Of course I knew I would be meeting some of Clarence's associates for the first time, and I wanted him to be proud of me. I wore a gold jersey knit with brown accessories which people had told me looked especially good.

I always enjoyed driving with Tom, a handsome, genial man in his sixties. From the very first time I had ridden with Clarence in the limousine, I had been aware of the easy relationship between the two men. Both served the FBI in different capacities. The bond of being special agents beneath their other duties had built deep respect between them. They were friends, not necessarily driver and chief.

For many years Tom had driven for J. Edgar Hoover, who had required him to wear a chauffeur's cap. That item had long vanished from his wardrobe when I met him.

Being with Mr. Hoover, I felt, must have been rather like living with a legend, his power having been so deeply embedded over such a long time. Surely his outer image must have been greater than the man who projected it.

As we rode along, Tom said, "Were you ever in the old FBI building, Shirley?"

"No," I replied.

"It was built around a center courtyard," Tom said. "There were two exits. One day the one we always took to leave was under repairs, so it was necessary for me to drive out the other way.

"As I started out, Mr. Hoover handed me a letter to mail.

" 'Mail this!' he said. 'There's a mailbox right outside.'

"Now, I didn't want to point out to the boss that he hadn't noticed we were taking a different route. All I thought I better say, as we came to the curb, was, 'There's no mailbox here, Mr. Hoover.'

"From the back seat Mr. Hoover growled, 'By god, we'll find out what happened!'

"Such was his power, that next day, at the second exit, there was a mailbox."

Mr. Hoover, he told me, was so accustomed to having his own way, to having all paths open before him, that he was easily frustrated. One day when they were coming up the ramp from the underground garage beneath the old FBI building, he had had to stop the car at the top to wait for an obstruction to be moved.

From the back seat, Mr. Hoover had ordered, " 'Drive on, Tom!' "

"I can't, sir," Tom had told him.

"Why not?" Mr. Hoover demanded.

"There's a truck in the way. It has a boom on it and a cable attached to a large block of cement." They were tearing up the street, Tom told me, and a huge section of a cement divider was being removed.

"Blow the siren," Mr. Hoover commanded.

Tom played a delaying game. "I can't, sir."

"Blow the siren!" again came the demand.

"In a moment, sir."

From the back seat came a final exasperated, "I'll give you two minutes, and then *blow the siren!*"

The tales of the first Director's absoluteness of decision and his assumption of correctness seemed endless. He would always tell Tom exactly which lane of traffic to drive in.

Frequently Mr. Hoover was accompanied by Clyde Tolson, his assistant. On one occasion while Tom was driving the two men, Mr. Hoover fell asleep in the back seat.

Mr. Tolson quietly told Tom to change to another lane.

The swerve of the car, while gentle, was enough to arouse Mr. Hoover, who demanded to know, "What are you doing in this lane, Tom?"

"Mr. Tolson asked me to get over," Tom replied.

Without glancing out of the window to check traffic, Mr. Hoover growled, "I don't care what Tolson told you, get over into the lane where you belong."

Being the driver for Director Hoover had never been dull, Tom admitted.

In downtown Washington, we drove to the garage beneath the new J. Edgar Hoover Building. As we entered, the guard on duty stopped Tom, who had to identify himself before proceeding further. I thought this was really exercising caution, since the guard must have been used to seeing Tom at least three or four times every workday. Nevertheless, not even Tom got into that garage without identifying himself and explaining who was in the back seat. Whatever the criterion was, we apparently passed, and Tom drove on down a steep roadway to a second basement below. As we passed numerous cars in the enormous garage, Tom first turned right and then left. He stopped the car in front of an enormous dark-brown metal door, the width of a three-car garage. Getting out, he took a key from his pocket, and on the side of a garage pillar, found a lock and inserted the key. Before me, the huge door slowly lifted. Tom slid back under the driving wheel, and we drove in. My eyes were wide open, staring at everything about me.

Before assisting me from the car, Tom again got out, turned another key, and the enormous door slid back down, enclosing us in the garage-within-the-garage. Parked alongside were two backup cars. Over to the left, diagonally across the corner, was a glass-enclosed office with a desk, chair, and telephone. It reminded me of a soundproof room in which a director might sit in a recording studio. To the right was a pair of steel doors. I hadn't had any idea what I might expect in this fortresslike structure, or of the people within it, but the mark of J. Edgar Hoover, with his penchant for total security, was everywhere.

While I stood on a small platform waiting, Tom entered the office and made a phone call, announcing my arrival. Then he opened one of the two big steel doors, and we passed through a narrow hallway carpeted in blue. This led from the private garage to a special elevator. Again Tom took out a key, again a different one, punched the elevator button, and turned the key. The door to a small private elevator opened before us. Against its back wall was the colorful seal of the FBI. As we rode up to the seventh floor, Tom explained that this was the Director's private elevator. For other people who used the garage below, there were four other elevators. This floor, he said, housed the offices of the Director, associate director, two deputy associate directors, some of the assistant directors, and numerous staff.

Clarence greeted us in the Director's dining room. With him were two deputy associate directors, Thomas Jenkins and James Adams.

I had the distinct impression that I had entered a man's world. The room was beautifully paneled and had a fine view of the Capitol, but there were no frills. A table was set for lunch with rectangular plastic place mats bearing the FBI seal. The dishes and napkins were white. There were several empty tables beyond, and I was told forty people could comfortably be served lunch there. This was the room, I was later to learn, where once each week the Director and eighteen assistant directors gathered for breakfast and an executive conference. At its far end there was a small seating area with a couch and comfortable chairs.

Lunch was a hamburger patty, country fried potatoes, and a lettuce and tomato salad, with rolls, served by Perry Lacuesta, whom Clarence introduced to me as Perry. As a special treat, because a lady was present, dessert was fresh strawberry pie. Clarence insisted this was for me, but knowing the way he loved desserts, I suspected he was using me as an excuse. Coffee was served, but there were no liquors or wines, or any fare which would interfere with a good day's work. I was surprised by the simplicity of the meal, almost its austerity. I had heard that Director Hoover and his top assistant, Clyde Tolson, had lunched nearly every day either at the elegant Mayflower Hotel or at Harvey's fine restaurant. Not this group of men! They arrived in the morning and barely saw the light of day outside those walls until quitting time.

During the meal I noticed that Jim Adams did not seem to look upon me with any great indication of pleasure. I wondered about that. As the meal progressed, Clarence explained many things to me about the FBI, the room, various men, their positions. Finally he happened to mention that I was an ex-nun. As usual, this announcement captured attention. Mr. Adams was across the table from me, and I observed that he gave me a particularly interested look.

After lunch Clarence took me to the kitchen to introduce me to Ray Cabacar, the chef. Both Perry and Ray had worked in wardrooms aboard navy ships, Clarence said, and knew how "to keep working men healthy and happy." The kitchen was an odd-shaped room surrounding an enormous butcher-block table. Two windows looked out toward the Capitol. All the furnishings were institutional appliances, highly functional, and in somber shades of beige and brown. On my trip through the halls with Tom, I had noticed this overall beigeness. Carpets, walls, ceilings, everything was beige. There were no decorations or pictures, except in the dining room. Surely, I figured, no woman was ever consulted as to the choice of appointments.

My tour led next to Clarence's office, which was approached from one direction through another pair of steel doors. Tom Jenkins carried this key. Actually, Clarence's office was at the end of an enormous suite containing his personal reception room, a room for two secretaries, a telephone room, and Tom Moten's office. The man in charge of the reception room was Bob Jones, who might have been mistaken for a professional football player. He had huge shoulders packed beneath his well-tailored suit. His other functions, besides receiving the Director's guests, included acting as personal courier and as a backup driver.

The telephone room housed a large switchboard which was staffed by three men who worked staggered hours from 8:00 A.M. until whatever hour the Director left at night. (While he was in Washington, away from Ruby, during her illness in Kansas City, he had regularly worked until 9:00 every evening.)

In the main reception room, the information on the walls quickly attracted attention. Three plaques in wood and bronze contained the names of FBI agents killed in line of duty during American wars, those killed in FBI service, and the third, with the fewest number of names, was the Heroes' Plaque. This was a new organization commemorating two agents who died while making an arrest in Washington. As a person with only marginal information of law enforcement, I was surprised to see what seemed to me, considering the vast extent of their daily service, the small number of names on the tablet for those who had died in FBI service. Here was an agency over fifty years old, and of its thousands of members in their frequently dangerous assignments, there were listed twenty-six names. I thought this spoke very well for the agent's preparedness to protect both himself and his co-workers.

We sat in Clarence's handsome office with its ample desk and large, comfortable chair, his momentos and family photographs grouped about, as we waited for the photographer to arrive to take my picture.

While we were chatting, I said to Clarence, "I wonder about Jim Adams. Does he approve of me?"

Clarence laughed. "You don't have to worry about Jim Adams, Shirley," he said. "He is very loyal to me. I haven't told any of the men about my relationship with you, but I was watching Jim's face during lunch. I'll bet he was thinking, 'Here it is July 1976, and we have more than enough problems in this Bureau, and the Director comes in here with a blonde. Now who knows what that means? Is this a girl friend? Is this someone he wants to marry? At her age she is probably divorced and has a couple of kids, and they're probably on marijuana, and we'll have to run a check on them. . . .' So probably the best piece of news Jim Adams received all day," Clarence continued, his hazel eyes twinkling, "was that for fifteen years you were in cold storage in a convent."

A week or so later we had our first invitation to dine at the home of an FBI agent. Our hosts were Jim and Ione Adams.

19

Proposal
With a Loophole

"Take a look at those cornices over the window, Shirley," Clarence said.

We were sitting in the kitchen of his Grosvenor Park condominium, from which I could see into the plainly furnished living room where he was pointing. Projecting out over the top of the draperies were two scalloped wooden valances painted an olive green. They appeared to be constructed of plywood. I was not impressed by their decorative quality.

Clarence had purchased the apartment three years earlier when he had moved to Washington while Ruby was ill. The draperies had been bought from a previous tenant. In those days he had not had time, nor had Ruby had the strength, to make many attempts at decorating. His apartment meant only a place where he could fall into bed, sleep, and rise to work again. On rare occasions, Ruby was able to be with him, but those were times more for togetherness than for tiring shopping trips.

"Those valances are going to cause a lot of trouble," Clarence said. "You may be embarrassed by it. I want you to think very carefully about what these continuing 'revelations' and the furor that occurs around them may mean to us."

The valances, he said, had been a joint idea of Ruby and a friend who had been visiting with her. The women had felt they would make the apartment appear more homey. But after Ruby had decided how she wanted the valances, she had not been well enough to shop. She had returned to Kansas City without ordering them.

During her absence Clarence measured for the drapery boxes and asked Tom Moten if he would see about getting them made. This did not seem unreasonable, since, for security reasons, Tom or some other agent would have to be in the apartment when the valances were installed.

When they were in place, Clarence asked Tom what he owed for them.

"Oh, that's all right, boss," Tom had said. "The exhibits section made them."

Clarence asked at the exhibits section for a bill. He was told there was none. Leftover lumber and some extra paint from another project had been used.

"All right," he said, "but I'd rather not have it that way. In the future, please don't."

The valances, he figured, probably cost about ten dollars. Still, he did not like to conduct his affairs that way. He told Tom that if he asked for anything for his personal use in the future, to buy it from a retailer.

In defense of the employee who unwittingly caused Clarence trouble by building the valances, one should remember that for decades the slightest whim of Director Hoover had been immediately granted. To hammer a few boards together probably seemed like nothing at all. Remarkable extremes had been exerted for Mr. Hoover's pleasure.

One evening when he was in California, Mr. Hoover had a date with a movie star. He wished a particularly romantic setting for the occasion and was disturbed to find out there would be no full moon that night. His agents, ever on the alert to serve him, outdid themselves assembling a palely lighted moon which they hoisted to a treetop a safe distance away from the Director and his date so that it gave the effect of a real moon!

ह~

Sitting across from me in the kitchen, Clarence said, "The matter of the valances will certainly come up. There is a discrepancy in the accounting department of the exhibits section. I have personally authorized an investigation. Even though I did not order the valances, and offered to pay for them, their construction is a matter of record." He shook his head. "John Dunphy, the exhibits section head, is in serious trouble."

I was concerned. I hated to see Clarence upset. It seemed to me he had quite enough worries without this added burden. But that was one reason I was with him, to share his problems and attempt to lighten his concerns where I could.

Shortly after that he had a business trip for several days. On the way home through Kansas City he was able to stop over with his daughter, Mary, Scrappy, son Kent, and his wife, Donna. In his absence, I returned to North Carolina, where he wrote to me.

August 7, 1976

My dear,

. . . The past two days have been about the most eventful ones I have experienced in many years. The discussion with the kids, the conference with the doctor, the phone call to you, and the discussions about the pending tv appearance and press conferences all mounted to bring me to the peak of impact. I was tremendously pleased by the reaction of the children, and your reaction to the news. It is as if a great load has been lifted from my heart. I was so anxious to have things turn out well, and now I could dance the Fairmount Stomp without a quiver of discomfort, because I am up in the clouds and walking on air. I love all of you, and to realize we are all together, is a dream come true.

All the children had about the same reaction, but with different expressions of their feelings. Kent, about whom I frankly was somewhat dubious, came through like a champion. "Whatever makes you happy, Dad, makes me happy." What a guy—and Mary, with her question, "Will she be good to you?" Not a single remark about age, background, or other extraneous matters. They all said, "We like her looks, and hope we can see her soon." You are truly going to get a new family you will be delighted to be with. They deserve a nice girl like you.

The doctor I consulted with was superb in giving me true facts and clear explanations. I feel I am in good hands with him, and have no reservations now about what I am going into. Dr. Kraft will be there too, and together they will form a fine team for me to rely on.

The briefing for the tv appearance may be short of the mark as to what will be asked, but at least I will be somewhat prepared. I do hope you tune in, and are not too harsh in your criticism. . . . So much is happening to me, I am whirling around. June 12 to August 7 is not such a long time, but my, what can be squeezed into such a time-frame is amazing.

You sounded like you were having a good time shopping around for wallpaper. I hope you find what you want. My preference is purple with yellow stripes slashing diagonally across the surface. Some red border to quiet the general effect. Or, if you don't like that combination, how about black stripes instead of yellow. And to think you can get my help for practically nothing!

I miss you very much, but I can see you in my mind's eye so clearly it is as if you were with me. Happy, I know; radiant for sure, and full of ideas about the future. . . .

I love you,
Clarence

Hanging over our heads like a Damoclean sword was Clarence's upcoming surgery. From the very first day when we had talked of marriage, he had been firm about its consequences. We would be married, he had said, his jaw tightening in a way which, I had learned to know, meant arguing would do me no good, only if the surgery was successful. The decision was totally his. If the operation did not work, if he was crippled by it, as could easily happen, he expected me to turn my back and walk away from him. Just like that! It was an order!

Clarence insisted that I go to see his Washington doctor with him and hear what he had to say about his condition.

"I want you to see just what kind of a pig in a poke you are getting," he said.

The doctor explained Clarence's X rays to me. He had a complicated back. As one ages, the spine can bend. Clarence's was curved, and some vertebrae were fused. His back problems had started long ago, while he was in his twenties, when he had slid into third base during a ball game.

The doctor described the upcoming surgery, and then he added, "Even if this surgery is totally successful, in the future, other vertebrae can deteriorate, and there could be other problems."

I saw the X rays. I heard the doctor. I knew the condition. But I was not shaken. I would take my chances on Clarence.

ॐ

He has games he plays, and I began to find myself a key chessman on his board. We flew to Kansas City together a few days before the scheduled operation, changing planes in Cleveland. This was the first time the FBI agents saw me traveling with their Director.

In Cleveland the SAC and two other agents met us with a wheel-chair to escort us to our next airplane. Clarence introduced me to them as "Miss Shirley Dyckes," but gave no indication as to who I was. He enjoyed watching the professional investigators try to figure me out, and did not want to deprive them of their fun by immediately giving the answer. Only a few clues proved adequate.

In Kansas City we were met by a similar group who wheeled Clarence to the waiting limousine, as I walked alongside. After I had seated myself in the back seat, the SAC handed me a manila envelope.

"The boss's mail," he said.

I blinked, and thanked him very much.

I must have been mistaken for a secretary!

As we rode along I held the envelope on my lap. I wouldn't have dared open it. I could imagine all sorts of dire information inside, and even danger. Later, I learned that the mail he recieves en route is always slit and preread before he gets it. Only once, to my knowledge, has he received a dangerous letter. Of course letters or packages which are suspect go through a routing system and are X-rayed or scientifically examined. The "dangerous letter" had been opened by a secretary. It contained an infected tick. Fortunately for the lady, as the letter had rolled through a post office sorting machine, the tick had been crushed, and was dead.

ॐ

The following ten days were the most exhausting of my life. I accom-panied Clarence to the hospital for his preliminary examination and met his doctors. They immediately began explaining to me the pros and cons of his case. Even though some of the possible projections they made were distressing to hear, I felt it was better to understand the situation as thoroughly as possible, rather than to fear the limitless unknown. The doctors were reasonably confident. I was grateful to them for speaking frankly with me.

Still, while visiting with Clarence in his room on the evening before his surgery, I could not hold back my tears. I began to cry. He sat up in bed and shook his finger at me.

"Shirley," he said, "you are nothing but a baby. You like to pretend you are a big, sophisticated lady who can cope with all manner of trials, but you're not. You are like a little flower that wilts if the climate isn't right."

Tom Moten was with us that evening. During the entire period of the Director's confinement, there was at least one agent always on duty outside his door. As Clarence had entered the hospital, he had had to surrender his gun and all his credentials. For several days he would be under morphine and could not possibly be responsible for these things. They were taken to the Kansas City FBI office and locked in the safe.

Without his gun, helpless in bed, alone, Clarence would have been totally without protection. One might wonder why there would be concern for his safety in his own "hometown," where he was popular with thousands. At that time, it was a fact little acclaimed in the newspapers that under Clarence Kelley, the Bureau had successfully seen over 5,400 members of organized crime convicted and jailed, an all-time high for the nation. Among this group were a number of the Kansas City organized crime syndicate.

When it came time for Clarence to be wheeled to surgery, the FBI agents accompanied him to the door. Within the operating room, scrubbed and gowned, was the surgeon for the Kansas City police force watching over him.

I sat in a small private annex throughout the operation with Clarence's children and Tom. We sipped coffee. I guess I must have appeared tense and drained.

Tom leaned over to me and asked, "Would you be interested in a coffee royal?"

From his pocket he produced a miniature bottle of Bourbon, and as I nodded my head yes, he shared its contents between our cups.

Later, in the coffee shop, Tom said, "I love that man, Shirley."

Tom and Clarence had known each other since their early days as FBI agents at Quantico, when Clarence had taught arms instruction.

"You know," he said slowly, "I spent some time with Ruby. She was such a fine lady, but so sick. I told her I was thinking about retiring, but she made me promise that I would watch out for Clarence." He studied me with a look of pleased confidence. "When you two are married and settled," he said, "I'll retire."

Tom was the first special agent to fully recognize what Clarence and I meant to each other.

ᔔ

Clarence came through the surgery with flying colors, though he had a long recovery period ahead. The prognosis was eighteen months until he would be totally fit again. But he *would* be well! The all-but-unbearable weight on my heart was lifted.

During the twelve days he remained in the hospital, I played many backgammon games with the agents on duty. It was fun watching the flowers arrive and reading the get-well wishes Clarence received. There were greetings from President Ford, Leon Jaworski, and L. Patrick Gray, among many others. Attorney General Edward Levi came to see him, staying only long enough to say, "Don't worry about anything. Just get better."

Bill Reed, acting as courier, flew in every couple days with a locked satchel of official papers.

I was aware of only one instance of an official acting toward Clarence in what I thought an inconsiderate way. The second day after surgery, Stanley Pottinger, a member of the Justice Department in charge of the criminal division, arrived for an official conference. Clarence was still very much under sedation complete with tubes and artificial feedings. Bill was in Clarence's room during the meeting. Mr. Pottinger took forty-five minutes to state his business. Outside, I was enraged at this man's intrusion at such a time. Months later, in Washington, Mr. Pottinger, in talking with Clarence, referred to this meeting. Clarence had no recollection that it had taken place! Fortunately, Bill had realized the condition of the patient and had made sure that the Director made no authoritative statements. Not only was I distressed over this misuse of his strength, which Clarence needed to speed his recovery, but I wondered about the judgment of a man who would call on the head of an intelligence department so soon after he had undergone major surgery. Anyone, it seemed to me, would have wondered whether whatever Clarence said at that time would stand up in a court of law.

After nine days, Clarence was out of danger. He told me, "Go back to Washington and find a place for us to live."

A weary, but happy woman, I boarded an airplane for the East.

While Clarence was in the hospital the newspapers were filled with articles on supposed illegal break-ins by the FBI before Clarence had become Director, and reportedly into his years as chief of the Bureau. From his hospital bed he could only reply that he could not flatly deny them.

On his return to Washington, he faced this and many other problems. One of the most simply solved was a personal one.

He called me on his return.

"Say," he said, "when we decided to get married, I forgot to ask you something. Would you like a diamond engagement ring?"

I hadn't even given the matter a thought! Faced with it, I thought of something better I would really like.

"Thank you," I told him. "I'll take an Oriental rug instead."

We chose the rug together, a fine Chindia, which he happily explains to friends was a poor bargain on his part. He would have gotten off better if he had bought me a diamond ring.

At this time also, we made a down payment on a Washington condominium, which would eventually house the rug.

On August 31, while shopping for new fall clothes at Saks in Chevy Chase, I phoned Clarence to see what time he was picking me up for a party that evening.

When he heard my voice, he asked, "Have you seen the evening paper?"

"No."

"Pick up a copy, and call me back."

I found a drugstore and bought a paper. The headline banner of the Washington *Star* read in huge letters, "Did FBI Decorate Kelley's Apartment?"

The further I read in the account, the faster adrenaline pounded through my veins.

"Informed sources," it read, "said that investigators received allegations recently that the bureau's exhibits section constructed plywood drapery valances for at least two sets of windows in Kelley's apartment, built custom cabinets for use in his kitchen, and performed other general interior decorating services within the first year after he assumed directorship."

I was furious.

I found a pay phone and dialed Clarence.

"That man is a liar!" I all but shouted. "Not only does he imply that you have an elegant apartment thoughtfully decorated, but to say that you have custom-built cabinets is to speak of thousands of dollars! Anyone could tell that those tin things in your building are standard equipment! Not only that, he implied you had more than those two windows done! The only statement he made that is correct is that the valances are made of plywood. If I were you, I would never talk with that man again! I would never again let him in the FBI building!"

Clarence, who had been upset, now began to be amused by my fury.

"Wheew! What a fireball you are!" he said. "How do you expect me to keep the press out of a government building?"

"Clarence," I insisted, "a lie is a lie! If I were you, I'd sue them! Anyone reading that article will think the FBI spent thousands of dollars on your apartment."

"Sue?" he asked. "What do you mean 'sue'? I'm a government employee. I can't sue the press."

"You're an American citizen," I stated. "You have your basic rights."

He laughed. "That sounds very good, my dear. Oh, the privileges of being a private citizen!"

The "valance affair," as Clarence had predicted, had indeed come to light. John Dunphy, head of the department, was indicted and tried. In the end, he was found guilty of taking some lumber from the exhibits section to build a birdhouse. Originally, the newspapers made it clear that Mr. Dunphy had been convicted on "a *lesser misdemeanor* charge of unlawful conversion of government property on August 13, in exchange for his testimony before a federal grand jury regarding alleged wrongdoing involving other present and former FBI officials."[*] In one instance I heard a radio news report say that Mr. Dunphy had been tried and convicted for taking a little bit of lumber, while Clarence Kelley was getting away so easily with the valances installed in his apartment. This announcer implied that Clarence had had no feeling for the convicted "little man," while he, the boss, went untried. How unfair!

Clarence had the valances appraised. In themselves, they were not much. But due to the fact that the workmen had not believed his initial measurements, and erred when they took their own, the total cost of the installation, mostly for labor and travel time, was computed at $335. Clarence willingly paid.

---

[*]*Washington* Star, *September 29, 1976, A-3.*

For the next few days Clarence was a popular whipping boy for the press. Into the headlines came a thunderous statement from a voice with a southern accent. Democratic candidate for President, Jimmy Carter, asked what he would have done to the Director of the FBI if he had been President, said, "I would have fired him."

President Ford and Attorney General Levi "weighed Kelley's future at the FBI."

I was planning my own personal future with Clarence Kelley.

Three weeks after his surgery, we returned to Kansas City. Clarence had been invited to be the speaker at the forty-seventh annual Mexican Fiesta, which would be held at Crown Center Hotel, sponsored by Our Lady of Guadalupe Church.

During the afternoon we visited at the home of Dr. Jacob and Phyllis Kraft, longtime friends of Clarence's. Jake had been one of his doctors during his surgery. While there we received a most unexpected surprise. A message was delivered to Clarence. President Ford had cleared him of any wrongdoing in the case of the well-exploited valances! We were exuberant! It was a tremendous relief to have this speculation officially lifted.

In days to come the Justice Department also issued a statement clearing Clarence. This was published nationwide, but somehow was overlooked in the editions I saw of one of his main detractors, the Washington *Star*.

Word really traveled fast! As we left the Kraft house, we were met at the front door by a bevy of television cameras and reporters.

We dropped Clarence off at the house he and Ruby had bought, and I returned with Mary and Scrappy to their house to dress for the evening.

Clarence arrived sometime later accompanied by Special Agent Al Rotton. Both Mary and I were surprised to see that Clarence was apparently wearing a new style in tuxedos. The front of his trousers was so draped and flowing that they looked rather like a judge's robe below his formal jacket.

"What happened?" I asked. "You can't go out looking like that!"

Clarence, like a schoolboy caught in mischief, opened his jacket. "I forgot," he said. "I've lost forty pounds. When I put this tuxedo on, there was a big space between it and me."

Mary and I viewed him.

His suspenders ensured him against disaster. There was a problem, however, as to where to hang his gun. It was usually suspended from a hook in the top of his trousers. Across the top of his pants numerous safety pins had been placed, each bunching in as much fabric as it could hold. Under this hung the gun. All had been covered up by his black satin cummerbund. While the rest of the family stood about and chuckled, Mary and I repleated the tucks in a more fashionable and more permanent manner—we hoped! At last the guest of honor and distinguished speaker for the evening was properly attired for the occasion and rode off in grand style in a seven-passenger limousine.

This was a most unforgettable evening. For one thing, it was a dinner party at which I almost did not get fed. Clarence sat with the city fathers at head table, and the wives were seated at a circular table directly below their husbands. We women chatted and had a marvelous time, though we thought dinner was rather slow in being served. After a time, everyone else in the dining hall had not only received their plates but had almost finished eating. I looked up at Clarence and indicated to him that no one at our table had received their dinner. Laughingly, he offered to toss me a bun.

Mrs. Charles Wheeler, the wife of the mayor, called to him, "This is a terrible thing, Clarence. You may get the idea Shirley is a cheap date. You don't even have to provide her dinner."

Actually, what had happened was not that we had been overlooked by the waiters. They had indeed been observant. They had noticed that no one at our table had dinner tickets! Honored guests or not, no ticket, no dinner! Eventually the oversight was taken care of, and as the others enjoyed their desserts, we were served our entrées.

Clarence had been invited not only to speak but to accept a gift from the Spanish-American community of Kansas City. Funds for this gift had been raised among the citizens whose lives and property had been saved by Clarence when he had refused to permit looting and burning during the Kansas City riots of the 1960s. In the name of the Spanish-American people of the city, Dick Herrera presented to Clarence a six-foot oil portrait by artist Frank Szasz of Kansas City, who had been commissioned to paint it. It was truly a remarkable likeness. Clarence accepted it in the name of the Bureau.

In his speech of presentation, Dick Herrera recounted a personal story of Clarence Kelley and why he was so beloved in his hometown.

Mr. Herrera's own father, he said, had been a Mexican immigrant. When he had grown old and was dying in the hospital, Clarence had called on the senior Mr. Herrera, whose son he had known many years.

Dick Herrera said, "I will always remember the radiant smile on my father's face as he said to me, 'Here I am, a poor immigrant. Who would ever think the Director of the FBI would take time to shake my hand and speak to me. What a wonderful country America is.' "

Clarence's speech had a surprise beginning for him and a dramatic end for the audience. Unbeknownst to all but Clarence, as he rose to take the microphone, the pins at his waist buckled beneath the weight of his gun, and his loaded revolver slid down and landed on the carpet with a faint thud! This speech was more intimate than usual. Clarence felt at home with the people of Kansas City, and they had honored him with the truly remarkable portrait. At its conclusion he waved the applause to silence.

"I would like to share something with you, my good friends," he announced. "A lovely lady, Miss Shirley Dyckes, who has helped fill the void which came about at the loss of my wife, has consented to marry me."

This was received with even more applause than his speech! News reporters and cameramen who had been about to leave the hall scurried back for pictures and copy. Well-wishers thronged the stage. Clarence scarcely had time to lean over and grab up his gun and reattach it before he was mobbed. The Mexican Fiesta all but started up all over again!

Thus I entered a life of headlines and flashbulbs, sharpened pencils eager for "a word," and television cameras that ground on front, back, and side views, with little regard for one's preparedness to be photographed and flashed nationwide.

I was faced with a choice which must be made sooner or later by the wife of every public figure in the United States, most of whom mature through the political process alongside their husbands, and ease into the situation gradually. For me, it was a right-now decision I must make—whether to be a private homebody with my views on current issues quietly retained, or to fully share in my husband's life, meeting situations which involved him, feeling and considering their meaning, and reacting, perhaps vocally, to them.

I chose the active course. Surely few lives in America connote greater visions of adventure than those of the men of the FBI. And I might share the life of the chief himself! There were injustices to face, contributions to make, and always, the excitement of people and events which were making history! I was delighted that Clarence wanted me with him on his trips to FBI field offices, gaining firsthand knowledge of the structures and function of the Bureau, and witnessing in person the particular stamp of openness and member participation which was becoming a Kelley trademark.

Of all the cities to begin my learning in—we first went to Miami!

As a girl growing up in Miami, I had been made aware of organized crime through the presence in the city of gangland czar Al Capone, who, after his release from prison, resided there. But generally I had the idea that crime in America was kept under control by Mr. J. Edgar Hoover and his FBI. I felt safe in our home on its quiet street where a couple times a day a police car would slowly cruise by, indicating protective surveillance.

Years later, when I left the convent and returned home to Miami to prepare for my trip to Europe, my parents were living in a beautiful walled-in area called Bay Point. Close by, on Biscayne Boulevard, was a building I had seen many times. Housed within it, though I never noticed, was the local division of the FBI.

Late in September, Clarence and I flew to Miami to attend the convention of the International Association of Chiefs of Police. Bill and Janet flew down with us. Clarence and the Reeds stayed at the Fountainebleu Hotel, while I visited with one of my sorority sisters, Joanne Thompson Gratton, now the mother of four teen-agers. Coincidentally, across the street from her lived the third leg of the childhood triumvirate of which Joyce and I had been a happy part, Caryl James Cullem. Caryl's husband, Jim, had as a young boy the ambition of becoming an FBI special agent, but because of a neck accident, he had gone into business and was a vice-president of the Ryder Trucking Company. Reminiscing was great fun.

In Miami I first visited an FBI field office. Julius Mattson, the SAC, showed me through the extremely plain but large building wherein the personnel were moving efficiently about. Julius told me there were three hundred special agents assigned to Miami, plus the clerical staff. Most interesting to me was his statement that across the United States all FBI offices are laid out in the same arrangement. Thus an agent immediately knew his way around any office. In an organiza-

209

tion which frequently transferred its agents from city to city, this similarity facilitated some of the adjustment to new surroundings. Of course all agents were not continually on the move. Some, who had special talents or background, found themselves in one location for years.

I had a marvelous time in the city of my childhood, remeeting many old friends and introducing them to Clarence. We were feted at luncheons and dinners. Fifteen or so of my friends gave me a bridal shower at Joy Parker Eldridge's home. Among my gifts were many kitchen gadgets and *three* cookbooks. One might have thought they already knew Clarence and his penchant for good food!

჻

During an afternoon reception I was attending in Clarence's suite, I was called to the telephone. Though I did not recognize the name of the person given to me, I was assured it was an old Miami friend.

When I picked up the phone, a woman's voice asked, "Hello, is this Shirley Dyckes?"

"Yes."

"Are you having a good time in Miami?"

I inquired who she was, and the woman identified herself as a writer for the Washington *Star*. She was phoning from Washington.

"Why are you calling?" I asked.

"Well, you know why . . . " she said.

I replied, "I really don't want to give any interviews. Thank you very much," and hung up.

This incident did not stop there. When I returned to Washington, where I was still teaching school, a member of the Board of Education called to say that a reporter had called and wanted to know in what school I was teaching. The board member did not think it was good for the children to be exposed to publicity which might come to me. Shortly afterward, the school receptionist was phoned by the same newspaper person, who asked at what time school would be out.

This interference in my private life annoyed me. I had told the reporter that I would not give her an interview, and I had no desire to be hunted down at my job or to have cameras and reporters upsetting the routine of the school children or staff.

Later, I found that this same reporter had phoned my father in North Carolina, my sister in Michigan, Father Xavier in New York, a student I had taught in Massachusetts, and had contacted numerous friends and acquaintances at the Watergate and a saleslady at Lord & Taylor's.

One of my friends told me she was approached: "Everyone tells me good things about Shirley. Certainly she was no angel. What was she *really* like? What do you *know* about her?"

Many friends called me long-distance to say they had been contacted by this reporter who appeared to be hoping to discover some lurid past. Since those she contacted were my friends, the article that finally appeared in the newspaper was favorable to me.

At about the same time, I read an article in her newspaper which accused the FBI of harassment of a woman by having asked the woman's neighbors about her conduct *ten years ago!* Yet in 1976 this reporter did the identical thing to me!

During the Miami visit with Clarence I had my first experience of being accompanied by bodyguards. Wherever we went, we were never alone. I was becoming accustomed to Bill Reed or Tom Moten or the SAC of a city always being with us, but this coverage was more close. Clarence was always accompanied by at least two FBI men. They kept him always in sight. Even while he slept, a pair of them were stationed outside his door. It began to be clear to me that there was another world in Miami other than the one I had known and enjoyed. While Clarence attended convention sessions, I visited with my friends. Whenever he joined me, he was accompanied by two agents, always watching us, always observing. Later on, I would find out why the Bureau was especially nervous for Clarence that weekend!

Joanne gave a large cocktail party for us in a private room of the Riviera Country Club. My friends knew Clarence's position, but still they were not prepared for the appearance of the FBI bodyguards. True to the image the FBI seems to engender, these men were clean-cut, well dressed, "crisp"-looking. But my friends were appalled to realize that these gentlemen not only were armed but could shoot to kill.

Clarence was in Miami to attend the IACP convention and to deliver two speeches. He spoke to the IACP and a group of journalists attending a seminar on criminal reporting.

His speech to the IACP contained some serious basic information and statistics on the FBI which I was interested to learn. He mentioned the calls for change and the reassessment of the role of the FBI in America. Some excerpts which impressed me were:

. . . law enforcement has always responded to the need for changes. Let me challenge our critics to point to any other public service that has progressed so far and so fast and performed so well in the last twenty years . . . . There have been criticisms of law enforcement in the past, and times of immense difficulty—we have always overcome them.

The number of convictions resulting from FBI investigations in fiscal 1976 established an all-time record.

Clarence stated some of his Forty Points—the "Kelley changes" he had proposed for the continuing upgrading of the Bureau. In July I had attended a graduation exercise at the National Academy for FBI in Quantico, Virginia, with Clarence. There were then 7,100 police graduates of the academy active in law enforcement in the United States. More than 1,150 were serving as chief administrators in their respective agencies—as police chiefs and sheriffs, as heads of state patrols, and other agencies. In the past five years 5,000 people had graduated from the academy. That figure equaled the entire number of persons graduated in the previous thirty-eight years!

To further the opportunities and job expectancy within the FBI, a management training program had been instigated which would provide road maps best suited to the talents, skills, and aspirations of every FBI employee.

Clarence made further comments on FBI activities.

In the field of organized crime, we continue to target on major gambling and loan shark activities.

Last fiscal year we disseminated information to federal, state, and local authorities resulting in numerous arrests and the confiscation of nearly $41,000,000 worth of narcotics.

The FBI is now heavily involved in public corruption cases . . . to aggressively bring to justice these public officials who are corrupt, regardless of their position.

Another specific area of investigation . . . is white collar crime . . . we have concentrated our efforts on those fraud cases which are conspiratorial in nature, those which closely resemble organized crime and racketeering activities, particularly in terms of scope, and their impact on consumers, and our social fabric, generally.

. . . our new investigative emphasis . . . is a program we call "quality over quantity." . . . In terms of the future of the FBI, I consider this shift the most significant achievement of my administration . . . we are reorienting our thrust, and committing long-term resources to serious criminal conspiracies—quality cases as opposed to quantity cases.

Clarence spoke of his days as police chief in Kansas City when officers regularly picked up scores of interstate cars in the course of routine patrol. By contrast, he said,

Today the FBI is concentrating on auto theft ring cases operating on a multistate or international basis. We are not investigating every instance of a stolen car crossing a state line. By reason of our proficiency, we can now emphasize those cases wherein a significant part of the criminal activity lies in the second state. It is not an abdication of our responsibility, but rather the fulfillment of a more appropriate federal role.

The involvement of the FBI from the smallest crossroad community in the United States to its relations with similar bodies in foreign nations around the world seemed mind-boggling to me. It was systematized, computerized, neat! New developments were happening on every front, and being put into use. A system for collecting and filing gun riflings intrigued me. This information would immediately be available to every local crime laboratory. Rather like the human fingerprint file, only for guns!

Both the atmosphere and Clarence's words as he addressed the group of journalists in Miami frightened me.

As we walked toward the banquet room where the luncheon would be held, representatives of the news media were assembled, waiting for us. I began to feel that this was no ordinary meeting. They followed us, television camera turning, microphones in our faces, flashbulbs splintering the light, as they asked Clarence many tough questions. The closeness of bodies, as they crushed near to catch his words, to record our faces, was terrifying to me. I found I was shaking. Clarence's hand in mine was like a raft in a vast sea.

The guests were already seated when we arrived. Clarence was ushered in between bodyguards. I was seated at a round table next to the door with an FBI agent on either side. As the door closed behind us, Special Agent Leo McClarien, a tall man with appraising eyes in his strong-boned face, placed himself before it. Only then did I learn that this was the final session of the journalism seminar for reporters on organized crime. This meeting was one of a long-studied and carefully built-up attack against organized crime in America.

Clarence spoke forcefully to the journalists, encouraging them to do their good work and to call on the FBI for assistance. His opinion of the criminal element astonished me. "They aren't as smart as most people think they are. In fact, many are just plain stupid. Some people go into crime because they aren't capable of making a success in a normal way." I was shocked by his words. I had always been intimidated by the thought of crooks. I found myself wishing he wouldn't be so explicit about organized criminals. I had seen *The Godfather* and didn't like thinking about my darling becoming a concrete example of what happens when the mob gets mad.

Listening to Clarence, I was both thrilled and frightened. He seemed very much in command, but also very much an enemy to those with high stakes in the underworld. Clarence might not be frightened for himself, but I had enough fear for both of us! I would have to learn fast to face it with assurance and calm.

As soon as he finished speaking, we left the hall, heavily escorted. Awaiting us were three cars, a lead car, a backup car, and a baby-blue Lincoln Continental limousine with Leo sitting at the wheel. This fabulously luxurious car had formerly belonged to Jackie Gleason. When Clarence was in town, its current owner lent it for his use. This limousine, of course, was not armored.

My first true measure of how concerned the Bureau was about Clarence's televised speech on organized crime was when Leo drove off with the limousine's back seat empty. Clarence and I piled into the backup car. All the way to the airport I worried about the baby-blue limousine which had been meant for us, fearing it would blow up with Leo driving.

Janet and I returned to the Washington area where I had to teach school. On the flight up I kept thinking, "In six days, I will be Mrs. Clarence Kelley."

214

During the Miami visit I had had a good look at the life that lay ahead. In the future it would circle around whatever Clarence became involved in. Yet, as I thought about it, throughout each day, he had found time for me. Life with him would always be active. He would take me along with him, and I would have to race to keep up.

Six days.

We had not told any of our friends our wedding date. It would be a quiet affair, with just our immediate families present. There wasn't time or energy to spend on an elaborate wedding.

Who cared about that?

What was important was *us!*

20

Promises
and Promises

At the time of our engagement Clarence was politically a headliner in news circles. The addition of my life to his added another dimension for press exploitation. That I had served as a nun seemed to provoke an unusual amount of curiosity.

When we began planning our wedding, I hoped it could be a private ceremony. Marriage, to me, was a sacrament between only two people. Our families should be there to share our happiness. But what did the rest of the world really care about those few minutes in a church?

We were fortunate that my parents lived on their quiet farm. Its vicinity offered a perfect place for privacy. In the hills, only a half hour's drive away, was an exquisite Catholic church, St. Margaret's, in Maggie Valley. Its rustic building of stone and wood was set high on a wooded hillside with sweeping, panoramic views beyond its walls of glass. It had been a gift to the community from Father Timothy Murphy, who after a full life in business in Detroit had retired. At that time, being widowed, he had entered a seminary and been ordained a Catholic priest. Near the church, he had had a handsome building erected to house priests who wished to vacation or make retreats. In return for this benefaction, Father Murphy asked that the priests serve in any requirements of the church during their visits. I had attended services at St. Margaret's several times and been thrilled by its inspirational setting.

First, however, we must meet with the requirements of both the state of North Carolina and the Catholic Church. The latter had the more detailed procedure! Cardinal Baum, whom Clarence had known in Kansas City, assisted us with our preliminary arrangements. In our wish for privacy, we requested that the usual announcement of marriage bans on three consecutive Sundays prior to the wedding be omitted. Since Clarence's schedule would not allow time for a premarriage meeting with the priest in North Carolina, we met with Monsignor Arthur, the pastor of St. Patrick's Church, located two blocks from the FBI in Washington.

The evening before the appointment, I checked with Clarence to make sure we had all the necessary papers to present.

"The Church is particular about its records," I reminded him. "We have to be able to prove our eligibility to marry."

Clarence assured me everything was in order, including the requested copy of the death certificate of his first wife.

Next day I met Clarence at St. Patrick's.

Monsignor knew I had been a nun, and in our premarital discussion we spoke of this. Then Clarence presented our credentials, and we began filling in forms.

After a moment Monsignor said to me, "When did you leave the convent, Shirley?"

"In June 1969," I replied.

He riffled through the papers before him. "I find no record of your dispensation here."

I was stunned! I had forgotten all about the details of *my* eligibility!

I phoned St. Mary's Convent in South Bend and asked a sister to mail me a duplicate of my dispensation. When I thanked her for this service, I asked her to let me know what fee was involved. I would send a check.

"Oh," she replied, "after all, you gave the community fifteen good years, I think we can afford this!"

The day before the wedding, we flew to North Carolina. Tom Moten drove us to the airport, accompanied by my wedding gown and a new, custom-tailored, guaranteed-to-fit suit for Clarence. I was not about to put up with any more safety pins. Though I should have known that with this man, there would still be surprises ahead!

On our way down George Washington Parkway, beside the Potomac, on that first day of October, Clarence held my hand in his, and I was quite sure the whole world was right beside me, or all that mattered of it.

Clarence said to Tom, "We're on our way to be hitched." He stopped, then went on in the sly, laughing-at-himself way that I found delightful in him. "I'm getting nervous, Tom. My bachelor days are sliding away. Remember the nice dinners the two of us used to have at Billy Martin's? Have you any advice for me now?"

From the front seat, Tom responded, his words slow, but warm. "Boss," he said, "you've got only two choices. Either go through with this or commit suicide!"

We were met in North Carolina by my parents. For the first weeks of my engagement, they had continued to express an understandable hesitancy about the age difference between Clarence and me. They agreed with me that he was a fine man, but it was a shame, they said, that he wasn't ten years younger. It took particular adjustment to have me about to marry a man a year older than my mother.

Final concern over this had been neatly taken care of during a recent visit north. When we met my parents outside the Madison Hotel in Washington, Mother had extended her hand to Clarence and said, "Hello, son."

Clarence laughed and said heartily, "Hello, Lillian."

A relaxed relationship flowed between us. In months to come, I would hear my father comment how fortunate I had been to find such a good husband. As for himself, he would say, "I am lucky to have a new brother."

The afternoon was one Clarence and I had been anticipating. His family met mine. Joyce and John, and three of their four children, eighth- and ninth-graders Susie and Stephanie, and John III, arrived. Stanley, the second son, they told us with dismay, had stayed home to play football. Scrappy and Mary, with six-year-old daughter Kelley, and eight-year-old Kent, and Kent and Donna arrived. We were so busy saying hello to everyone there was no time to rehearse the wedding. After reviewing the happy group, Clarence summed it handily. "They all look intelligent and able to find their way down the aisle."

We had stopped at the courthouse, on the drive to the farm, and obtained our marriage license, but had not met the parish priest who would marry us. Father Burke phoned during the afternoon, and we discussed the ceremony. Clarence was a member of the First Christian Church, and we asked that the service blend both our faiths. Further, I told him, Clarence was only six weeks out of back surgery. It was difficult for him to stand, or kneel, for long periods. Father said that this could easily be accommodated by having four chairs placed in the sanctuary, where we and our witnesses might sit.

At dinnertime, the fifteen of us sat down together and shared one of my mother's feasts. It seemed like a combination Thanksgiving-Christmas to me. Seeing everyone together, rejoicing for Clarence and me, was wonderful. However, I noted a little reserve from my normally bouncy nieces Stephanie and Susie. The girls had always been close to me. During visits with them at their home near Detroit, we had had many free-spirited good times together. That evening they seemed a little long-faced.

I asked Stephanie what the problem was.

"You've always been our Aunt Shirley," she said. "You were fun to be with. We loved you because you were a little kooky. Now you are going to be an old married lady like all the other mothers."

I assured her I had no intention of changing. "I'll always be your Aunt Shirley," I said.

Beside me, Clarence said, "Don't you worry, Stephanie. She'll be kooky like she's always been!"

I watched as the girls gave Clarence a new look. They recognized a bond between the Director of the FBI and themselves—my kookiness.

I awoke on my wedding day to find the sky overcast, the horizon-encircling views of the Smoky Mountains obscured by clouds.

We breakfasted lightly and then dressed for church.

I loved my wedding gown. It was simple. Utterly feminine. White organza with bands of lace palely embroidered with flowers. Elegant, yet practical. I would be able to wear it to parties on summer evenings. And it was especially mine. I had chosen it. It had never been worn before.

How many lifetimes distant my earlier convent marriage cere-mony seemed. I was no longer the same person. The Bible says, "For everything there is a season." That is how I viewed my life. I had experienced two Catholic vocations. As a nun, I had given my whole heart to religious life. When it no longer fulfilled me, I had left it and chosen single life, finding happy adventure in discovering myself to be independent and capable of contributing to the world through teaching. On my wedding I would enter the third vocation. I had no hesitation.

In the full-length mirror in my room, I viewed myself happily, as I counted over in my mind the "something blue, something new" saying for brides. Beneath my long skirt, I wore a lacy blue garter. A friend had given me a finely embroidered white handkerchief I would carry.

Mother came into the room with something in her hand. It was her gorgeous deep-cut cameo. She pinned it at the neck of my gown.

"I just felt it needed that little touch," she said, smiling at me. "But I want it back."

"Thank you," I said, hugging her. Through my head ran the rest of the bride's requirements: "something old, something borrowed . . ."

I was ready.

Two cars with Clarence and the rest of the family arrived. Clar-ence got out of one to greet us. I was pleased to see that his new dark pin-striped suit fit elegantly. No safety pins! In spite of the tradition that a groom does not observe his bride on their wedding day until he sees her approaching down the church aisle, we had a quick word together.

The half-hour drive to St. Margaret's was along unmarked country roads. Daddy and Mother and I, and two pots of white chrysan-themums, led the way, followed by Kent and Clarence and their family. John and Joyce and their children were in the third car, following closely. Otherwise, on the winding roads, they might never have found the church. I kept glancing back to make sure they were not lost. John teased me about it later.

"Shirley, with me riding shotgun in the last car, there was *no* way your bridegroom was going to get away."

We approached the lovely church up a last incline of dusty, mountain gravel road and gathered on the sidewalk. Mother carried the

220

chrysanthemums inside and placed them on the altar. They were all the decoration necessary.

Joyce, in a short oatmeal-colored dress, the skirt brightly embroidered with mushrooms worked in yellow yarn, and holding a bouquet of yellow daisies, radiated happiness. I had not been able to be in her wedding, but now, at last, she could be matron of honor in mine.

Kent was his father's best man. He came up beside me in the vestibule and asked, "What do I do, Shirley?"

I laughed. "Don't ask me, Kent! You've had more experience than I. This is the first wedding of this kind I've ever been in."

Beside the gathered family, two FBI agents were present, the resident agent, Cosby Morgan, from Asheville, and assistant director in charge of external affairs Donald Moore, from Washington. Two members of the press were present at the chapel when we arrived. One was from the Waynesville *Mountaineer,* and the other from the Asheville *Citizen Times.* Our wish for privacy was respected. They did not pursue us with questions. No professional pictures were taken inside the church, though both John and Scrappy unobtrusively clicked away with their cameras throughout the service.

When the family was assembled in the front pews, Clarence and Kent and Fathers Burke and Murphy took their places. The wedding began. Kelley, in her flower-girl dress, walked daintily down the aisle, carefully carrying her basket of rose petals. In the awe of the moment, she forgot to scatter a single one. Behind her, young Kent proudly carried the ring on a satin pillow. Daddy escorted me down the aisle.

From two sides, the beauty of God's creation became a part of the chapel through its walls of glass. The sun had come out, and its light streamed across the hills and through the gently moving branches of trees. We met before Father Burke as he stood against the windowed backdrop of far-reaching mountains and sky. As he spoke, I watched one small fluffy white cloud float past. The priest's words, Clarence's presence, the loving company of our families, and the natural beauty of St. Margaret's mingled within my mind to create a special sense of blessedness.

After Father Burke had read from the Psalms and given a brief sermon, we stood to pronounce our vows. Clarence placed a wide gold wedding band on my finger. Surely joy such as I had never known was with me.

Father Murphy, that dear white-haired man in his eighties, smiled at me. It seemed a special benediction when he said, "Happy the bride the sun shines on today."

We turned to go down the aisle and met wide-eyed wonder on little Kelley's face. In her hands she still held her basket of flower petals. "All right, Kelley," we said. "Now is the time to throw your petals."

She led us from the church, happily scattering her blossoms.

We had another hour or so together as a family at a wedding breakfast Mother had arranged at Mountain Valley Country Club, overlooking rolling countryside, dotted with apple orchards, and smooth swards of the golf course. Then Clarence and I returned to the house to change into travel clothes for the flight back to Washington.

Of all the places in the world in which to find privacy for our honeymoon, we chose the Watergate! My apartment, with its locked hallways and screening television cameras, was the only place where we could stay without two bodyguards standing beside our door. If I had had girlish visions of a wedding trip, this was not quite what I had had in mind. Clarence lightened my dismay by agreeing that we would have an extended honeymoon in the Loire Valley of France as soon as he left the Bureau. I am looking forward to that.

Promises! Promises!

21

Mrs. Clarence Kelley

Three into one, plus two into one, made an interesting equation. We had between us three places to live, the contents of which must fit into a one-bedroom condominium for two people.

We had fourteen days to put together our household. Our apartment would be ready for occupancy then. I don't mean that Clarence had a vacation; we both worked all day, for I continued teaching until mid-October. Evenings and weekends we cleared out his Grosvenor Park condominium and my Watergate apartment. In Kansas City, Clarence's house was for sale. By January these three households would become one. The total of what we "could not live without" would become part of our lives together. To give an example of one of the problems involved—I had four closets stuffed with clothes. Clarence had an equal number at his apartment. Four plus four equaled eight. The sum must be divided among the four closets at our new dwelling.

A similar situation concerned dresser drawer space. There was too much of everything. Something was going to have to give. I decided I would. I would begin by giving away some of Clarence's neckties. He had three drawers full of beautiful, expensive ties, many never worn!

After carefully weighing the merits of each, Clarence bundled up one third of them and gave them away.

Marriage was a drastic change for me. When I lived alone, I put something down and it stayed there. No one *else* put anything down. In my two-room apartment at Watergate, I cleaned, cooked, and entertained when I felt like it. I was in the habit of doing many personal chores in the evening, after returning from teaching school or dinner.

Marriage changed that. I had a husband who felt at home. He *moved* things. He left things about. He expected services. He wanted meals. He made plans for my time. If he was not home every night at 6:30, his driver had already picked me up and deposited me at the FBI building, to accompany him to some function. I loved Clarence. He was the most entertaining companion imaginable. He was absolutely delightful to listen to and be with. But he had some fixed ideas about food and clean laundry. He liked both!

We traveled. That was fun. But we never returned from a trip without our suitcases bulging with clothes to be laundered. Clarence frequently wore two shirts a day. As a single person, I had easily been able to manage my laundry once a month. Now it was at least once a week! This included many drip-dry shirts to be collar-rubbed, washed, and retrieved from the dryer before they developed permanent wrinkles. No wonder my mother, who had faced laundry before Dacron was invented, used to say, "A bride should quickly burn the first shirt she irons—then there will be no complaining about sending them to the laundry!"

Clarence's wardrobe was enormous. So were his shoulders. They made it almost impossible to buy clothing without alterations. This was a way of life for him. If you gave Clarence the name of any city where he had ever been assigned, he would be able to give you the name of a good tailor. Beyond this factor, in the four months I had known him, he had lost forty pounds. As a result, when I became Mrs. Clarence Kelley, I discovered that my elegant husband had brought me a most unusual dowry. He had a drawer full of undershorts, each neatly pleated and secured on either side of the front with large, strong, safety pins! They were carefully folded and stacked in his drawer. It seemed out of character for the Director of the FBI to have anything pinned on him! I was tempted to toss out the entire lot. I began systematically replacing them in smaller size and finer quality.

Mrs. Clarence Kelley

Clarence never bothered to ask me the price of anything I purchased. He had the attitude "You get the paycheck. You pay the bills. You take care of what is necessary."

One day, in mentioning his new undershorts, he learned that I had paid $4.50 for each of them. He was astounded. What a terrible waste! An unnecessary expense! I had thrown money away!

In response, I stated that I certainly thought $4.50 for the underwear of the Director of the FBI was not out of line.

Clarence thundered, "I see no relationship between my position and the quality of my underwear!"

I stood firm.

He has since become accustomed to his under-elegance.

In the mornings I had only three duties to perform. I must provide Clarence with orange juice, coffee, and his necktie-for-the-day.

His day began with a 6:30 alarm, after which he went through a series of back-strengthening exercises. Each morning he had a working breakfast at the Bureau. While Edward Levi was attorney general, they breakfasted together once a week. Other days he would meet with out-of-town visitors or members of the press, Congress, or the executive department. Every week there was a working breakfast with the eighteen members of the Executive Conference, who, with Clarence, ran the FBI.

Since I did not cook breakfast, and Clarence was only home for lunch on weekends, and we had dinner or evening engagements at least five nights out of every seven, I could easily have forgotten how to cook. The one evening we were home, each week, we almost always had guests. Sundays, we attended church, frequently meeting friends afterward for brunch at the Sheraton-Carlton Hotel. Home cooking became so inconsequential that we turned our dining room into a den. Its walls were almost totally Clarence—his mementos, pictures, awards, cartoons, ranged from floor to ceiling! Some of the apartment was me, with my "engagement ring" Chindia rug, yellow silk moire wall coverings, antiques, and paintings. We surrounded ourselves with what we liked. If asked what style we favored in decorating, I would have answered, "Just us."

After I stopped teaching school, I found myself increasingly involved in Clarence's life. In the first year of our marriage that included fifty trips. I visited twenty states, Great Britain, Sweden, and France. In the same period, Clarence made sixty-two trips. Each trip generally included stops in several cities where FBI services were performed, speeches made, and occasions attended on related police work and crime prevention.

In Washington, Clarence frequently invited me to join him during business-related events at lunchtime. Often these events included Bureau tours in the afternoons or a trip to the National Academy at Quantico, Virginia. My rule on attending daytime Bureau functions was if wives and daughters were present in Clarence's party, I would attend.

At home I had endless letters to write. Although we had not expected wedding presents and had spread the word that with our combined households there was nothing that we needed, every day, from September through January, gifts arrived. Each was acknowledged. Every week, from every trip, I would accumulate a list of fifteen or twenty notes to write in thanks for thoughtful courtesies extended to us. I could have used a secretary, but preferred personally to write notes. Clarence's office took care of all his official correspondence.

I am sure Clarence's marriage to me required a few adjustments at the office. Although his first wife, Ruby, had called him upon occasion, she had not been a frequent interruption. As our program was heavily stepped up by my social availability, I came to know the office personnel very well. Clarence was anxious for me to entertain visitors to his office for a very specific reason. He felt that the J. Edgar Hoover Building belonged to the taxpayers. A certain amount of his time should be given to greeting people. In fact, he saw himself as a salesman for the FBI. He was pleased to have as many as possible tour this American institution.

From all over the country, people wrote to Clarence. Many sent him suggestions on how to improve the Bureau. Others sent tips on neighbors they suspected were criminals. Occasionally women sent him love letters. One day I walked into the office to find his secretary smiling broadly, shaking her head, over a letter. It was from a woman who imagined herself married to Clarence. She had written, "Come home, the children and I miss you."

He received gifts. At Christmas, he was likely to be given handmade items. I saw a hand-knit muffler and gloves some admirer had made for him. They were returned to the agent in her area, who personally delivered them back to the woman with the Director's gratitude and message that he could not accept gifts.

Clarence is an announced chocoholic. From many states, people sent him brownies and fudge. He had an ongoing contest he called his Fall Fudge Festival. People not only sent sweets to him, but included the recipes. He had quite a collection!

Of course all packages passed through a routing system. If for any reason their contents were suspect, they were X-rayed or examined in the laboratory.

Clarence's appetite was well known. Not only did he know a tailor in most American cities, but he had a cross-country knowledge of good places to eat. On a trip to San Diego with him, a city which I had heard greatly touted, I expected to be dined at the elegant Fountainebleu Room at the Westgate or some similarly marvelous place.

When asked his preference for dining, Clarence answered readily, "Let's go to Tijuana for tacos!"

We did.

In San Diego we had one of the few unpleasant experiences I have known with Clarence. In the early hours of the morning, we received a phone call. A door to a room down the hall from ours had been kicked in, we were told. The caller wished to know if the Director would like to step out into the corridor and discuss the matter.

Obviously, Clarence was not interested in stepping out into the hall to talk with this "helpful" stranger. He turned the matter over to the two agents sitting in the living room of our suite.

At another time, in Birmingham, Alabama, while in our hotel suite, I was awakened by what sounded like a thud on the door. I jumped out of bed and ran to the door to the living room, where the guard was sitting. Peeking around the corner, I asked, "Did you call me?"

"No, Mrs. Kelley," he replied. "That noise was from across the hall."

I crept back into bed, to lie beside my good buddy, who had soundly slept through the whole thing.

ॐ

My private life with Clarence would not have been possible without his gun. Frightening as that loaded weapon was, it was a friend. His need for self-protection was imposed on him by his title. There were few, if any, who had direct malice in their hearts for Clarence Kelley. Yet next to the

President of the United States, his office received the greatest number of threats each year.

In choosing our apartment, this had to be considered. I wanted a condominium large enough to accommodate two people comfortably, but small enough for me to maintain by myself. With these requirements filled, we would not have to have anyone else regularly in the house, beyond the two of us, at any time. Our door had to have a special lock, and our apartment only one exit. It must be high enough from the ground to make access impossible from the outside. Its balcony must be separated from any neighboring balcony to provide protection.

I was fascinated when the men came to install our telephone. We had two phone systems, one, the typical household line, and the second, direct to the FBI switchboard. This latter had a "scrambler" on it. It carried an electronic device which made it impossible for anyone between the speaker and the FBI to make intelligible the sounds on the wire. Because of this interference, it was noisy and not particularly pleasant to use. The regular phone, Clarence warned me, I should always presume to be tapped. Legal or not, this was possible in several ways. We were always aware of our conversations on the private line.

When these phones were installed, two men from the telephone company arrived, as well as a man from the FBI who "swept" the room. He was from the electronics department and knew how to make sure no bugging devices had been planted in the phones or about the apartment. He also had the job of sweeping Clarence's office after visitors had left. Periodically, at the Director's request, when I was not at home, he "swept" our apartment. To my knowledge, the guests to our home had a clear record. Such precautions were something Clarence had to do for the good of the country. It was fine to talk about what the government could, or could not, legally do, but some other countries did not have the same standards. Even some groups of Americans had been known to plant devices.

As for the gun, I never went to sleep without checking to see if it was on Clarence's bedside table. I was probably one of the few women in America who went to sleep at night with extra cartridges on my nightstand.

We were such a normal-looking couple. How many people swimming or relaxing by our apartment house pool ever thought that in my handbag, while Clarence swam, was his loaded gun?

He went nowhere without it. If he stepped to the trash room, he was armed. If I went to the laundry in the evening or on weekends, he accompanied me, gun at his hip. It must have startled my fellow tenants to enter the laundry to see me busily sorting and folding clothes, while beside me, his satchel propped up on a chair, his black folders spread out before him on the table, the director of the FBI sat, drawing on his pipe, doing his office work. But alert! He missed nothing.

I had a shrill alarm which I always carried with me. Sounded close to one's head, it could break an eardrum. Its scream would attract the attention of anyone within a block.

At the time of the Claudine Longet tragedy, Clarence decided that I should have a few lessons on how to handle a gun. He gave me basic instruction. He was so used to firearms that he often forgot how frightening the appearance of a gun was to many people. He recalled the time when as a young agent he had been called in on a case with a machine gun in his hands. After the arrest was made, while all the terrified spectators were still in the room, he had casually laid the machine gun down on the counter. Before him, the people remained frozen with horror. When Clarence saw their faces, he picked up the gun and with an embarrassed "Oh, pardon me," departed.

He told me also of an incident in Houston. As he was getting out of his car, his gun came off its hook and fell to the sidewalk. A well-dressed lady was passing by. Seeing the revolver on the pavement, she leaned over, picked it up, and handed it to him.

"Pardon me," she said. "Did you drop something?"

She continued walking as though nothing had happened.

"That," said Clarence, "could only have happened in Texas!"

People have asked me how we were able to retain our closeness when we traveled so much and attended so many meetings. One answer was that I *was* able to travel with Clarence. I believe he made only ten overnight trips without me in the first year of our marriage. Trips that I took with him were at our personal expense. It was necessary to keep accounts of those expenditures. They amounted to over ten thousand dollars. That was one of the fees for admittance to public life. I was grateful that we were able to manage it. If we had had children to raise on his after-tax salary, it would have been difficult.

Our other secret weapon against doldrums which might have beset our marriage was our intercommunication system. If we were not side by side, we would find each other across a room, and smile, or he would give me his long eye-glinting wink. In an unobtrusive way this message could be paragraphs long. Many times when he was on a speaking trip outside the city, sitting in the front seat with the driver, he would put his arm behind the seat for my fingers to touch his hand with a little squeeze.

We were both of minds that appreciated worthwhile endeavors, and hence, I was not jealous of the consuming responsibility he had as the Director of the FBI. He was on twenty-four-hour call. When problems arose, our life together was interrupted.

An element that made our public life particularly pleasant was the kind of persons that most of the FBI agents were. They were fundamentally intelligent, unobtrusive, and had great senses of humor. We shared many hours with them. Prime among these were Clarence's drivers. Tom Moten, true to his word to stand by Clarence until we were married, retired in February. He was roundly feted by his co-workers, who presented him with a fine fishing rod. His replacement was a rugged individual with a name I felt fitting to his assignment—Joe Battle. Bob Jones, from the office, acted as a substitute driver. These men not only drove but they assumed alertness for Clarence, so that he could study his papers or relax while driving to his next appointment.

Although women were present on some occasions, most of the time that we traveled, I was accompanied by two or three men. As we arrived in New Orleans, a little girl caught my eye. She stared at me, then turned to her mother.

"Look at all the men, Mommy!" she exclaimed as I walked by with Clarence and the purposefully paced agents.

I smiled to myself. Some change from the convent!

When we were first married, I could normally count on Saturdays and Sundays as our own. In January this changed. Clarence announced that he planned to retire the following year, and suddenly his speaking schedule increased. Between Easter and the middle of August we had only one free weekend.

I was always happy if on Friday evenings we could be home and alone by nine o'clock. I loved to watch *The Rockford Files*, a TV series of super-clever crime-busting.

On our one free Friday night in June, I was well into the program, when the phone rang. I glanced at its blinking light and saw the call was coming from the FBI switchboard.

"It's for you!" I said, picking up the instrument.

The voice announced its caller and asked to speak with the Director. I handed Clarence the phone and bounded to the TV to turn down the sound. My hero, Jim Rockford, was in a very tight spot. I wanted to give him all my assistance by watching intently. The volume down, I sat close to the set.

"James Earl Ray has escaped from prison," I heard Clarence say.

I clung close to the TV as he continued to chat. Finally he hung up, and I was able to increase the sound volume. Against the background of Jim Rockford's troubles, Clarence told me his.

In a few minutes the phone rang again. I leaped back to the set to help Rockford solve his case.

Clarence answered the phone.

This procedure continued until the end of the program. At its conclusion, I told Clarence I hoped he would be better able to help the next hero, Quincy, than he had Rockford.

As Clarence talked, explaining the tense situation in Tennessee, I kept one ear and one eye on the TV happenings.

"I wish I could go down there and get into the case," he said. "Of course the SAC in Knoxville can handle it perfectly well. . . ."

I could see he was itching to toss a shirt in a suitcase and take off. But I knew that was against his principles of management. Stay out. Let the local authorities handle it.

He had many more calls during the night. A member of the Justice Department called to say they were interested in what was going on, but gave no comment or advice. Neither the attorney general nor the President nor any member of Congress called, either out of curiosity or to prod. It was assumed that the Director had control of the situation from the federal aspect.

Throughout the long night, only one detractor phoned: a member of the Committee to Investigate the Assassination of Martin Luther King. His message to Clarence was "not to kill Ray." I particularly found the insinuation that the FBI agents would shoot needlessly to be insulting. On the other hand, I certainly did not want any FBI agents to accept shots from Ray, if he were armed, without taking precautions to defend themselves! I was furious.

As I tried to get some sleep that fitful night, I realized, there I was, in the midst of a real live whodunit, with my husband actively involved in the tracking down of a most wanted criminal, and I had been aggravated because I had been distracted from my one-hour fictional program! The world of fantasy seemed a lot more satisfying than the real thing! It was comforting to know, when one turned on the knob of one's TV, that within the hour the hero would get his man. As Mother Regina had said, I liked things "all neatly tied up with pink ribbons." I found it inconvenient and annoying to have a real criminal escape on Friday evening so that it was reported to my husband during the hour of my favorite show. And ahead lay a weekend of continued interruptions. Real life could not wrap up a crime in an allotted hour, much less one with frequent times out for commercial announcements.

Our marriage would have been close to idyllic if the automobile had not been invented. We were each convinced that the other was a terrible driver and could enumerate the reasons why he/she was a menace on the highway.

Kent said of his father, "Driving with Pop is a thrill a minute, isn't it, Shirley?"

Clarence's problem, I felt, was from lack of recent experience. For the past fifteen years, he had had a driver. So he *was* the chief of police in Kansas City and was authority par excellence on traffic control—it was actual driving, not statistics, that counted! With the wheel in his hands, to my mind, he was a threat, although he had never had an accident. He was almost equally dangerous as a "side seat driver." I did not find it conducive to relaxation and skillful automotive operation to have reeled off to me, as I approached a traffic signal, the exact number of seconds that particular light would remain red, as opposed to the length of time the light on the route I had *not* taken would have remained red.

As soon as I took control of the car, my mild-mannered, easygoing husband turned into a bossy autocrat. He fastened his seat belt and reverted to being a cop. From where he sat on the side, he was convinced I was overlapping the middle line. He would tell me so, not once, but several times, in the length of a block.

On the other hand, when I rode in the passenger seat, I was certain he was about to shear off fenders and door handles. He came so close to parked cars I expected to be thinly sliced.

Mrs. Clarence Kelley

Fortunately for our marriage, these journeys into incompatibility happened only once a week. Every morning Clarence's driver-bodyguard called for him, transported him about all day, and returned him safely to me at night. Most of our evenings were filled with official and Bureau-related events. The agent driver drove.

Clarence and I had only about one night a week as private citizens. It was outings on these occasions which endangered our marriage. There was no hope of compromise for our predetermined convictions. We were equally convinced that disaster-at-the-wheel lay in the hands of the other. Fortunately, or otherwise, since Clarence's spinal operation, I usually drove.

Mary and Kelley and young Kent came to visit us. As a recent kindergarten graduate, Kelley had learned about "Ham Ham" Lincoln and insisted on seeing her favorite statesman on his big marble chair at Lincoln Memorial.

The five of us drove through the evening traffic toward the memorial. There were certain places in Washington, D.C., at which, at certain hours of the day, it seemed impossible to arrive! This turned out to be one of them. We approached the monument from Rock Creek Parkway, looped around through streams of vehicles, and the next thing I knew, we had been shunted off to the road across Memorial Bridge to Virginia! Such a thing could happen to anyone, I assured my companions. The evening was yet young. "Ham Ham" would wait for us. We would try again.

Back we went, coming by a circuitous route through the parklands, and again approached the monument where we hoped to park and walk up the many steps to pay our respects.

What to my wondering eyes should appear, as I edged through the next intersection, but all the traffic was going in the wrong direction! I was proceeding, and cars were pouring toward me, honking their horns. They kindly divided, like the miraculous Red Sea, to let me pass through.

Clarence became upset.

"You are going the wrong way!" he shouted.

I had already figured that out.

"Turn around! Go back!"

In the middle of a solid stream of traffic?

There was no turning back. I navigated against the tide and found myself again headed onto Memorial Bridge, Lincoln Memorial shrinking in the distance behind me.

"Get over to the curb!" Clarence shouted. "Pull over! Get out! I will drive!"

"Clarence," I said, "it is not lawful to stop on a bridge."

"Stop! Get out of the driver's seat! You are a menace to society! We will all be killed!"

I continued to drive. "There is no way to stop in this traffic."

Clarence, beside himself, lost his remaining cool. "Ruby!" he shouted. "Mary!" Desperately he sought my name. "Shirley!" he yelled, "pull over!"

From the back seat, I could hear Mary giggling.

In spite of his muttering, I drove along George Washington Parkway to Rosslyn, where, on a wide, quiet street, I told Clarence he might drive, if that was his inclination.

He assumed command, and we proceeded across Key Bridge for a third try at Lincoln Memorial.

"So," I said. "I am *not* the first woman you have yelled at. 'Ruby! Mary! Shirley!' "

Kelley and Kent may not have understood, but at least our tones had changed. We all laughed together.

Clarence, I think, would have great difficulty trying to pass in disguise. The breadth of his shoulders and the shape of his head are markedly individual. In life, he looks exactly like his photographs. He is an easy figure to cartoon. Because he looks so like his portrayals, he is easily recognized wherever he goes. We have had many heartwarming encounters with strangers who were well-wishers, and some have been unforgettable.

One day we were walking along Western Avenue in Chevy Chase. A young man, halted by traffic, saw Clarence and leaned out his car window to call. "Who are you?" he asked. "I *know* you are important. I know you! Who are you?"

Clarence told him his name.

"Far out!" the young man yelled. "And I even said hello to you!"

With that, he drove off.

I loved it! Ah, fame!

"I know you! Who are you?"

22

A Trip and Tips

"What do you do when you travel with the Director?" interviewers frequently asked.

I visited FBI offices, attended functions, and continued to learn about the FBI by listening to conversations and speeches. On a trip to Jackson, Mississippi, I found a cause I could personally espouse.

Clarence had set up a series of four meetings in four cities. The SACs who ran the FBI offices throughout the United States were each to attend the one most convenient to his locality and time schedule. A team of assistant directors and supervisors from headquarters would be present at all the meetings. These sessions were a part of the participatory management techniques Clarence had introduced to the Bureau. Mr. Wilburn DeBruler, the assistant in charge of planning and inspection, played a leading role. Clarence attended every meeting. It was his desire to produce feedback from the SACs by placing himself open to direct questioning from them. He believed that a variety of viewpoints often resulted in a better service.

When one considered the prior history of the FBI, this was a radical change. For years there had been a unilateral chain of command. Clarence found it necessary to encourage the men to speak their minds. Some found it difficult to combine their respect for the office with the freedom to challenge. To the uninitiated, this role of the loyal opposition may seem difficult to comprehend. Under the previous Director, J. Edgar Hoover, it had been, "Do it my way or get out!"

A story is told of one occasion when Mr. Hoover was asked by Clyde Tolson, his assistant, if he agreed to censuring a certain agent. In his request, Mr. Tolson inadvertently had not stated the agent's offense. Mr. Hoover replied in writing, "I agree. What did he do?"

During the two and a half days in which Clarence met with his men in Jackson, I was entertained by the FBI wives. Several of them had come from other cities. I was invited with them to a pot-luck luncheon by the wife of the Jackson SAC. Wives of local agents were also present. The home of the Jackson SAC was brand-new. They had moved into it only two weeks earlier. The grounds were not yet landscaped, and no draperies hung at her windows. This aroused amused understanding among the other wives, who, themselves, were frequently uprooted and placed about the country like chessmen on a vast board. One of them started reminiscing about the problems of draperies when she moved. It seemed that remaking the draperies to fit each new house in the city to which they were assigned was a major undertaking. Another wife commented that this topic was considered so paramount by one wife she knew, she was writing a book of her life in the FBI. It would be titled *The Drapes Don't Fit Again.*

In the afternoon we had a special tour of the governor's mansion in Jackson. I had met Governor Cliff Finch the evening before and been charmed by him. My dinner partner had commented, nodding toward the new governor, "You see that fellow. He won his seat by identifying himself with the common man; overalls, pitching hay, and all that. His logo was a lunch pail. I thought to myself, 'This fellow will never fill the job,' but he has turned out to be a hardworking, down-to-earth, excellent governor."

The executive mansion had recently been restored, and as I toured its splendid rooms, I felt the people of Mississippi were most fortunate to have such a fine historic landmark. Apparently Mississippians were proud of it too. The mansion was open to them twenty-four hours a day! In the middle of the night, one might ring the bell and be admitted, and courteously shown through. The elegant structure with its high ceilings and beautiful floors and its priceless antiques was truly a house "of the people." When the governor and his lady were not entertaining in the official dining room, members of Mississippi associations could reserve it for their own enjoyment. Any Mississippian who wished to spend the night in one of the spacious bedrooms with its canopied or four-poster beds could do so! One of the FBI wives was a Girl Scout leader. She told us another troop leader whom she had heard of had taken her troop for an overnight camp-out in the elegant residence. The girls who could not find accommodations on the ample beds had unrolled their sleeping bags on the floors.

During the Jackson session, Clarence was interviewed by a local TV station. Three or four agents and I sat to the side in the suite as the meeting was taped.

In walked Judy Denson, a woman in her thirties, whom I would probably never have noticed in a crowd. Within a half hour, this woman made a lasting impact on my life.

She moderated a women's talk show called *Coffee With Judy*. Quickly she brought the discussion with Clarence around to a subject which vastly interested her. Within the past month, in Jackson, she said, women had been raped on a grocery store parking lot, in a shopping center parking lot, and in a movie theater. Fear of assault was beginning to dominate the activities of women. Recently, Judy had called a woman friend to ask her to accompany her to a movie. Her friend had declined. She was afraid to go out on the streets of Jackson at night. Judy had become incensed. Her friend's freedom was impaired.

She had done some investigating and come up with some sobering facts. Seventy percent of all crime against women in the United States is committed against them in their everyday, local areas, during the hours when their children and husbands are away.

I was shocked. Sitting, watching the taping, I realized I had only three chances out of ten of getting any help from Clarence if I were attacked. There I was, married to the first cop in America, and I had no better protection than anyone else.

I had grown up in the South. I had been taught that, for the most part, a man will protect a woman. Women were not taught techniques of protection. They were told to stay inside, lock the doors, don't go out. That was "protection."

I am not one to stay inside and hide.

This young woman, who was currently dedicating her time to the assistance of the women of America, impressed me deeply. She had managed to interview local law-enforcement people on her program and the crime resistance agent in the Jackson office. She had shown educational movies on how certain crimes were perpetrated, and there she was, interviewing the Director of the FBI for her morning ladies' show.

I felt, "Here is a person who can make a difference in making America safe for women, instead of allowing crime to run free over us."

Clarence had expressed to me his belief that crime rates can be drastically reduced in America. The moment will come, he thinks, when the average American will put his foot firmly down and say, "I will not tolerate this anymore! Here is an advocate!" Over half of his recent speeches had been on crime resistance. But it was Judy who convinced me that what Clarence was recommending in a crime resistance program was not just the stress of the obvious but the core to controlling a certain type of helpless victim crime.

I left Jackson, Mississippi, no longer fearful of personal attack, and determined to learn how to take care of myself.

When I returned to Washington, I called John Coleman, the man in charge of crime resistance for the Bureau, and said, "John, in my travels with Clarence I am exposed to countless people. What can I do to help the cause of crime resistance? Is there some message I can pass on as I talk with people?"

He replied, "Yes, there is."

For starters, he gave me two simple tips. The first interested me especially. More than half the cars stolen in the United States are unlocked. Many of them have their keys in the ignition. Never leave your car with the motor running while you run into a store to pick up something. Not even if you think you will be gone "just a second."

Secondly, when you park your car in a parking lot, make sure, when you leave it, that it looks as though a man drives it. Investigative files show that rapists frequently case parking lots watching for potential victims. They recognize cars driven by women. The articles left in an automobile are like a self-portrait of the driver. The rapist waits, not for a certain woman, but for the driver of the car.

As Mr. Coleman talked, I was only mildly impressed. I thought of my own car and wondered who would care about it. I had hoped he would give me some big, secret weapons which I might share. His advice seemed sound, but obvious.

Later that day I went down to the garage and viewed my car as a stranger might. There was a white plastic umbrella tossed on the back seat. Squooshed behind the driver's seat was a small white pillow. At a glance, anyone could have told a woman drove my car. I returned upstairs and did as John had instructed. I got one of Clarence's hats and took it down and laid it on the front seat. I hid my little cushion under the seat and locked my umbrella in the trunk. By these simple actions, I had considerably reduced my vulnerability to crime under certain circumstances.

I am a person who cannot scream when I am scared. I cannot make a peep. By pushing the simple button on the shrill alarm that I carry, I may possibly still be attacked, but I will gather a wide audience! Actually, the screamer is so unpleasant that the most likely reaction is to get away from it as quickly as possible. When I was a guest on the *Good Morning, America* show, I activated the shrill alarm and commented on crime resistance. At the FBI building, the phones were jammed with calls from all over America with requests for further information and where one might purchase a shrill alarm. Wherever the program was shown, it created interest.

Since the Jackson trip, I have paid close attention to references made to crime resistance. I attended the congressional hearing when Clarence testified on the subject. This program had received much criticism within the Bureau. There were those who felt that the purpose of the Bureau was to investigate crime, not prevent it. Clarence did not argue with this basic philosophy, but he felt that the whole purpose of criminal justice was to make people's lives safe. Since no one else picked up the banner to inform people on how to prevent crime, and he felt it needed a crusade, as long as Clarence was in the Bureau he emphasized this problem. In each of the fifty-nine FBI offices across the country, one or two agents were assigned to this phase of crime. There have been some astounding results.

In twenty-two months a New York firm had lost $800,000 in merchandise. The FBI agent in charge of crime resistance was called in, since it was a problem involving interstate traffic. During the next five months, as the recommendations of the agent were followed, the total theft was reduced to $17,000.

Another agent told me that his jurisdiction had included an airport which had suffered a $300,000 loss in baggage and freight. After he had analyzed the problem, he suggested changing certain routines and procedures. In the three months after these were made, the airport had not had a single theft.

A point made in favor of such programs is that they do not involve large sums of money or installation of expensive new equipment. Frequently crime may be prevented by rescheduling people and a reorganization of routines.

The importance of crime resistance is primarily to save lives, but there is another tremendous benefit which affects us all. The enormous cost of theft is passed on to the consumer. When someone walks off with a case of beer, the consumer must eventually pay a higher price for the rest of the shipment. Theft saps away some of the quality of life.

In my awakened enthusiasm in crime resistance, I was pleased to learn that in the past two years the program had created several study groups. Five cities were chosen and one type of crime was closely analyzed in each city.

Crimes against the elderly were high in Wilmington, Delaware. The task force studied these crimes in depth. A high relationship was found between truancy from high school and theft. It was brought out that elderly people are most frequently the victims of teen-age attacks. With close cooperation from the school board, and the local police working with the FBI, they were able to catch and punish offenders, and thereby decrease the crime wave in the city. The study showed the vulnerability of the elderly. Older women were encouraged not to carry pocketbooks. They were advised to buy clothing with inside pockets where they could carry their money. Manufacturers received suggestions about producing a ready-made pocket which might be sewn into garments at home. Clothing manufacturers were encouraged to place inner pockets in their styles most likely to be purchased by the elderly.

In the cities where a specific crime area had been studied, there were striking reductions in that crime. When Clarence and I were on an airplane, a man asked to speak with us. He was from the governor's office in Virginia. He explained to Clarence how rewarding they felt the crime resistance program to be. One, regarding schoolchildren, had been started in Charlottesville. At first the teachers had felt it to be a waste of time and had been reluctant to get into it. At the completion of the project, they were most enthusiastic. It had had excellent results. Not only had crime decreased among the students, but their attitudes had changed. They had new respect for authority.

One of the finest accomplishments of the Bureau in this regard, Clarence felt, was a proposal on crime resistance which he sent to the White House for the President's study and action in June 1977.

The proposal encouraged the White House to hold a conference on crime prevention which would bring together leaders from various sections of society—educators, the church, civic organizations, business, labor, women, and the media—to replicate them to take action similar to the actions taken in the task forces in the cities and other crime resistance endeavors. This would be accomplished by using crime resistance personnel, both federal and local.

On that same trip to Jackson when I first became a pressing advocate for crime resistance programs, I had some further adventures.

We departed Mississippi for St. Louis, Missouri, with a stopover in Memphis.

I had never visited that city and was sorry we were only going to change planes there. Eagerly watching from the window, I saw the mighty river winding below.

Clarence leaned over my shoulder.

"I had a lot of problems when I was the SAC down there."

"I know," I said. "You left the Bureau from Memphis."

"That's right," he said thoughtfully. "I was one of the youngest men ever to leave the Bureau and get a full pension." He buckled his seat belt as the light came on.

"You see those plantations out there, in the distance?" he asked, pointing into space. "That's where the problem was. Blacks had been given the right to vote by the Constitution, but many plantation owners threatened to fire them, or cancel their credit in the stores where they purchased their staples, if they registered for the coming election. The Justice Department sent men down to inform any citizen that if he was threatened in any way in the use of his suffrage, he should notify the FBI immediately. My office was swamped," Clarence said.

"I had several hundred cases which had to be resolved by election day if those people were to be allowed to vote. Requests for additional help were unsuccessful, though every move I made was closely followed.

"At that time I had been in the Bureau almost twenty-one years. I decided I did not want to be subject any longer to the questions posed to me about why certain conditions existed. Not that I objected to questions. I objected to a lack of suggestions as to what should be done. I left the FBI. I was forty-nine and had so much unused vacation and sick leave stored up that though it was still some months until I would be fifty, I was able to retire."

I could hear the sadness in his voice over the remembered lack of support to his leadership, but I felt I heard strength, too, as he looked to the future.

A Trip and Tips

ಶ

In St. Louis, Clarence spoke at the graduation exercises of the Police Academy. Twenty-four men and six women became new officers.

Prior to the ceremony we attended a reception for the police commissioners and our party. I met Colonel Theodore McNeal, of the St. Louis Board of Police Commissioners, and his attractive wife, Virgie. Mrs. McNeal had dark hair and pale gold-brown skin. I thought she might be southern European or Latin American, but, she told me, both she and her husband were black. I was surprised. She could easily have passed for white. She had a beautiful face with a gentle sweetness about it. I could not imagine that she had ever had to cope with a problem in her life.

At the time, early February 1977, I was feeling particularly beset by problems. The new administration had taken over Washington, and Clarence was under continuous attack.

I listened to Colonel and Mrs. McNeal, and by the end of the evening, I again felt a change in my outlook on life. Something beautiful was projected into it.

Ted McNeal had been in public service most of his life. He and Clarence shared many years of mutual respect. As I chatted with him, I told him I was an ex-nun. He told me he was not a Catholic, but held a soft spot in his heart for the Church. He had started out working as a Pullman-car porter many years ago. He had been one of the first to attempt to unionize porters and received much opposition for his efforts. At one point in his organizing, he had gone to Louisiana to talk with reporters. For no cause of which he knew, he had been thrown in jail. It was possible that, unknown and unfunded, as he was, he might have languished there for an indeterminable time. However, someone notified the local Catholic bishop of his plight, and he had been released.

Ted McNeal said, "A white man. A man I had never met. That bishop saw me as a human being whose rights were being violated. He came to my assistance. I owed my freedom to him."

He went on to say that out of gratitude, he went out of his way to give his time to speak at Catholic churches.

Mrs. McNeal joined in our conversation and introduced me to a term I had never previously heard—"passing over." It is used when a person with a partly black bloodline, but fair skin, renounces his heritage and enters a white community to "pass" as one of them. She illustrated this by telling me an incident of a friend of hers, which had happened many years ago. At that time black women were not allowed even to try on merchandise in a store. They were never employed as clerks. Her friend, who was beautiful and had very light skin, applied for a job. She was not trying to prove anything. She needed the income. Her husband, who was several shades darker than she, could not pick her up at the store. She would have been fired. It was necessary for her to meet him elsewhere.

Mrs. McNeal told me she had chosen years ago to be what she was and accept the consequences. She spoke without resentment. There was a serenity and inner strength exuding from this couple which added greatly to my appreciation of life.

I was in the midst of inner, personal turmoil. For the past month I had heard many unfair accusations of my husband. The President wanted to get rid of him. The attorney general had promised to fire him, and no one seemed interested in studying the facts of the case.

Clarence had friends who were willing to champion his cause. Noted lawyers were telling him he was being unfairly maligned. Clarence would not hear of their making a public case for him. One gave due honor to lawful authority and continued one's course.

Bitterness had been eating away at me as I saw him proceeding, lips pressed, against daily onslaught.

I looked into the serene face of beautiful Virgie McNeal and saw a woman who had suffered more wrongs in life than I would ever know. How insignificant were my feelings! Through this fortuitous meeting, I gained a fine new perspective.

23

Behind the Scenes

Clarence and I were married during a trying time in his career. It was a month before the presidential election of 1976. Not that the outcome of the election should have had anything to do with the position of the Director of the FBI. Clarence's appointment had been unanimously approved by Congress with no time limit except that he retire at age seventy. He was sixty-five years old. Nor did his political affiliation enter into it. He was an Independent. Still, the Democratic candidate, Jimmy Carter, had sworn to fire him, a statement which was headlined throughout the country, which lost at least one registered, lifelong Democrat to the ranks. The day I read that statement, I wrote the National Committee of the Democratic party a letter of resignation.

Another press release about that time from the Carter camp stated that "high unemployment rates in the Nixon and Ford administrations were a reason for rising crime among young people." It added, "Other reasons are the public example set by Watergate, disclosure that the CIA abused powers, and the disgraceful action of the FBI."

Newspapers carried on with the theme, "the peccadillos of Clarence Kelley, the director of the FBI . . . essentially part of a continuum of Republican corruption . . . when you see the head of the FBI break a little law but stay there, it gives everyone the idea that crime must be okay."

Even after the Department of Justice issued a statement which filled twenty inches of newsprint in the Washington *Post*, headlined "FBI Director Kelley: An Effort to Be Honest and Careful," and included the statement, "It is our view that Mr. Kelley should remain as director of the FBI," there was little letup.

In November Mr. Carter won the election by a small margin. A pilgrimage to his home in Plains, Georgia, immediately began. Congressmen, senators, and outgoing members of President Ford's cabinet were invited to the southern town to brief the incoming President on their departments. During the two-and-a-half-month transition period between administrations, funded from the American taxpayer's pockets for two million dollars, many on the Hill felt it would be helpful if the air could be cleared between the President-elect and the Justice Department. Neither Attorney General Edward Levi nor Clarence was invited.

At this time America was facing some glaring domestic issues. At the time of my engagement to Clarence, the announcement had shared the front page with a story of a hijacked jet. Jimmy Hoffa had been kidnapped and was missing. The Coachella school-bus kidnapping had taken place. The FBI was investigating the Roselli murder. There were questions of Cointelpro, the illegal break-ins laid to the FBI, probes of Socialist Workers party problems, and an investigation into the bombing murder in Washington of a former official from the Chilean Embassy. Plus many others. It was surprising to me that the President was not interested in Clarence's views on these matters or of those of the attorney general.

It is possible that the President-elect thought that the incoming attorney general would handle these matters. That did not seem consistent with his minute interest in such details as to where the White House secretaries would park their cars! It seemed to me that even if Clarence were to be replaced, his opinion might be worth an hour or two of the man's time.

The new year arrived, and no acknowledgment of his presence was made by any of the President-elect's staff. Invitations to attend the inauguration of President Jimmy Carter were issued. For the first time in the history of the United States, the outgoing cabinet was passed over. This snub also included the Director of the FBI.

At a Mardi Gras Ball in Washington, shortly after the inauguration, I heard a side angle to this. A young woman from Louisiana approached Clarence and pointedly inquired if he had been invited to the inauguration. When he replied in the negative, she said, "I thought that was probably the way it was. We were very upset in our town. An invitation was received by a Georgian, possibly from Plains. He was an inmate of our jail at the time." This citizen was disturbed that the inauguration had not included those who had already served their country. The turnover seemed to be a turn-out.

ह्य

In the four years Clarence had been in the Bureau, he worked under four attorneys general, Elliott Richardson, William Saxbe, Edward Levi, and Griffin Bell. His comment, collectively, was, "All good men, for which the nation should be grateful."

Clarence reported directly to the attorney general and the deputy attorney general. Whenever a new attorney general was chosen, he was briefed on the working of the FBI by its Director. Explanation of the vast, complex machine of the Bureau was time-consuming. At the same time, Clarence was frequently drained of his time by the press, which, when it could not find current complaints, dug as far back as half a century for its headlines. The most far-fetched of these, it seemed to me, was an inquiry into a matter concerning Helen Keller in 1926! Not only was Helen Keller deceased, but at that time, Clarence had been only fifteen years old! The seemingly annual turnover of attorneys general, and the attentions required by the press, used much of Clarence's time which he felt could have been used for direct work on his job.

When Clarence was sworn into office, Elliott Richardson was attorney general. I had heard him speak and considered him a patrician, a man of elegance and style. By contrast, his successor, William Saxbe, was the salt of the earth. Clarence's face always lit up when he referred to Bill, whose down-home mannerisms of a country boy were a coverup of his brilliant mind.

In 1975 Clarence got another new boss. The new attorney general, Edward Levi, was quiet and scholarly. He was in office at the apex of Clarence's press-exaggerated troubles.

I became accustomed to the ring of the FBI extension phone in our apartment. Clarence would respond, and I would hear, "Yes, put him on . . . Yes, General . . . Yes, General . . . No, no, General

. . . No, I don't feel bad . . . You're my lawyer, General . . . I'm with you . . . Thank you for calling, sir."

The background for these responses would invariably be a story in the press that had portrayed Mr. Levi as criticizing Clarence. Most of the time the attorney general's message had not been accurately transmitted. At other times, he would phone to see how Clarence was taking what had been reported. How did he feel about it? There was one word which continually marked Edward Levi's character—kindness.

Clarence and the attorney general breakfasted together once every week, a "your house or mine?" arrangement, sometimes at the Bureau, sometimes at the Justice Department. There was a constant flow of information between the two men.

Being a person with inherent respect for authority, who made no moves within the Bureau without the knowledge of the attorney general, Clarence was obedient to his boss on all occasions, except one. On one point, he was adamant.

Edward Levi was the first Jewish attorney general the country had had. In his first week in office, he received a threat on his life. Security guards were not necessarily assigned to attorneys general. Some are, and some are not, protected. It was felt, in this case, that both Mr. and Mrs. Levi should have round-the-clock protection.

One evening we entertained the Levis in our favorite Georgetown restaurant. It was around Christmas. Edward had only one more month to serve under President Ford.

During dinner, he asked Clarence, "Please, just this last month, can't I get along without a bodyguard?"

Clarence's loud, firm reply startled me. "No, General! As long as I am the Director of the FBI, and you are the attorney general, you will have a bodyguard." Clarence then turned to me. "I can't let a mild-mannered man like Edward Levi, who isn't used to firearms, be unduly exposed to danger in his position."

Mr. Levi dropped the subject.

On January 20 Edward Levi submitted his resignation to President Carter. An interim attorney general, Richard Thornburgh, who had been assistant attorney general in charge of the criminal division of the Justice Department, assumed the position. I had met Mr. Thornburgh in New Orleans, in December, when he had flown down to give a speech at a testimonial dinner for Joseph Sylvester, the retiring SAC of the New Orleans office.

Among the divisions of the Justice Department are the FBI, which investigates and presents the results of its findings, and the criminal division, which is the major prosecuting arm. It is necessary for the two to have a good working relationship. Clarence and Dick Thornburgh got along well.

At this time I was upset by what I considered a lack of common courtesy extended to my husband by the newly elected President. I felt that if Jimmy Carter had been the president of a large corporation and had chosen to ignore the head of a department which had problems, offering it neither constructive criticism nor support, his stockholders would have reason for complaint.

Then I tried to think of the situation from another angle. It might be that the President viewed the position of the Director of the FBI differently. Every President chooses his own cabinet. Clarence was a high-ranking man in the Justice Department. It might logically be concluded by President Carter that if he could choose numbers one, two, three, four, etc., in each department, why was it that in the Justice Department alone, the FBI Director stayed in spite of the will of the President?

There was certainly reason for this thinking. But the purpose of the FBI was to investigate the criminal element in the United States. That has nothing to do with politics. No victim of crime is ever asked his political affiliation.

Whenever the head of an organization is replaced, it can be expected that there will be a lag in efficiency while the new personnel becomes adjusted and informed on the job. America did not need to have a pause in combating crime while the directorship of the FBI swung with political winds. That was one reason Congress had placed an age limit on the job. This period of time (in Clarence's case, a maximum of eight years) would allow enough scope to permit the choice of a Director who would not be politically oriented. That was why, in spite of the position being made so uncomfortable for him as to be almost untenable, Clarence insisted on staying on. *The Bureau would not be politicized.* To my mind, preventing the Federal Bureau of Investigation from being politicized was Clarence Kelley's most important contribution to history.

President Carter sought, and finally chose, the fourth attorney general under whom Clarence would serve, Judge Griffin Bell. During the Senate judiciary hearings on his appointment, Mr. Bell stated that when he became attorney general, he would fire Clarence Kelley.

However, in the Carter White House, an understanding had been reached with Senate majority leader Robert Byrd (Democrat, West Virginia). The Director of the FBI would only be removed for cause.

There was none.

Senator Byrd had been the author of the bill, passed in 1973, which stipulated that the Director of the FBI would serve ten years, or until the age of seventy, unless there was adequate cause for his removal. Candidate Bell's statement so enraged the senator that he threatened to suggest that Bell not be confirmed. He informed Mr. Bell that the hearings would not continue until the candidate-attorney general went to Clarence Kelley's office and ironed out their differences.

It was under these circumstances that Clarence had his initial meeting with Judge Bell. He was assured by Bell that there was no cause for his removal.

Among others in the Senate who were upset by the proposed removal of Clarence were Senators Robert Dole (Republican, Kansas) and John Danforth (Republican, Missouri). They threatened to stage a filibuster on the Senate floor to prevent the appointment.

Senator Danforth requested an interview with Judge Bell. At its conclusion, he requested the judge to phone Clarence, in his presence, to discuss the Director's future in the FBI. Before the candidate hung up, Senator Danforth took the phone and ascertained that Clarence was satisfied with the arrangement.

During those two weeks in January, to my mind, the outstanding lawyer in the nation was Senator Robert Byrd. The subject under consideration was not one of personal friendship, though there was admiration between the senator and the Director. Senator Byrd was acting from a law-enforcement point of view and for the continuing good of the country. If the FBI was to remain free from political involvement, the precedent must be set in January 1977.

On January 26, by a Senate vote of 75–21, Judge Griffin Bell became the fourth attorney general under whom Clarence would serve.

At the swearing-in ceremony for the new head of the Justice Department, President Carter was present, as were Clarence and the top men of the Justice Department. The President and the attorney general entered through a rear door. Mr. Carter made a brief address, including reference to a physical happening of the morning. The large front door of the Justice Department, which had been locked for years, had been "thrown open."

"That door had to be locked," the President said, "because of a chasm that developed between our own government and many of our people." He called that decision during the Nixon administration "a symbolic separation of both disaffected people, and disadvantaged, from the core of Justice."

At the conclusion of his words, the President and the new attorney general did not step forward to shake the hands of the men of the Justice Department. They turned and walked away.

As to the symbolic door—Edward Levi had considered opening it. Upon inquiry, he had discovered it would cost about thirty thousand dollars a year in additional funds to supply proper security. For whatever reason, since the opening of the door, there have been some startling happenings within the halls of Justice. A rape occurred within the first six months. Newspapers report children playing noisily in the corridors. Vandalism has increased.

$$\approx$$

President Carter's inaugural address promised peace in our land during his administration. Within six weeks of that speech, in downtown Washington, halfway between the Justice Department and the White House, the mayor of the nation's capital, Walter Washington, was blockaded in his office, while elsewhere over one hundred people were held hostage by an armed group of American citizens!

I was home, expecting to drive to Philadelphia with Clarence to attend a SAC regional meeting. He called. We would delay the trip a day. He did not know when he would be home. I was to stay in the apartment and keep the door locked.

About 8:00 P.M. I learned from headquarters that Clarence was in his car and could not be contacted. He and the attorney general were out looking over the situation. I was fit to be tied! It was the most serious danger for Clarence I had experienced. It made me furious with Jimmy Carter! Why had he sponsored that "put the armored limousine away" policy? What right had the President to endanger the lives of people who were trying to do their jobs? Clarence out there without even bulletproof glass! The President had not deprived *his* family of that sort of protection!

250

I vented my frustration by calling my mother in North Carolina.

"Fifty days," I said, "and Mr. Carter has set such a tone of permissiveness that the mayor is barricaded in his office. A city councilman has been shot."

Mother replied, "Don't talk like that. You never know who is eavesdropping."

"I don't care!" I said. I wanted Clarence safely home.

While I waited, I listened to Chris Curle's excellent TV program. The topic was TV reporters' responsibility toward the hostage situation.

A guest on the show, a psychiatrist, noted that while the Detroit *Free Press* had been on strike, certain kinds of crime disappeared. Sensational suicides, such as jumping off from bridges, ceased. The victim knew his act would not receive newspaper coverage! A hostage situation, this doctor said, usually involved someone looking for widespread media coverage. This person had usually had many failures. The media should get across the message that hostage situations are rarely successful. To instigate one is courting another failure.

The following day I drove to the FBI building with Clarence, a trip which normally took twenty minutes, but because of police cordoning the streets, and detours, required an hour.

I sat quietly, waiting for the signal to leave for Philadelphia. Around me I heard discussion of police SWAT teams and the FBI SWAT team and the possibility of help from the Marines, which would require special permission from the President. Clarence spoke of getting plans for the three illegally held buildings. Jim Adams mentioned the increased seriousness of the situation, as the instigators became more depressed as tiredness and despair grew. Always, the critical factor was to save the lives of the innocent people involved.

Dick Held, the associate director, came in to talk of the FBI building. Tours for the day would be limited to those who had driven long distances from their homes. There would be no off-the-street visitors. Clarence recommended that since there would be fewer tours, two guides should attend each one. One to lead and one to follow, to watch for anything irregular. I thought of all the guns on display and the many drawers of bullets on file.

The day was tense. Always Clarence was aware that the crime was an in-city one. The police were in charge. The FBI must be alert, its resources at the ready.

At last we were able to leave for Philadelphia. I was glad to leave

Washington, relieved to put distance between Clarence and the grim situation there. Then I faced one myself. It was too late to drive. We must fly. The only way we would be able to get to Clarence's meeting on time was by small chartered plane.

The next day I read in the newspaper that we had "flown in the bureau jet." Don't you believe it! The entire Justice Department has no jet airplane.

I had never flown in a small airplane, and I had sworn I never would. They frightened me! But what was I to do? Let Clarence go off into the vast blue in that tiny airplane without me? I buckled myself in and hung onto him the entire trip. Pressed to my other side was the aircraft door. I was certain it was going to pop open any second!

Since then, I have had other rides in small aircraft. I have discovered they are sources for spectacular views of the world.

Only in certain instances was I provided with a bodyguard. That was at the discretion of the local SAC, who knew the cases the agents were working on, and the disposition of the city.

On one occasion in New York City I was accompanied to Lord & Taylor's by a woman agent. She was in her thirties and exquisitely dressed in a black faille suit with a white silk blouse. She was blonde and made a stunning picture. I complimented her on her choice of clothes and teased her about the effect she must have on the office with her gorgeous wardrobe.

She laughed. "I am working on a fabulous case," she said. "My job is to impersonate a serious collector of art. Meanwhile, I am trying to find a stolen painting. All my clothes are from designer salons. I buy them with my own money. But what an excuse to shop! When your husband isn't here, I am picked up in the Bureau limousine. Another agent impersonates my chauffeur, and I go out on the job!" She laughed. "I used to be a teacher, but this beats teaching any day!"

Later I heard that she had made her case.

A woman agent, who wore a size five dress, met me for lunch in Chicago. She told me of a time she and another female agent had gone to lunch. Her friend had left her gun in the office.

During the meal her friend had seen a hefty six-footer about to reach into her pocketbook. There was not only money in the purse but her gun.

The unarmed agent screamed, "Thief! Thief!"

Her small-sized friend turned round and grabbed her huge assailant, who was about to run. The man found he had a screaming female on each arm. He had expected intimidated women, instead of two that locked on him like a pair of human handcuffs, yelling, "Police! Police! Get the police!" He started to give them a barrage of obscenities.

The size-five agent said to me, "I told him, 'Shut up. I am the FBI.' He was so undone, I didn't even have to produce my gun."

I was pleased to learn that under Clarence, the number of women agents in the Bureau had risen from twenty-nine to seventy. Among them several had married other agents since entering the Bureau. Usually married agents were placed on different squads in the office so that they were not together all day.

In Houston I was accompanied by a woman agent who was about to marry another agent. We attended a TV show on which I was interviewed. During the program I introduced her as an agent who was about to marry an FBI man. Interest in me dropped as attention was focused on her.

Had she met her friend on the rifle range? she was asked. "No," she replied, "on the jogging field." They had trained together and been graduated in the same class.

It was especially interesting to me that quite a few women agents were former schoolteachers who had become dissatisfied with teaching institutions and turned to the FBI.

ॐ

Clarence did not submit his resignation on January 20, as did many other government officials. He did, however, announce that he would retire in January of the following year. This statement was not acknowledged by the White House. Throughout the spring and summer of 1977, he never knew when he might be informed that he was out of a job. Other matters kept him so busy that he had no time to worry about that.

In February the President announced formation of a nine-member search committee to find a replacement for the Director of the FBI. It was composed of a cross-section of American minds and experience. Irving S. Shapiro, chairman and chief executive officer of E. I. du Pont de Nemours & Co., was its chairman. Other members were Justice Susie M. Sharp, from North Carolina; Mary Wall, wife of a Methodist minister, an early supporter of Jimmy Carter, from Illinois; Joseph F. Timilty, from the Massachusetts State Senate; Judge Cruz Reynoso, from California; Thomas Bradley, mayor of Los Angeles; Charles Morgan, a Washington, D.C., attorney; F. A. O. Schwarz, a lawyer from New York City; and Clarence.

Throughout the spring and early summer, this group met twelve times, for a total of ninety hours, in an effort to find a successor. Usually arriving in Washington on Thursday evening and staying through noon on Saturday, they sacrificed time from their regular jobs and cut short their weekends with their families. I was aware of the cost to the country of the airplane fares and hotel bills involved, but more significant was the diversion of abilities from other occupations to this search.

President Carter, in his openhanded way, had extended an invitation to anyone in the United States who thought he might make a good Director to submit his application. From clerks to company presidents, the résumés poured in. The original list numbered 235. Week after week the committee assembled. The candidates under consideration were reduced to fifty and, finally, to five.

President Carter accepted the search committee's list, added two names of his own choosing, and after some weeks of delay, scrapped the entire selection.

In August 1977 he announced his choice of a man whom he had asked to accept the job eight months earlier, but who had turned him down—Judge Frank Johnson.

24

'Mid Pleasures and Palaces

One summer afternoon, standing in the formal garden of the British Embassy, I was made especially aware of the sweeping variety of my life—Miami, the convent, Pericles, Washington, D.C. I had met so many people from such different backgrounds.

I extended my gloved hand and was greeted by Princess Anne of Great Britain. She was taller than I had expected. There was an insulating reserve about her, but she was beautiful! Her pale, smooth complexion was flawless, her voice gently modulated. What woman does not thrill to royalty? I was delighted to be in that young, radiant presence. But, I wondered, could her life be as exciting, satisfying, and pleasurable as mine?

❦

We were the guests of Ambassador and Mrs. Ali Hedda for a seated dinner at the Tunisian Embassy. There I met Shirley Temple Black, who was then chief of protocol for President Ford. Through the years I had had many occasions to admire her in her public life, but like millions of Americans, her name always brought to mind the bright image of a toe-tapping, curly-headed moppet.

During dinner she recounted having met Mr. Hoover when she was a little starlet. An agent had invited her to shoot his gun at the pistol range. Shirley had accepted, squeezed her eyes shut, and pulled the trigger. She missed the target completely, shooting high in the air. Her brother had proved to be a better shot. He had become an FBI agent.

ॐ

There had been so much discussion about gifts public officials might exchange that by the time Clarence and I were married, the practice was down to a trickle. No gift might be privately accepted which was valued at more than fifty dollars. As a result, there was a brisk trade in ashtrays, pewter plates, and cuff links. This consideration of price could make it difficult for sincere well-wishers to express themselves upon a meaningful occasion.

We had not been married long when we were invited to the South African Embassy for dinner with Ambassador and Mrs. Roelof Botha. Clarence considered Helene's buffets among the best on Embassy Row. It was there that I tasted my first cook-sister, a pastry original in South Africa. It was a sweet, flaky, twisted oblong with a sticky top which I found incredibly delicious.

The spacious house was furnished in native woods, many of which were dark and carved. Clarence had been intrigued on previous visits by their unusual names, such as monkeywood. After we had sipped some South African wine, he led me to the living room to show me a remarkable breakfront made of stinkwood, a richly dark, heavy wood, which had almost the hardness of teak, with beautiful, bright graining running through it.

After dinner, as the other guests were departing, Helene delayed us. "Please wait a moment," she said. "I have a little something for you." She disappeared and returned with a wooden box in her arms. Across its top and carved along its sides were stylized African faces. She continued to hold it as she said, "It is a gift for you, and I want you to notice, it is not finished. Until you have worked on it, it is not a salable article. We have checked with the State Department. It is not worth fifty dollars. See," she said, opening it, "it is rough inside. You must line it. The wood is not oiled. You must get oil, and oil it. There is no hardware. That you must furnish also. In this condition, you are allowed to accept the box." Still, she held it tightly in her hands.

"If something happens that the government tries to take it away from you, you must send it back to me. I do not want it kept in the national storeroom for gifts."

With that firmly stated, she handed me the box.

I, too, felt it was a shame to place such small treasures in the national storerooms where they were rarely seen. I have not finished the handsome box. I do not want any excuse for having to relinquish it.

Clarence and I attended a Crime Resistance meeting in Phoenix shortly after the election of 1976. We met and entertained newly elected Democrat Senator Dennis DeConcini and his diminutive, blond wife, Susan, and Eldon Rudd. The latter's first words to me were "Hello, Mrs. Kelley, I'm an ex-FBI agent, and newly elected to Congress." Later I heard that as a legat,* Eldon Rudd (Republican, Arizona) had had a brilliant career in Mexico.

Among the facilities we visited in Phoenix was the Lions' Club project for the blind. Part of this complex was a special pavilion where blind students who were about to enter college, but who had not learned independence, came to live while they trained to handle their domestic needs. It included a large Braille library which had an extensive service for delivering tapes, records, and books to the blind in their homes. From its kitchens hot meals were served to the blind. Having worked with the blind children of Pericles, it was particularly interesting to me to compare notes on the two facilities.

Clarence frequently encouraged me to speak at FBI field offices, gatherings which included the entire staff of frequently one or two hundred people. I was delighted to share any views pertinent to the occasion and always included thanks for kindnesses extended to me. I was aware that I had not come up through the ranks as the other wives were doing. Some husbands held risky jobs. I had come late into the life of the FBI, when the going was easier. I shared with the field offices the great feeling of respect and confidence which I saw Clarence receive as we traveled about the United States and attended international functions in Washington. Because other agents were not as easily recogniza-

---

*Legal attaché—the agent in charge of the FBI office in a foreign country.

ble as Clarence, this could not be as apparent to them; but such regard, I felt, was meant for the entire organization, not merely its Director.

At the luncheon honoring Crime Resistance Week, Senator Barry Goldwater, the senior statesman of Arizona, introduced Clarence, who made the keynote speech. I was in seventh heaven to find myself seated beside the senator, a personal favorite of mine. I was also an admirer of the thinking of Milton Friedman, who had served as economics adviser to Senator Goldwater when he had been the Republican presidential candidate in 1964. I told him I had respected his choice.

"Remember, Senator Goldwater," I asked, "when you said then, thirteen years ago, that the Social Security system would run out of money?"

"Yes." He grinned his famous smile, his eyes creasing at their corners in his suntanned face. "I remember. Now they believe me."

Senator Goldwater felt that Clarence was doing a great job at the FBI.

"He took over a rather beat-up agency at a critical time in our history," he said. "I say it is thanks to him we still have the agency which is so important to the preservation of decent things in our country."

I must have been glowing like the Arizona sunshine as I heard his words. It was so *good* to hear praise of Clarence, and from such a source!

"Clarence brought a lawman's background to the organization and transferred it to the morale of the people working in the FBI," Senator Goldwater said. "I think we can say, thank God we had him at that time. Otherwise, those who don't want our country protected would have had their wishes granted, and we would have, in effect, been standing naked to our enemies."

With Clarence I toured the offices of the *Arizona Republic*. Inquiry into the death of Don Bolles, the investigative reporter for the paper who had died in his car after it had been booby-trapped, was in full swing. Bolles had been investigating corruption and land fraud in Arizona. Because of the killing, security was exceedingly strict. Even Clarence had to go through inspection and clip a visitor's pass on his lapel. It was a pleasure to meet Nina Pulliam, the small, trim editor of the *Republic*, and listen as she and Clarence discussed the Bolles tragedy. Until the death of her husband, Eugene, her desk had abutted his as they worked together.

During the plane trip home, Eugene Smith Pulliam, who happened to be aboard, introduced himself to Clarence as Mrs. Pulliam's stepson, and the editor of the Indianapolis *News*. He inquired about the accuracy of an article recently published about Clarence in the family's *Arizona Republic*. I thought that a most refreshing approach to journalism! Later, when an interview of me by *Republic*'s Dorothy Gopel was published I found it unerring in tone, as well as wording.

As a result of the presidential election there were many farewell parties in Washington, as officials prepared to depart. We attended a delightful one for George Bush, the retiring chief of the CIA, and his self-confident, all-American wife, Barbara. I marveled that George, a tall, attractive man with a boyish grin, who was known to be rather quiet and restrained, was so easy to chat with socially. He had been chairman of the Republican party until he had been summoned to become director of the CIA, a job which he assumed with little prior knowledge of the workings of the vast and intricate bureau. In the short time he had held the position, he had done such a brilliant job that a chief of the French intelligence had flown over to express his particular regard for him at his farewell party.

We met at the Alibi Club, which was located in a townhouse on a Washington side street. The select group of men who composed the club's membership had, through the years, contributed mementos of their lives and travels to the decor of the club. Stepping into the building was like entering a curiosity shop. It was jammed with a most remarkable assemblage of toys, statues, clocks, and furniture. Its tables were loaded with memorabilia. The walls were covered with framed pictures, some of which had movable parts. I saw a lad in one who rolled his eyes. Another caught a fish. It would have required several visits to study it all.

After cocktails we were seated around a large oval table in a room which was a kitchen with both a stove and a fireplace. Kettles and utensils of many vintages hung on its walls. No place mats or cloths were used. The decorations were drinking mugs shaped like famous statesmen or heroes. Mine was Sir Winston Churchill. I was seated beside Judge Richardson Preyer, Democratic congressman from North Carolina, who had just completed his fifth term and was heading strongly into his sixth. His effervescent Emily was seated next to Clarence, which suited him just fine. For a wedding present, Emily later gave us a copy of the *Congressional Cookbook*, which included two of her recipes, one for chicken, the other featuring chocolate—both Clarence's favorites! Along with Clarence having favorite tailors and restaurants in cities across the country, he also had categories of the cooking abilities of his hostesses. As some people remembered birthdays of strangers, Clarence never forgot a favorite dish he had eaten, and he always reserved a warm spot in his heart for its creator.

As we sat about after dinner, chatting, the thrust of the conversation turned to the question, Was America discrediting herself, or actually committing suicide, by so fiercely attacking its own intelligence communities for actions which were commonplace in the international intelligence community? The visitor from France, whose name I will not give you, said he never talked to the press, nor the Parlement, and only on rare occasions with the President.

Clarence commented, "What marvelous working conditions you enjoy!"

A few nights later at a party, I was in a group where an African diplomat said he felt our government was foolish in making such a fuss over matters such as the surreptitious entries that it was suspected the FBI had been making, or whether mail had been opened for examination.

"In our country," he said, "if we think someone is suspicious, we intercept their mail. We open it and read it. If there is nothing in the letter that indicates a conspiracy against the government, we seal it up and send it on its way. Where is the citizen's right violated? He gets his mail!"

Life never slowed down for me in Washington. One evening we had been invited to Senator and Mrs. Henry Jackson's for dinner with one of the senator's aides, Don Donohue, and his wife, Barbara. It was snowing so hard we weren't sure we could drive the short distance. Do you think a blizzard would interfere with the senator's evening jogging? My, no! He arrived a little tardily, still buttoning his jacket as he came downstairs into their all-white living room, his step jaunty, his cheeks ruddy from his frosty run.

Clarence was too involved to be able to attend the Bob Hope Special in Kansas City, a benefit for Baker College, at which he was to have been an honored guest. He asked me to represent him.

"You mean, I will meet Bob Hope in person?" I asked. Of all the movie stars that ever were, I considered Bob Hope the greatest!

I flew to Kansas City, and with Mary and Scrappy, and Donna and Kent, attended the show. Mrs. John Rhodes, wife of the Arizona congressman and an enthusiastic Baker alumna, and former Republican Senator Harry Darby (Kansas) were also honored guests. In his inimitable style, Bob Hope, supposedly in his seventies, moved about the stage for nearly an hour, rapidly quipping jokes without obvious cue cards.

Donna said to me, "When you go up on the stage to meet Mr. Hope, see if he has the cues written on the floor. They must be someplace. Nobody could remember all that so fast!"

When I went up, I looked, but even though I had learned to be more observant since becoming the wife of the Director of the FBI, I couldn't find any cues.

A picture was taken of me beside Bob Hope. I considered myself to be sophisticated. No one overwhelmed me. But do photographs lie? The picture published next morning in a Kansas newspaper had me open-mouthed, star-struck by my favorite comedian.

∾

I was also a great admirer of Leon Jaworski and was delighted to meet him. He reminded me very much of Clarence—a Rock of Gibraltar with a healthy head of gray hair. I felt he would be easy to trust. No wonder Clarence liked him! Mr. Jaworski was the guest speaker at a testimonial dinner for Joe Allbritton, who had recently become owner of the Washington *Star*.

I asked Clarence why we were attending a banquet to honor a man whose newspaper had written such terrible things about him.

He explained to me that the publisher frequently has little control over what is published in his newspaper. He delegates authority to his editors, who choose articles which will find readers and increase circulation.

As we entered the Mayflower Hotel, we met the Allbrittons, who greeted us warmly. Obviously Mr. Allbritton was an admirer of Clarence. In those bleak days of February 1977, we were carefully counting

Clarence's friends. In the new administration his fans were not outspoken, though across the country, they seemed legion. In restaurants, on sidewalks, in airports, they rushed up to him to offer him words of encouragement and support.

At last I met a lady whom I had really wondered about. Whenever Clarence spoke of this person, it was with enthusiasm. She was beautiful, charming, cosmopolitan. She even had a title! There was genuine fondness in his voice when he mentioned her name. In the days before we were married, she was the only one of whom I felt any jealousy. She was Baroness Garnett Stackelberg, a contributing editor to the Washington *Dossier*. Clarence, that rogue, had never mentioned that the baroness was firmly attached to the baron! We met frequently at embassy parties and were entertained in her home. I found her to be an animated, delightful person. On our introduction I confessed the unease Clarence had caused me and the relief I felt to find she was married. If she had not been, I told her, I would never have stood a chance.

We welcomed to Washington a new CIA director, Admiral Stansfield Turner, a rugged, handsome man with an engaging personality, and his wife, Pat. I instantly admired Pat. Her husband's new national prominence was not about to faze her a bit! As a rare treat, and as an ideal way to acquaint Admiral Turner with the men he might wish to contact, dinner was served in the FBI building.

Our other guests included Dick and Elizabeth Held, Jim and Ione Adams, and Tom and Elizabeth Leavitt of the FBI, and Henry and Angie Knocke of the CIA. After dinner we relaxed around the table, conversation centering on the inside stories of the undercover operations held in various cities across the United States with the cooperation of the LEAA,* FBI, and local police departments. In Washington three of these successful operations were called "Sting," "Got Ya Again," and "High Roller."

In the Sting operation the lawmen worked out of an old warehouse. One agent pretended he was looking for a hit man. Applicants

---

Law Enforcement Assistance Administration.

for the job came to him bragging of their talents and the number of murders they had committed. The scene was recorded by closed-circuit television cameras and on tape.

One official in the operation injured his back while preparing the stage setting for his part of the work. Since moving was painful for him, he was set up as "the godfather." Enthroned on a well-placed chair, he loftily interviewed applicants for various "jobs."

The program was vastly successful, resulting in the convictions of about 150 unsavory citizens in the Washington area. It was followed shortly by Got Ya Again, and later, for higher stakes, with High Roller, which was based in an expensive suite of an elegant hotel.

Sting was the first undercover venture to surface which involved the joint cooperation of LEAA, the FBI, and the Washington, D.C., police. At the time of High Roller, James Golden, LEAA, Nick Stames, FBI—Clarence did not wish to crowd the limelight, but gave it to his Washington field office SAC—and D.C. police chief Maurice Cullinane appeared with U.S. Attorney Earl J. Silbert on a television program and spoke freely of their mutual endeavor.

I had met Jim Golden at the Mardi Gras Ball, where he had been exultant about the effectiveness reached by the three organizations working together. At that time, he told me, "Clarence did it! He got us to work together. It could never have happened without him!"

Any tribute to Clarence was of course another star in my heavens, but I also knew what he was saying—in the Hoover Bureau, it could not have been a joint-team operation.

LEAA has successfully financed twenty-two Stings in fifteen cities, the FBI and the police working together to break up rings that cross state lines. Since it was necessary to have personnel in these cases who could not be recognized by the local crooks, the FBI moved its men from all over the country to areas where their faces were unknown. They posed as bartenders, or hit men, or for whatever personality the situation required, and in which a local policeman might have easily been identified.

In Buffalo an operation centered around an antique shop well stacked with recording devices. It netted over $250,000 in recovered stolen goods. In Jacksonville, Florida, $1.2 million was returned in stolen goods and 111 suspects indicted. The cost to the law departments was minimal. Eighty percent of the recovered property could be identified and returned to its rightful owners. Insurance and credit card companies joined in expressing their gratitude for relief from some of their most costly problems.

As Clarence and our FBI guests chatted on about this, I saw a question growing in Admiral Turner's eyes. He asked, "What about the publicity? Doesn't it hinder following operations?"

Clarence replied, "Not really. Most thieves don't read newspapers. They just aren't smart. Many Americans seem to forget that. They have too much respect for criminals. That is why they are so frightened of them. With these Stings we have actually injected some humor into rounding them up. Making them look foolish will contribute toward their demise. Part of the plan is to make the criminal wary, to give him the idea that the police can be anyplace and every place.

"Experts in crime study," he went on to say, "feel that people are less inclined to seek a life of crime if they are worried about informers in their midst."

A recent, effective example of this was the attempted kidnapping of Mr. and Mrs. J. Willard Marriott. The person approached for help by the man planning the crime was an FBI agent working undercover.

As Admiral Turner bid us good night he invited us to dine with him at the CIA. I was thrilled. "And will your after-dinner entertainment be stories of the CIA and what you are up to?" I asked.

He laughed, but said he didn't think that would be possible.

One person in Washington whom I had been most anxious to meet was President Ford. He had been a loyal supporter of Clarence's, and someday I hoped to thank him. At the time of our marriage he had been involved in his election campaign. I did not have an opportunity to meet him until the following spring, when he was no longer in office—and I almost missed that!

We attended the Invest in America luncheon in the Senate caucus room in Washington when the former President received the American Eagle Award for 1977 for outstanding service to the American people. Senator John Danforth, the young Republican senator from Missouri who had won the seat of retiring Democrat Stuart Symington in 1976, was our host.

After the luncheon, Clarence and I started downstairs toward his waiting car.

I said, "Aren't you going to wait and say hello to Mr. Ford?"

"No," Clarence said. "Not with all those people waiting. He'll have hands to shake for half an hour."

"But I've never met him."

"My gosh," Clarence said. "I'd forgotten that." We stepped back inside the building.

When Mr. Ford stepped out of the elevator accompanied by his Secret Service guards, Clarence shook his hand and presented me.

I was delighted to meet that smile head-on. Gerald Ford seemed to have a younger-brother Eisenhower charm about him. I congratulated him on his Eagle Award and commented that I had been sorry that Clarence had not been present in Kansas City when he had received the Harry Truman Good Neighbor Award earlier in the year. (Clarence had received it in 1976.) We chatted for just a moment and then walked out of the building.

The street was filled with traffic. Parked along the curb were several black limousines gleaming, dustless, in the sun. Behind them was a seven-passenger dark blue Cadillac. I took special note of it as Mr. Ford got in and drove away. Perhaps, I thought, that was the difference between working and retirement—in retirement one rode in a blue limousine.

ॐ

Clarence felt that we should entertain the Search Committee, and we sent out invitations to dinner at our apartment.

Though I was not from Missouri, as was Clarence, I had a "show me" streak which he very well knew. In dealing with my occasional stubbornness, he never tried to change my opinion with dogmatic statements but wooed me with finer techniques.

One evening a week or so before the Search Committee dinner, he suggested that it would be nice if we included the attorney general, Griffin Bell.

I was not overjoyed. Judge Bell certainly had the right to state his opinions of Clarence, but they had found no favor with me!

Clarence sat across from me patiently giving me his "I'm waiting for your answer and I expect you to react nobly" look.

Studying his face, which I truly love to please, I finally replied, "Okay, he's your guest."

Nothing more was said about the attorney general's possible visit until the evening before the party. The May weather was balmy, and we were dining outside on our balcony. Clarence began talking about Griffin Bell. This man, he said, had not given him a bit of trouble. He had not seen him as regularly as he had seen Edward Levi, but whenever there was something he needed to discuss, he called Judge Bell, who always said he would come over to the Bureau and discuss the matter before the day was out. His consideration and cooperation, Clarence felt, had been outstanding. "Anyone who steps into the job of leader of the Justice Department has a lot to learn, regardless of his past successes. Griffin Bell has been most cooperative with me, Shirley."

"I'm glad," I said, "that conditions in the Justice Department are beginning to thaw out." Thoughtfully, I ate my dessert.

In my travels I had been hearing favorable comments about the attorney general. I had heard him praised several times. Agents in Savannah had mentioned the good relations between the Bureau and Judge Bell. Clarence's testimony, as we sat together on the porch, had been moving. Yet I had been deeply hurt by Griffin Bell's denunciation of Clarence before he ever interviewed him. In the book I had begun writing that spring, I had detailed my outrage over the initial relationship.

"Clarence," I said, "I am still going to dedicate a full chapter of my book to him."

"Suit yourself," he said.

The following evening, after everyone else had arrived, the doorbell rang. As I opened the door, a courteous southern voice said, "Good evening, Mrs. Kelley. I am Griffin Bell."

I think I had expected an ogre, but a gentleman walked in. The second remark he made warmed me to him. In the greetings of the other guests, someone remarked on a particularly harsh newspaper criticism of the attorney general.

"That really upset my wife," the judge said.

I felt, "Welcome to the club, Mrs. Bell!" Mary was home in Georgia attending her mother, who was ill.

At dinner I was seated on Judge Bell's right at a table for four. Los Angeles Mayor Tom Bradley, and state Justice Susie Sharp, who had earned her law degree in 1928, were my table companions. Susie, Griffin Bell, and I discovered mutual friends in North Carolina. Tom and I had a lively discussion on educational standards. Conversation was easy, and I found myself totally relaxed with my former nemesis from the Justice Department.

There was great goodwill among all. Committee members made several favorable comments about Clarence. Dearest to my heart was one: that by far the most qualified person to direct the FBI that they had met or interviewed was Clarence Kelley. Judge Bell was complimentary of the Bureau. Clarence stated that he had had the finest cooperation from the attorney general. Members of the committee voiced their appreciation for the opportunity to serve on it and of all they had learned about the FBI. When the party ended, and the attorney general said good night to me, he leaned over and kissed my cheek.

After the door had closed behind the final guest and my two helpers had gone home, I made myself a tall glass of ice water. Clarence was already in bed. In a few minutes, I followed him.

While he attempted to sleep, I sat up on my side of the bed, sipping my cold drink, thinking.

"It's late," Clarence said. "Why don't you go to sleep, Shirley? Tomorrow the Search Committee starts again at eight o'clock."

I looked down at my beloved husband. "How can I go to sleep," I asked, "with a conniving husband who knew that if Griffin Bell came into this house, I would like him? You have destroyed an entire chapter in my book! But," I said, "I'll still tell it the way it was!"

Clarence opened his eyes and looked at me, "I knew you were an honest woman, Shirley. Now, please, turn out the light."

ﻙ

In August Clarence and I flew to Europe to attend an Interpol meeting in Stockholm, accompanied by FBI agent Don Moore and his wife, Charlotte. We stopped in London on our way. That was the first time in the history of the FBI that its Director had attended an Interpol session or visited FBI foreign field offices.

I hadn't been in England long before I began to wonder if we had gotten off the airplane in the wrong country—possibly Kuwait! Or maybe I was having an Arabian Nights' dream! I had never seen so many Arabs outside of a Rudolph Valentino rerun!

While traveling, I had frequently found another view of the country's people and life when I had my hair done in a local beauty parlor. I made an appointment in the salon in the Churchill Hotel, where we were staying. I was the only non-Arab in the shop! Not only the other customers, but all the help were Arabic. Several fashion magazines on the table were printed in Arabic. On the streets I had noticed many Eastern and Mideastern people. Many were staying in our hotel, and a large number of the patrons of the restaurants we frequented were Arabic. I was told that many fine old English country houses were being bought by visitors from the Middle East who were suddenly wealthy with oil money.

While Clarence and Don met with the heads of British intelligence from Scotland Yard and MI-5 and MI-6,* Charlotte and I saw what we could of London and had a fine ride a few miles down the river on the Thames police boat. It was only another ripple on the water when we got there, but it was fun to float about on meridian longitude zero degrees, the site of the setting of "Greenwich mean time," which had been determined by international agreement in 1884.

Clarence and I, who had only been to the theater at home three times since we were married, found time to visit Haymarket Theatre for a production of Somerset Maugham's *The Circle,* followed by supper at Leith's. Surely Clarence entered that restaurant in his book of favorite places to eat! Not only did it have desserts served by trolley so that one could take several choices, but appetizers were served the same way. Until that point I had been concerned that Clarence might be suffering from jet lag, but when I saw his selections, I knew it would never catch up with his appetite!

Returning to our hotel, we passed Claridge's. Our driver waved toward it and said, "You've probably heard of that hotel. President Carter had the Embassy book its rooms for his visit. They put in extra telephones and security and made many arrangements for him. A delegation from another country, who also contributed heavily to the British economy, wanted the hotel at the same time, but they were turned down for the prior reservation. Then when Mr. Carter arrived and heard the price of the rooms, he refused to allow his entourage to stay there. Now Claridge's is considering what action to take with the American government for the $25,000 loss of revenue."

In England Clarence was given a prize most highly to be desired by the head of an investigative agency; but also, most difficult to obtain. Peter Matthews, Chief Constable of Surrey, presented him with a black

---

*MI-5: *Military Intelligence Security Service.* MI-6: *Military Intelligence Secret Intelligence Service.* Both services are within the British Ministry of Defense. They were established in Great Britain about 1909.

high-domed bobby's hat. A treasure indeed for a former cop! To own such a hat without a proof-of-ownership certificate was illegal. Accompanying the gift, properly certified, was the necessary paper. A handy thing to have! Wearing such an item, or attempting to hide it under one's coat, would have been pretty obvious.

We flew to Stockholm where representatives of Interpol and officials involved in drug abuse and other types of police work which crossed international lines were assembling from 104 countries. Attending from the United States besides us were customs officials and H. Stewart Knight, the head of the Secret Service, Joseph Blank, deputy director of Civil Aviation Security, Neil Benson, chief postal inspector, and Bill Kish, the legat in charge of the London office whose territory included the British Isles and Scandinavia.

Our arrival in Stockholm was heralded by an almost total absence of the American flag. Along the roadways and over the bridges flew the flags of many nations honoring the Interpol meetings, but the only American flags I could spot were at our Embassy and the one over the entrance to the elegant Grand Hotel overlooking the water across from the royal palace. Our nation's lack of position of honor in Sweden dismayed me.

But Sweden was certainly generous to its visitors. Eight hundred of us were treated to a long luxurious boat ride through the Archipelago, over blue and sparkling seas, around the islets where sharply green trees clutched at crevices in the outcroppings of almost solid rock. It was a glorious day, colors of sea and sky and slant-roofed houses were as fresh as though just splashed out of a paint box. We were served a sumptuous smorgasbord. I enjoyed watching the people from nations around the world as they wondered about the foods they were choosing. I could not understand their words as they described them to each other, but I could see the delight in their eyes and smiles as they tasted the variety of flavors. I wondered how often such hospitality was shared. Surely our group was not the only recipient of such opulent generosity. I was amazed that we could be entertained so lavishly by a country with a population of only 8.25 million.

Sweden was full of surprises. Most astonishing to me was its immigration policy. Sweden accepted all aliens without restriction, including political dissidents and criminals. I heard it estimated that there were 800,000 aliens within its boundaries, all of whom might receive welfare immediately upon arrival—about four hundred dollars a month!

In the United States, when a fugitive from federal justice left the country, it was the duty of the FBI to notify foreign governments. Sweden had been reluctant to hand over such people who had sought her shores. Clarence told me he would be delighted if they kept all of them, but it was a national obligation to notify the governments and ask extradition of such illegal entrants. As an example, I heard of a suspected murderer of a girl in Washington, D.C., who had fled to Sweden. The FBI notified the Swedish law-enforcement agencies, but they refused to return the alien. The man then kidnapped a Swedish girl and tied her to prevent her escape. She was able to free herself and jumped from a window to safety. Obviously it was not to our advantage to have such a citizen back on our shores, but as a fugitive from justice, it was our obligation to pursue him.

I saw the King of Sweden from too far away. It would have been fun to be able to meet the handsome young monarch, born in 1946. He was exceptionally popular with his countrymen, though the remnants of his political power were stripped from him on January 1, 1975. He was still considered the head of state, but performed only ceremonial functions. At the opening session of Interpol, to which wives had been invited, the King was ushered in, but was given no speaking part in the program. For decades the ruling Social Democratic party had had on its basic program the abolition of the monarchy. So far, I heard, it had never found it politically opportune to raise the issue at the polls. King Carl XVI Gustaf and his German wife, Silvia, were much in the papers while we were in Sweden. The recent birth of their baby daughter was bringing them special love from their "subjects."

Among the British delegation to Stockholm were two Toms, both affiliated with newspapers, Tom Tullett, crime bureau chief for the *Daily Mirror* and *Sunday Mirror*, and Tom Sandrock of the *Daily Telegraph*. When Bill Kish introduced me as the wife of the Director of the FBI and mentioned that I was a former nun, both Toms looked at me and grinned broadly.

One said, "You aren't Carrothers, are you?"

"No," I said, "my name is Shirley Kelley."

There seemed to be a private joke between the two correspondents.

The other Tom said, "There are nuns, and there are nuns, and an investigative reporter has an obligation to identify the subject!"

Then they told me the story of Carrothers. It seemed a man of that name had been an undercover agent with British intelligence during World War II. On one of his assignments, he had been disguised as a nun in complete habit. In order to reach his destination, he had boarded a loaded troop train and had ridden out from London tightly packed in amid the soldiers.

Passing through a tunnel, the soldier seated beside the supposed nun had become rather romantic. At his advance, the demure nun, in firm tones announced, "Hands off, fellow! I am Carrothers of MI-5!"

We were entertained by the chargé d'affaires, acting Ambassador Jack Perry and Mrs. Perry, for cocktails in the spacious rooms of the beautiful American Embassy with its large windows overlooking lawns, gardens, and a river. There we met many honorary Swedish consuls. These were American citizens of Swedish ancestry or birth who had kept close association with Sweden and who acted as consuls for Sweden in their home cities in the United States. Also present was stately blond Countess Wachmeister, wife of the Swedish ambassador, a recognized artist in both her native country and the United States.

The following day Mr. Perry again entertained the American delegation to Interpol. I was seated next to Hans Melin, Kemmissarie, who was in charge of aliens for the Swedish police, an official who, I discovered, was something of a national hero. Years before, during a visit by Mrs. Harry Truman to Stockholm, he had thrown himself in front of her to save her life. In so doing, his back had been broken, but the First Lady had escaped unscathed. Naturally I inquired about the alien situation with Mr. Melin and learned much about the Swedish experiences supporting nearly 10 percent of its population who are alien to it.

Though the politicians might be trying to rid Sweden of its monarchy, they certainly knew how to treat their guests like royalty! Interpol's final evening as the guests of the minister of justice, Sven Romanus, was at Stockholm's landmark Town Hall. That sculptured-brick building dominated the skyline with its green copper roof and shining gold ornament-topped tower. It was so contemporary in appearance one felt it had been designed tomorrow—but it was over fifty years old!

I felt like a queen as I entered its wide, roofed courtyard. I had chosen to wear a red and gold paisley gown, front draped, rather in the style of a medieval princess. It was perfect for the magnificent setting in which I found myself.

Dinner was served in the Golden Hall, which was reached by a wide marble stairway. The walls of the room were completely of small mosaics depicting scenes of Swedish life in exquisite colors set amid a background of countless gleaming gold mosaics. A breathtaking room! White-clothed tables stretched before me to its far corners, with places set for more than a thousand to be seated and graciously served. Swedish crystal goblets with twisted stems caught and twinkled the light. Flowers in late summer colors bloomed on every table. The scene was dazzling, and most dazzled was I! It was the room in which the Nobel prizes were awarded. Such minds, such creative imaginations, such industry, had been honored there!

I have never attended a dinner more elegantly served. At the back of the great Golden Hall, two huge doors opened, and smartly dressed waiters and waitresses bearing trays filed in and waited by each table until the furthest had been reached. At a signal, all began serving at once. This procedure announced every course and three wines! Observing the service was almost as entertaining as watching a play.

Throughout my several days in Sweden I had been avoiding one frequently offered delicacy—reindeer. To me, deer had always meant Bambi or those eight light-footed creatures harnessed to Santa's sleigh! At the banquet that festive night, the main course was—Rudolph! "When in Sweden," I told myself, "be a Swede." I tasted the meat, and it was delicious. Maybe that was why Swedish children put their shoes out for St. Nicholas instead of expecting rooftop visitors.

If you ever want to come home to the best in America, plan your return from abroad to land you in Miami, and from there, drive, fly, or hitchhike to Disney World. I had never guessed during all those years in the convent, or the following ones of my teaching, what I was missing by not visiting Walt Disney's Magic Kingdom.

'Mid Pleasures and Palaces

Clarence had an engagement our first day home to speak at a luncheon for one thousand people in Orlando, but I managed to sandwich in generous slices of Disney World fun around it.

There is indescribable joy to be found within the borders of that fantasy world. Delight glows on every face. Do only happy people go there? I had not known what to expect—a gigantic amusement park, I supposed. Disney World was far more than that. Everything was geared to beauty and attention to detail. Apparently nothing grew old or died. Paint appeared as though the brush that applied it had just lifted. Windows shone. Curtains might have just been hung, costumes lifted fresh from their boxes! The epigram for Walt Disney's creation must have been "Good Clean Fun!" Sheer and multiple ingenuity was everywhere apparent. I was overjoyed by the imaginative antics of the Pirates of the Caribbean. The Jungle Ride was utter delight, with surprise, amusement, and tiny terrors presented at every curve of the stream. Once was not enough for such treats. I wished I had time to ride again and again.

In the evening twelve of us were hosted by Robert Matheison, a Disney World vice-president, and his wife, aboard a pontoon boat on the lake. We floated about its mirrored surface sipping cocktails and eating hot hors d'oeuvres while we marveled at the man-made wonders created in God's tropical setting. For dinner we went ashore to Pioneer Hall to be entertained American style, Old West version. A cast of six sang cowboy songs and country music, their spirit so infectious that we clapped our hands and stamped our feet, we happy, square Americans.

I could not help reflecting on the countries we had just seen, and others from previous visits. It occurred to me that what most of the world seemed to miss was America's gusto for life, our enthusiasm, our love and admiration for humor expressed through clever technology. What other country could have created Disney World?

25

Happily Ever After

In late September 1977, Frank Szasz's full-length portrait of Clarence was officially unveiled at the J. Edgar Hoover Building. We met with friends, fellow agents, and officials for the quiet ceremony. It was thought-provoking to see my beloved "hung." The significance of the occasion brought to me for the first time the realization that for many generations Clarence would be a part of FBI and national history. Oil portraits of officials in public places, I had thought, were of Benjamin, Abraham, or George, but there was Clarence in the brightly colored, expertly rendered painting—an about-to-speak resemblance. My heart was bursting with pride that I was a special part of that moment with him.

I had known him less than sixteen months. We had been married not quite one year. There had been trials and honors. My mind ran a gamut of all that I knew about Clarence. I remembered a story his daughter, Mary, had shared with me, an incident of her childhood. The family had been making an automobile trip. Mary had carried her favorite, but old, pillow with her. At a motel, she had decided that she preferred one that was provided there to her own, and she made a switch. Twenty miles upon their journey the next day, Clarence had learned of the exchange. He had turned the car around and driven back to the motel to return the purloined pillow. *That* was the man whom the press had tried for so long to portray as a crook over the embarrassing incident of the misordering of the valances!

An early incident in our married life had given me a dramatic view of the harried, harrowing, and unheralded ways of the FBI. One evening at home Clarence received a phone call about an American girl who had disappeared in Europe, a brilliant, serious-minded young woman who had been studying abroad. European investigative sources had failed to locate her. Her mother, and later her father, had traveled to Europe in efforts to assist the search. The evening was lost as Clarence phoned the man in charge of the legats in the countries where the girl might be. He discussed the disappearance with Bureau lawyers to learn what jurisdiction the FBI had in those areas. The conclusion was finally reached that the FBI should proceed to investigate.

To me, listening on the sidelines, it seemed a tragic, hopeless incident. The trail must certainly be cold. I thought of the alleys and twisting, turning back streets of Europe's medieval-designed cities. Surely the girl was a needle in a time-tossed haystack!

Perhaps two months later I asked Clarence if anything had ever come of the investigation for the girl.

"Oh, that case," he said. "We found her quite some time ago."

"Alive?" I asked.

"Yes, though not in the best of health. Two Turks had kidnapped her and were secretly feeding her dope in her food. With proper procedures, she has been stabilized and is safely home with her parents."

He hadn't even told me!

Of course he could not bring home daily reports on his work, but I found his successes thrilling. On days when Clarence was being maligned by the press, he didn't have time to feel bad about it, but I did! When I heard of such cases, I asked myself, Which side would I rather be on? Did it matter what the press said? What was the value of a few empty words thrown irresponsibly around when there were men with the expertise to save lives?

The day-to-day satisfactions of agents who solved cases which brought lawbreakers to justice, or which uncovered plots to harm innocent victims, or sabotage, bombings, or incidents which might have international repercussions were far deeper and more exhilarating than the pangs caused by irresponsible words. Imagine the satisfaction known by the agent who located the Mackle girl who had been buried alive by her kidnapper and was found with only a straw in her mouth for breathing!

I could only be an ear to such events, but as they piled up day after day, I realized the greatness with which I lived.

Clarence's purpose when he became Director of the Bureau had been to make changes. It was necessary in some instances to change the impression from a JEH-FBI to a USA-FBI. The Bureau, internationally known for its fingerprint file, had been firmly under the thumb of one man. Within its domain this man was not questioned or crossed. Those who dared did not linger. On the other side of the fence, those who did too well and received too much personal recognition for their accomplishments were eased out. It had been a one-man show. Anonymity, except for its leader, had been considered a strength of the Bureau. It had only one voice, that of J. Edgar Hoover.

Agents told me that, in the Hoover days, appointments to leadership positions were not necessarily made from the point of view of merit or ability. If there was someone in the field who did not quite fit in, often times he would be kicked upstairs to a big job. "Send him off to Washington and get him out of our hair" was the theory of many men in the field.

Into this situation stepped Clarence. When he became chief of police in Kansas City, after twenty-one years as a special agent in the FBI, the comment had been, "He was an FBI man. He knows nothing about police work." Twelve years later, after having turned the Kansas City Police Department into a model agency, he became Director of the FBI, where at first he was looked down upon as "not one of us." He was "just a policeman." He came into a Bureau of men handpicked by his predecessor. For forty-eight years the Bureau had had remarkable success as the top domestic intelligence agency in the world. With such a record, what need was there for change? Twenty thousand people had to be made to feel the *need* for change before reforms could be put into practice.

A fact which the American public seemed to find fuzzy, and the press to have forgotten, was that the Director could not summarily dismiss employees, no matter how loud the clamor for a shake-up. Government employees and civil servants are protected by law from arbitrary firing. There has to be just and probable cause for such action. Neither is the Director allowed to reduce the position of a man in the Bureau without just cause. Clarence could, and did, strongly recommend that some agents involved in imprudent practices, and of retirement age, retire for their own benefit, as well as the Bureau's. At the time of the most severe press attacks on Clarence, he said to me, "No man in the Bureau will be embarrassed in front of his wife or children without positive evidence of cause being presented to me."

After all the long outcry of the media, one man in the FBI was indicted and fined five hundred dollars. One man was fired. Not a bad record for the fifty years of the Bureau! Yet as late as August 1977, a Herblock cartoon in the Washington *Post* featured a character wearing an FBI badge carrying a bag labeled "FBI crimes," with Mrs. Average Citizen sitting by with the legend, "I thought they were supposed to protect us." The attorney general was drawn looking at the situation in a perplexed manner.

Tricks were used. A TV interviewer adjusted a tape of an interview with Clarence, creating a deceptive account. I was made to wonder, were some members of the press corps fundamentally opposed to those who achieved leadership in government or business? Why did they knowingly hammer away at the basis of our economic and political system? I sometimes felt there were reporters who had almost malevolent purpose. I did not mean to place blanket blame, as there were many who reported honestly. But there were those several with nationwide and international coverage who seemed determined to present the worst possible picture of people and events. They were intelligent people, who were paid handsomely for their services. Toward them Clarence had a more benevolent attitude than I. He maintained that they were trying desperately to be Woodwards and Bernsteins, to make it big in reporting. If they guessed, and the guess was wrong, they had nothing to lose, since the law usually protected them. If they guessed and happened to be right, there was a chance they would get a scoop that would enhance their careers.

ॐ

Clarence was not a flamboyant man. He had a job to do, and he did it. He surveyed the institution of the FBI in July 1973, recognized its great points, and determined to provide changes to correct what he considered were its weaknesses. He had hoped to stay in office until he had completed his task. As I listened to the remarks being made at the dedication of his portrait, I felt a great sense of relief. His forty changes were in effect. By not resigning in the face of criticism, he had set the precedent of a Congress-determined term for the directorship rather than one of a position vulnerable to presidential whim.

For some time I had felt there were striking comparisons to be made between Clarence and former President Gerald Ford. Both made valuable contributions to their country in the period following Watergate and after the national turmoil caused by the Vietnam War. They were called upon to fill offices that had been subjected to criticism and disillusionment by many Americans. Both were men of personal integrity and stability, who lacked excessive desire for personal acclaim. They each appreciated the opportunity to serve the people of America and were aware that time alone would heal many wounds. They used their best efforts to steer a steady course while frequently receiving severe and unjust criticism. President Ford pardoned former President Nixon rather than allowing him to be possibly incriminated for actions considered by many as questionable, but not new to politics. For this President Ford probably sacrificed election to a full term of the presidency. Similarly, when past abuses and ineffective actions on the part of the FBI became public information while Clarence was Director, he could have made himself look good by chopping heads. He refused to bow to such pressure. Rather than seeking superficial, cosmetic changes which would be easily recognizable, he set about methodically rebuilding the FBI from within.

Even the incoming President, Jimmy Carter, paid his respects to President Ford for the service he had provided his country by uniting it during a uniquely difficult period in its history.

Of Clarence, John Goshko in the Washington *Post* grasped the truth of his position in his article entitled "Lame Duck Chief Is Reforming Tomorrow's FBI." At that time, Attorney General Bell said, "Regarding the changes Clarence Kelley has instituted, which are still in their embryonic stage, and require more work to ensure that their promise is realized, my impression is that 95% or more of what the FBI does is well done, even though for a lot of time they have been taking a lot of heat over things which happened some years ago and that actually involved only a small part of their work."

As for Clarence, to him it was the implementation of the changes in the Bureau that was important, not the man who made them.

During my year with Clarence in the FBI, I had come to a rather surprising realization. In those months I had been closer than ever in my life to the seamy side of America, yet I had growing confidence in America's future. Respect for authority was again being restored. In a year of controversy over his position, Clarence had received countless recognitions and awards, including his fifth honorary doctorate of law.* When he was honored guest at a Marine Corps review, I had been told that the marines had more applicants for officer training than they could accept. Similarly, the FBI had a waiting list of thousands of applicants. Across the nation other police groups told me the same story of eagerness to serve. There was a quickening interest in the country for the protection of its people and ideals through law and order.

At the unveiling ceremony I saw "my boy" in two guises. One was the man we were leaving behind, suspended on the wall, the one that for years Americans would see. That man felt that the Bureau was under good management. For the benefit of all Americans, we hope that his successor will break all Clarence's records, including to date over five thousand investigations which had led to the convictions of members of organized crime. We were proud that crime resistance had been recognized, and was being pursued, and felt content that the new openness within the Bureau would be continued.

The other Clarence at the unveiling, the live one, would continue by my side. He had several exciting plans—a new business in Washington, D.C., a visiting professorship at the University of Alabama, two books to write, and he had been asked to run for mayor of Kansas City. Opportunities for action seemed endless.

Meanwhile, there was a house to build in Kansas City. Clarence had his children and grandchildren to enjoy. That "instant family" which I had acquired merely by saying "I do" was an entire continent of enjoyment for me to explore. While Clarence was Director, there had been little opportunity to get to know them. With a house in Kansas

---

From Southeastern University.

City, we could be close to one another. On July 31, 1977, a new blessing had arrived. Kent and Donna had presented us with grandchild number three, Ruth Dyanthea Kelley. The possibilities for enjoyment seemed limitless.

Because of the unpredictable vagaries of human nature and circumstance, a life cannot be predesigned. When, at nineteen, I made my decision to become a religious, I began a life of service to others. I had not planned it that way. It happened. When I put myself into a situation, I believed in it with enthusiasm. The results were both gratifying and rewarding.

One faces many doors in life which may be opened or passed by. Destiny is influenced by those one chooses to proceed through. I crossed a campus and entered a convent; closed that door behind me and became an individual in another world; walked out of the Watergate and into the heart of a very special man. With Clarence, many new doors were opened to me, and now we stand on another threshold.

Acknowledgments

Joseph E. Battle
Homer Boynton
William W. Branon
John Coleman
Marguerite Devine
Sister Mary Louise Full
Werner P. Gullander
Thomas Harrington
Barbara Hauer
Peggy Hogan

Ruth McCord
Donald Moore
Patrick Murphy
Seymor Phillips
Janet Reed
Alta Southers
Ronald Thompson
Carl Webster
Patricia Williams
Larry Winters